The Ultimate 500 Crock Pot Re

Written by: Jamie Stewart

Copyright © 2016

All Rights Reserved

All rights reserved. No part of this book may be reproduced or transmitted in any form or by any means, electronic or mechanical, including photocopying, recording or by any information storage and retrieval system, without written permission from the publisher, except for the inclusion of brief quotations in a review.

Warning-Disclaimer

The purpose of this book is to educate and entertain. The author or publisher does not guarantee that anyone following the techniques, suggestions, tips, ideas, or strategies will become successful. The author and publisher shall have neither liability or responsibility to anyone with respect to any loss or damage caused, or alleged to be caused, directly or indirectly by the information contained in this book.

Table of Contents

PART ONE: BREAKFAST   6

PART TWO: LUNCH   66

PART THREE: DINNER 122

PART FOUR: FAST SNACKS   180

PART FIVE: DESSERTS 238

500 CROCK POT RECIPES

A crock pot is a modern kitchen tool which is used to prepare food in a traditional way. Nevertheless, the crock pot is much more than a regular kitchen equipment. It changes your attitude towards food, furthermore, it can change your lifestyle. Imagine this situation. You wake up, you are relaxed and you are ready to start a new day! Your hot and tasty morning meal is ready, all is perfect. Of course, you no longer have to imagine this perfect morning! It is possible with your crock pot! There is no need to stand around the pot, there is no need to stir your meal and adjust the temperature, and so on. The night before, you just put all your favorite ingredients into your crock pot and set this amazing kitchen tool. Moreover, many people claim that the meals are more flavorful and richer-tasting than food cooked on the stovetop. Crock pot is a perfect for everyone who likes to keep things simple in the life as well as in the kitchen. That's it, that's the magic of slow cooking you'll meet with your crock pot and this cookbook!

Six Surprising Benefits of Hands-free Cooking

Regardless of whether you own the crock pot or you tend to get one, you should know some advantages of this kitchen equipment. There are chefs that call them "irreplaceable" for many traditional recipes which our ancestors used to cook.

1. The crock pot is convenient for the average modern family. Nowadays, people are working more than 40 hours a week. Therefore, who has two hours to spend standing over the stovetop, making the meals for the whole family? From now on, you can make all the meals in an easy way. Prepare a stunning family salad, cook traditional meals, organize party dinner that will feed a crowd, surprise your kids with amazing healthy snacks! Many busy moms are working multiple jobs, so there is no time to cook some desserts for their kids. The good, surprising news is that you can cook almost all of your favorite desserts in the crock pot and you can indulge your sweet tooth with amazing crock pot recipes. Therefore, when you read this cookbook, you will become aware that you can make your favorite meals in a much simpler way. The book consists of five hundred recipes that are separated into five chapters: breakfast, lunch, dinner, fast snacks and desserts.

2. Great budget-friendly meals. The crock pot, as well as any slow cooker, is economical to use and the meals are less expensive. There are less expensive cuts of meat that are tough to chew if they are prepared in some conventional way, for instance, in the oven or on the stovetop. Cooking in a crock pot softens meat in a natural and effective way. You can use beef sirloin, bone-in pork chops, bone-in chicken thighs and the other cheap cuts of meat to prepare delicious meals while staying within your budget.

3. You can freely cook at any time of the year. Many people avoid cooking during the summer time for a few obvious reasons. It's warm and you prefer to spend your time outdoors! The crock pot does not heat up your whole kitchen, unlike stove and oven. Simply put all of the ingredients into your crock pot, set the temperature, and go out to have some fun! Besides the fact that your crock pot saves your hard-earned money, it also saves your time and energy. Using amazing crock pot you can also free up your whole kitchen (pots, stove, oven, etc.) for other types of cooking.

4. Simple is good. The crock pot is getting back to a simple and healthy way of life. During the years, manufacturers have improved technological features to make crock pots easier to use. So, the crock pot is designed to make gorgeous meals with very little hassle. That's for sure, you will feed even picky eaters and they will polish off their meals! You can take your crock pot with you on the camping and you can enjoy tempting fresh meals all day every day.

5. Learn a simple way to become a better cook. Anyone can become a great cook with the crock pot. You don't have to be a skilled kitchen professional. Simply follow these recipes and you will see a big difference. In this cookbook, you will find easy-to-prepare recipes that will meet the expectations of the most demanding guests and family members. Of course, there are recipes that are a little more difficult to prepare. Don't worry, there are step-by-step explanations that anyone can follow in his/her kitchen. All you need is a great love for cooking and your meals will disappear in a hurry!

6. Your crock pot can be left unattended. This is one of the biggest benefits of the powerful crock pot! If you want stunning and hot homemade meal for tomorrow morning, you can grab your favorite ingredients, put them into the crock pot, and go to bed. Further, you can set your crock pot with favorite food inside of it and go wherever you want. When you and your family get back home, you will have an extraordinary lunch ready to warm you up. The same goes for dinner, desserts and snacks. If you are planning a big party, it can be a true challenge for you and you can get so stressed. There's no need to worry, you have your crock pot. Plenty of healthy snacks, homemade candies, marvelous cakes and other great meals can be prepared in the crock pot. During that time, you can relax, you can decorate the room or you just can take a break. You will never, ever wait for your guests tired and exhausted. Awesome!

Tips for Better Crock Pot Meals

This cookbook will teach you to cook in many different ways such as roasting, baking, stewing, poaching, braising, etc. These recipes are carefully selected and created to provide you with all the necessary knowledge for perfect slow cooking. Here are some frequently asked questions with extra advice.

How to achieve a perfect thickness of your meal? If your meal is cooked but too watery, there is a trick that always works. Set the crock pot to high, cover with the lid and cook for 10 minutes. Stir in combined 2 tablespoons of flour and 1/4 cup of cold water for every cup of unwanted liquid. Then, stir 2 to 3 more minutes. When the recipe calls for tomatoes and you don't have fresh tomatoes, you can use tomato paste instead of tomato juice and the result is a denser sauce.

Do you need to stir ingredients during cooking? No. Forget the stirring. If it is specified in the recipe, you can stir ingredients. Crock pot uses indirect heat, so there is no risk of burning your favorite food.

Is there any pre-preparation? The crock pot is so easy to use. Anyway, you can throw all the ingredients in your crock pot and start cooking. It would be nice if you can brown the meat before cooking, but it is not necessary, of course. The same goes for onions, garlic, mushrooms and some kind of vegetables. Anyway, simply follow the recipe and you cannot go wrong. Keep in mind that root vegetables take longer than other vegetables; therefore, place them at the bottom of the crock pot. Vegetables can lose important nutrients while slow cooking. To prevent this, sauté the vegetables briefly before slow cooking.

Is this a healthy method of cooking? Yes. This is a low-fat method of cooking because you don't need to add any fat or oil in most cases. Of course, you had better cut the fat off the meat and remove the chicken skin. The most of crock pot recipes calls for vegetables, nuts, seeds, legumes and high-fiber foods; hence, you will be sure that you and your family eat healthy meals.

With five hundred recipes in this cookbook, you will find amazing dishes from appetizer, fast snacks and old-fashioned breakfast to stunning desserts. You will be able to prepare a variety of meat and meatless delectable recipes. As you can see, the crock pot is not designed only for soups and stews, as people usually think. Slow cooking will bring you much more pleasure than you can imagine. The crock pot and this cookbook will give you the joy of cooking at home and inspire you to cook more often!

PART ONE: BREAKFAST

Easy Sunday Beef Sandwiches

(Ready in about 8 hours | Servings 6)

Ingredients

- 1 jar of your favourite spaghetti sauce
- 3 pounds roast meat
- 2 bay leaves
- 5-6 peppercorns
- 1 cup beef stock
- Mustard for garnish
- Pickles for garnish

Directions

1. In your crock pot, place all of the ingredients. Cook on low for 8 hours.
2. Remove bay leaves and peppercorns and ladle over English muffins.
3. Serve with mustard and pickles and enjoy!

Lazy Man's Pizza

(Ready in about 4 hours | Servings 4)

Ingredients

- 1 pound hamburger, browned and drained
- 1 pound noodles, cooked
- 2 cups mozzarella cheese, shredded
- 2 bell peppers, sliced
- 1 onion, chopped
- 1 teaspoon granulated garlic
- 1 can beef soup
- 1 cup mushrooms, sliced
- 2 jars pizza sauce
- 1/2 pound pepperoni, sliced

Directions

1. In your crock pot, alternate layers with the ingredients in the order given above.
2. Cook for 4 hours on low; then serve.

Chocolate French Toast with Honey and Bananas

(Ready in about 2 hours | Servings 6)

Ingredients

- 1 large-sized loaf bread, torn into cubes
- 2 cups low-fat milk
- 1/2 teaspoon cardamom
- 1/2 teaspoon ground cloves
- 1 teaspoon ground cinnamon
- 1 tablespoon hazelnut extract
- 5 large-sized eggs
- 2 heaping tablespoons chocolate cream, plus more for topping
- 1 tablespoon butter, unsalted
- 4 bananas, sliced
- 1 tablespoon honey

Directions

1. Put the bread cubes into your crock pot.
2. In a large mixing bowl, combine, milk, spices, hazelnut extract, eggs, and chocolate cream. Whisk well to combine.
3. Pour this mixture over the bread cubes in the crock pot to make sure the bread is well submerged.
4. Cover the crock pot with a lid and cook on high approximately 2 hours.
5. Heat a saucepan and add butter. Add bananas and honey to the hot butter and sauté 3 to 4 minutes, turning once.
6. Divide chocolate French toast among six serving plates, add banana-honey mixture and enjoy with fat-free milk!

Melt-In-Your-Mouth French Toast

(Ready in about 5 hours | Servings 8)

Ingredients

For the French Toast:

- 12-ounce loaf bread of choice
- 2 cups whole milk
- 3 eggs

- 1/2 cup brown sugar
- 1 tablespoon almond extract
- 1/4 teaspoon ground nutmeg
- 1/4 teaspoon allspice
- 1/4 teaspoon turmeric powder
- 1 teaspoon ground cinnamon
- 1 cup almonds, coarsely chopped
- 3 tablespoons unsalted butter, melted
- 2 bananas, sliced

For the Sauce:

- 1/2 cup brown sugar
- 1/2 cup half-and-half cream
- 1/2 cup butter
- 2 tablespoons corn syrup
- 1 teaspoon almond extract

Directions

1. Preheat the oven to 300 degrees F. Line a crock pot with disposable crockery liner.
2. In a baking pan, place the bread cubes in a single layer. Bake for about 15 minutes or until the bread is golden. Then, replace bread cubes to prepared crock pot.
3. In a large mixing bowl, whisk together whole milk, eggs, sugar, almond extract, nutmeg, allspice, turmeric, and cinnamon. Pour this spiced mixture over bread cubes in the crock pot. Press bread cubes down with a spoon to moisten them.
4. In a small non-stick skillet, toast the almonds for a few minutes. Combine toasted almonds with melted butter. Pour this mixture over the ingredients in the crock pot.
5. Cover, and then cook on low heat setting for about 5 hours. Remove crockery liner and set French toast aside.
6. Next, prepare the sauce. In a medium-sized saucepan, over medium-high heat, cook the ingredients for the sauce. Bring to a boil, turn the heat to low and cook for 3 more minutes.
7. You can cool prepared sauce to room temperature or set in a refrigerator. Pour the sauce over the French toast, top with banana slices and enjoy!

Homemade Yogurt with Croissants

(Ready in about 8 hours | Servings 16)

Ingredients

- 1/2 gallon low-fat milk
- 1/2 cup milk powder
- 1/4 cup plain yogurt with active yogurt cultures, at room temperature
- 16 croissants of choice

Directions

1. In a saucepan, over medium heat, combine together milk and milk powder. Cook, stirring constantly, until an instant-read thermometer registers about 180 degrees F.

2. Next, cool at room temperature

3. In a bowl, combine together 1 cup of the warm milk mixture and the plain yogurt. Whisk until smooth. Next, slowly pour the milk-yogurt mixture into the saucepan, stirring constantly.

4. Pour prepared mixture into canning jars and place them in a crock pot. Pour enough lukewarm water into the crock pot. Water need to reach just over halfway up sides of your filled jars.

5. Cook on HIGH for 5 minutes. Then, allow to stand about 4 hours, until the mixture is thick. It's important to turn on your crock pot to high for 5 minutes, every hour.

6. Chill the yogurt at least 4 hours or until yogurt is set. Store in the refrigerator and serve with your favourite croissants. Enjoy!

Cranberry Coconut Steel Cut Oatmeal

(Ready in about 6 hours | Servings 8)

Ingredients

- 2 cups steel-cut oats
- 4 cups water
- 2 cups coconut water
- 1/2 cup almonds, chopped
- 1 tablespoon brown sugar
- 1/2 teaspoon ground cinnamon
- 1/2 teaspoon salt
- 1/4 cup dried cranberries
- 1/4 cup snipped apricots
- Shredded coconut for garnish

Directions

1. In a crock pot, combine together oats, water, coconut water, almonds, sugar, cinnamon, and salt. Cover; cook on low-heat setting approximately 6 hours.

2. Top each serving with cranberries, apricots, and coconut and serve warm.

Overnight Oatmeal with Dried Fruits

(Ready in about 6 hours | Servings 8)

Ingredients

- 2 cups steel cut oats
- 1 cup raisins
- 1 cup dried cherries
- 1 cup dried figs
- 8 cups water
- 1 cup half-and-half

Directions

1. Into a crock pot, put all of the ingredients.
2. Set the crock pot to low heat and cover with a lid.
3. Cook overnight or 8 to 9 hours.

Orange Poppy Seed Bread

(Ready in about 2 hours | Servings 12)

Ingredients

- Non-stick cooking spray
- 1/4 cup poppy seeds
- 2 cups flour, all-purpose of choice
- 1 tablespoon baking soda
- 1 tablespoon honey
- 3/4 cup brown sugar
- 1/2 teaspoon kosher salt
- 3 large-sized eggs
- 1/2 cup canola oil
- 1/2 cup sour cream
- 1/4 cup whole milk
- 1 teaspoon orange zest
- 1/4 cup fresh orange juice
- 1 teaspoon vanilla extract

Directions

1. Coat a crock pot with non-stick cooking spray.

2. In a bowl, stir together poppy seeds, flour, and baking soda, and set aside.

3. In another bowl, combine together honey, sugar, salt, eggs, canola oil, sour cream, whole milk, orange zest, orange juice, and the 1 teaspoon of vanilla extract. Add this orange mixture to poppy seeds mixture. Stir to combine and place in the prepared crock pot.

4. Cover and cook on high for about 2 hours.

5. Cool completely before serving time and enjoy with freshly squeezed orange juice.

Bacon and Veggie Quiche

(Ready in about 5 hours | Servings 6)

Ingredients

- Disposable slow cooker liner
- 4 slices bacon
- 1 tablespoon olive oil
- 1 red bell pepper, chopped
- 1 green bell pepper, chopped
- 2 cups mushrooms, chopped
- 1 cup spinach
- 1 ½ cups Swiss cheese, shredded
- 2 cups whole milk
- 8 large-sized eggs
- 1 teaspoon granulated garlic
- 1 tablespoon fresh basil
- 1 teaspoon fine sea salt
- 1/4 teaspoon cayenne pepper
- 1/4 teaspoon ground black pepper
- 1/2 cup biscuit mix

Directions

1. Line your crock pot with disposable slow cooker liner.

2. In a saucepan, fry bacon slices until crisp; drain and crumble.

3. In same saucepan, heat olive oil over medium-low heat. Sauté bell pepper and mushrooms until tender. Stir in spinach and Swiss cheese.

4. In a mixing bowl, combine milk, eggs, granulated garlic, basil, salt, cayenne pepper, and black pepper. Add this mixture to mushroom mixture in the saucepan.

5. Next, fold in biscuit mix. Replace prepared mixture from the saucepan to the crock pot. Scatter the crumbled bacon on top.

6. Cover with a lid; cook on low-heat setting for 5 hours. Cool slightly before serving time, divide among serving plates and enjoy!

Spiced Oatmeal with Nuts

(Ready in about 8 hours | Servings 4)

Ingredients

- 1 cup steel cut oats
- 1 tablespoon butter
- 1/4 teaspoon turmeric powder
- 1/2 teaspoon allspice
- 2 tablespoons maple syrup
- 1 cup dried figs
- 1 cup dried apricots
- 2 cups water
- 2 cups coconut water
- 1/2 cup half-and-half
- 1/2 teaspoon sea salt

Directions

1. Combine all ingredients in your crock pot.

2. Cover the crock pot with a lid. Cook 8 hours on low or 4 hours on high-heat setting.

3. Serve with chopped nuts of choice!

Ham and Cheese Family Delight

(Ready in about 4 hours | Servings 6)

Ingredients

- Non-stick cooking spray
- 1 cup whole milk
- 2 cups light cream
- 4 eggs

- 1 red bell pepper, chopped
- 1 yellow bell pepper, chopped
- 1 onion, finely chopped
- 1 teaspoon dried basil
- 1/4 teaspoon turmeric powder
- 1 teaspoon dried thyme, crushed
- 1/2 cayenne pepper
- 1/4 teaspoon ground black pepper
- 6 cups toasted bread cubes
- 1 cup cooked ham, chopped
- 1/2 cup hard cheese, cubed
- 1/3 cup dried tomatoes

Directions

1. Lightly oil a crock pot with cooking spray.
2. In a bowl, whisk together milk, light cream, and eggs. Stir in red bell pepper, yellow bell pepper, onion, basil, turmeric, thyme, cayenne pepper and ground black pepper.
3. Next, add bread cubes, ham, cheese and tomatoes. Add the mixture to the crock pot.
4. Cook on low heat setting for about 4 hours or until a toothpick (knife) inserted in centre comes out clean. Enjoy!

Halloween Bread with Cranberries

(Ready in about 2 hours | Servings 8)

Ingredients

- Non-stick cooking spray
- 3/4 cup canned pumpkin
- 1/2 cup half-and-half
- 2 tablespoons sugar
- 1 teaspoon ground cinnamon
- 1/4 teaspoon cardamom
- 1/4 teaspoon allspice
- 2 cups all-purpose flour
- 1 teaspoon baking soda
- 1 teaspoon baking powder
- 1/2 teaspoon salt
- 1/4 cup unsalted butter, cubed
- 1/2 cup cranberries
- 1/2 cup maple syrup
- 2 tablespoons butter, melted
- 1/2 cup chopped walnuts, toasted

Directions

1. Grease your crock pot with non-stick cooking spray.

2. In a mixing bowl, combine pumpkin with half-and-half, sugar and spices.

3. In a large bowl, stir together the 2 cups of flour, the baking soda, baking powder, and salt. Next, cut in cold butter. Add pumpkin mixture to prepared flour mixture. Gently stir to combine.

4. Fold cranberries into the batter.

5. Spoon mixture into your crock pot. Pour maple syrup and melted butter over the batter. Then, scatter the walnuts over the top.

6. Cook on high-heat setting for about 2 hours. Serve warm.

Bread Pudding with Dried Figs

(Ready in about 3 hours | Servings 6)

Ingredients

- 8 cups bread cubes of choice
- 1/2 cup dried figs, chopped
- 4 medium-sized eggs
- 2 cups whole milk
- 1/4 cup butter, melted
- 1 teaspoon honey
- 1/4 cup brown sugar
- 1/4 teaspoon mint extract
- 1/4 teaspoon ground cinnamon

Directions

1. Put prepared bread cubes together with dried figs into a crock pot.

2. In a large mixing bowl, whisk together eggs, milk, butter, honey, brown sugar, mint extract, and cinnamon. Pour this mixture into the crock pot. Toss to coat.

3. Cook on low heat setting about 3 hours.

Spiced Apple Bread Pudding

(Ready in about 3 hours | Servings 8)

Ingredients

- 4 medium-sized apples, cored and chopped
- 3 cups bread, cubed
- 3 large-sized eggs
- 3/4 cup packed brown sugar
- 1/4 teaspoon allspice
- 1/2 teaspoon ground cloves
- 1 teaspoon ground cinnamon
- 1 teaspoon nutmeg
- 2 (12 fluid ounce) cans evaporated milk

Directions

1. Lay apples and bread cubes in a crock pot.
2. In a bowl, beat eggs until frothy. Stir in remaining ingredients and mix to combine.
3. Pour prepared egg mixture over apples and bread in the crock pot.
4. Cook on high heat setting for 4 hours or until custard forms.

Grandma's Apple Oatmeal

(Ready in about 6 hours | Servings 8)

Ingredients

- Margarine, melted
- 8 cups water
- 4 cups applesauce, unsweetened
- 1 1/2 cups steel cut oats
- 2 medium-sized apples, diced
- Grated nutmeg to taste
- Cardamom to taste
- Ground cinnamon to taste
- 2 tablespoons honey

Directions

1. Lightly grease your crock pot with margarine.

2. Combine the rest of ingredients in a large mixing bowl. Pour this mixture into the crock pot.

3. Cook on low heat setting at least 6 hours.

Chocolate Kid Friendly Oatmeal

(Ready in about 6 hours | Servings 10)

Ingredients

- Non-stick cooking spray
- 10 cups water
- 6 bananas, mashed
- 2 tablespoons chia seeds
- 7-8 dried dates
- 2 cups steel-cut oats
- 1 teaspoon ground cinnamon
- 1/2 cup cocoa powder, unsweetened

Directions

1. Lightly oil a crock pot with cooking spray.

2. Mix remaining ingredients in prepared crock pot.

3. Cook on low heat setting approximately 6 hours.

Vanilla Blueberry Quinoa

(Ready in about 6 hours | Servings 6)

Ingredients

- 4 cups vanilla flavoured almond milk
- 4 cups water
- 2 cups quinoa
- 2 cups blueberries
- 1/4 teaspoon grated nutmeg
- 1/4 teaspoon ground cinnamon
- 1/3 cup flax seeds
- 1/3 cup brown sugar

Directions

1. Stir all of the ingredients together in a crock pot.
2. Cover with a lid; cook on Low for 8 hours or overnight.

Apple Orange Quinoa

(Ready in about 8 hours | Servings 6)

Ingredients

- 2 cups water
- 1 cup quinoa
- 1 tablespoon fresh orange juice
- 2 cups apple juice
- 1 tablespoon chia seeds
- 1 teaspoon ground cinnamon
- 1/4 teaspoon grated nutmeg
- 1 cup raisins
- 1 teaspoon vanilla extract

Directions

1. Combine all ingredients together in your crock pot.
2. Cover with a lid; cook on low heat setting 6 to 8 hours.

Easy Yummy Breakfast Casserole

(Ready in about 12 hours | Servings 8)

Ingredients

- `1 (32-ounce) bag hash browns, frozen
- 2 carrots, thinly sliced
- 1 yellow onion, chopped
- 3 cloves garlic, minced
- 1 pound cooked ham
- 2 cups cheddar cheese, shredded
- 8 eggs
- 1 cup whole milk
- 1 teaspoon sea salt
- 1/4 teaspoon ground black pepper
- 1/4 teaspoon crushed red pepper

Directions

1. In a crock pot, alternate layers as follows: 1/2 of the hash browns, 1/2 of the carrots, 1/2 of the onions, 1/2 of the garlic, 1/2 of the cooked ham, and 1/2 of the cheddar cheese. Repeat one more time.

2. In a mixing bowl, beat the eggs; then add remaining ingredients.

3. Pour this mixture into the crockpot; cover; cook on low for 10 to 12 hours.

Restaurant Style Hash Browns

(Ready in about 8 hours | Servings 10)

Ingredients

- 1 (32-ounce) bag hash brown potatoes
- 1 pound turkey bacon, cooked
- 1 jalapeño pepper, minced
- 3 cloves garlic, crushed
- 1 cup spring onions, diced
- 1 cup Cheddar cheese
- 1 cup whole milk
- 12 eggs
- 1 teaspoon salt
- 1/2 teaspoon ground black pepper
- 1 teaspoon dried thyme

Directions

1. In your crock pot, alternate layers as follows: 1/2 of hash browns, 1/2 of bacon, 1/2 of jalapeño pepper, 1/2 of garlic, 1/2 of onions, 1/2 of cheese.

2. Next, add layers as follows: 1/2 of hash browns, 1/2 of bacon, 1/2 of jalapeño pepper, 1/2 of garlic, 1/2 of onions, 1/2 of cheese.

3. In a mixing bowl, combine milk, egg, salt, black pepper, and thyme. Pour this mixture into the crock pot.

4. Cook on low for 8 hours or overnight.

Creamy Coconut Oatmeal with Pumpkin Seeds

(Ready in about 8 hours | Servings 12)

Ingredients

- 4 cups steel cut oatmeal
- 2 cans coconut milk
- 10 cups water
- 1/4 teaspoon cardamom
- 1/2 teaspoon ground cinnamon
- 1 teaspoon almond extract
- 3 tablespoons coconut sugar
- 1/2 cup coconut flakes, for garnish
- Pumpkin seeds for garnish

Directions

1. In your crock pot, place oatmeal, coconut milk, water, cardamom, cinnamon, almond extract, and coconut sugar.
2. Turn to low and cook for about 8 hours, or until creamy.
3. Garnish with coconut flakes and pumpkin seeds!

Vanilla Almond Steel Cut Oats

(Ready in about 8 hours | Servings 12)

Ingredients

- 2 cups vanilla flavoured almond milk
- 2 cups steel cut oatmeal
- 8 cups water
- 1 teaspoon ground cinnamon
- 1/2 teaspoon grated nutmeg
- 1/4 teaspoon ground cloves
- 1 teaspoon vanilla extract
- 3 tablespoons maple syrup
- Raisins for garnish
- Chia seeds for garnish

Directions

1. In your crock pot, place almond milk, steel cut oatmeal, water, cinnamon, nutmeg, cloves, vanilla extract, and maple syrup.
2. Set the crock pot to low and cook your oatmeal for about 8 hours.
3. Garnish with raisins and chia seeds and enjoy!

Yummy Winter Breakfast

(Ready in about 8 hours | Servings 12)

Ingredients

- Non-stick cooking spray
- 1 (26-ounce) package hash brown potatoes
- 2 cups sausages
- 2 cups Cheddar cheese, shredded
- 10 eggs
- 1 cup milk
- 1/2 teaspoon dried tarragon
- 1 tablespoon granulated garlic
- 1/4 teaspoon ground black pepper
- 1 teaspoon salt

Directions

1. Oil your crock pot with cooking spray. Place hash brown potatoes in the bottom of the crock pot.
2. Heat a cast-iron skillet over medium-high flame. Then, cook sausage until they are browned, about 6 minutes. Then, spread cooked sausage over the hash brown potatoes.
3. Place shredded cheese on top.
4. In a large mixing bowl, beat the eggs with milk until frothy. Add spices and whisk to combine. Pour this mixture over the layers in the crock pot.
5. Cook for 6 to 8 hours on low-heat setting. Serve hot!

Cheesy Hash brown Casserole

(Ready in about 8 hours | Servings 6)

Ingredients

- 4 Bratwurst sausages, cooked
- 2 cups hash brown potatoes
- 1 cup sharp cheese, shredded
- 1 cup whole milk
- 4 large-sized eggs
- 1 tablespoon granulated garlic
- 1/4 teaspoon ground black pepper
- 1 teaspoon salt
- 1 teaspoon dry mustard

Directions

1. In a saucepan, cook the sausages until they are no longer pink. Place hash brown potatoes in a crock pot.

2. Transform cooked sausages to the crock pot together with their grease. Lay sharp cheese on top.

3. In a mixing bowl, combine the rest of ingredients. Pour this egg mixture into the crock pot.

4. Cook on low for about 8 hours, or overnight. Serve with mustard and sour cream.

Thanksgiving Bacon Casserole

(Ready in about 10 hours | Servings 10)

Ingredients

- 1 tablespoon olive oil
- 1 cup green onions, chopped
- 1 green bell pepper, thinly sliced
- 1 red bell pepper, thinly sliced
- 2 cloves garlic, minced
- 2 pounds hash brown potatoes, frozen and thawed
- 8 slices turkey bacon, cooked
- 1 1/2 cups Gouda, shredded
- 10 large-sized eggs
- 1 cup milk
- 1/4 teaspoon cayenne pepper
- 1 teaspoon sea salt
- 1/4 teaspoon ground black pepper
- 1 heaping tablespoon fresh parsley
- 1/4 cup chives

Directions

1. In a cast-iron skillet, heat olive oil over medium flame. Sauté green onions, bell peppers, and garlic until green onions are softened. Stir in hash brown potatoes and cook for 2 more minutes.

2. Lay 1/2 of the onion-potato mixture in your crock pot; then, lay 1/2 of the cooked bacon and top with 1/2 of shredded Gouda cheese.

3. Repeat layering in the same manner.

4. Whisk eggs together with remaining ingredients; pour this egg mixture over cheese layer in the crock pot.

5. Cook on low heat setting, 8 to 10 hours.

Amazing Spiced Omelette

(Ready in about 2 hours | Servings 4)

Ingredients

- 6 eggs
- 1/2 cup whole milk
- 1 teaspoon sea salt
- 1/4 teaspoon freshly ground black pepper
- 1 teaspoon dried basil
- 1 teaspoon dried oregano
- 1 teaspoon dried thyme
- 1/4 teaspoon chili powder
- 1 small head of cauliflower, broken into florets
- 1 medium-sized red onion, chopped
- 1 garlic clove, minced
- 1 cup Cheddar cheese, shredded
- Chives for garnish
- Olives for garnish

Directions

1. Lightly oil the inside of your crock pot.

2. In a mixing bowl or a measuring cup, whisk the eggs, milk, and spices. Mix until everything is well combined.

3. Add cauliflower florets, onions and garlic to crock pot. Add the spiced egg mixture.

4. Cover; then, cook on high approximately 2 hours, or until eggs are set.

5. Scatter shredded cheese on top and place a lid; let stand until cheddar cheese is melted.

6. Divide the omelette into wedges, garnish with chives and olives and serve.

Overnight Western Omelette

(Ready in about 12 hours | Servings 12)

Ingredients

- 2 pounds hash brown potatoes
- 1 cup spinach
- 1 pound cooked ham, sliced
- 2 cloves garlic, minced
- 1 yellow onion, diced
- 1 red bell pepper, seeded and diced
- 1 cup Gouda cheese, shredded
- 10 eggs
- 1 ½ cup milk
- 1 teaspoon sea salt
- 1/4 teaspoon freshly ground black pepper
- 1/4 teaspoon chili powder

Directions

1. Lightly oil your crock pot with non-stick cooking spray.
2. Alternate layers in your crock pot. Place 1/3 of the hash brown potatoes; place 1/3 of the spinach; then place 1/3 of cooked ham, 1/3 of garlic, 1/3 of the onion and 1/3 of bell pepper.
3. Top with shredded Gouda cheese; repeat same layers two more times.
4. In a large-sized bowl, mix together remaining ingredients. Pour in the crock pot.
5. Cover with a lid; cook on low-heat setting for 10 to 12 hours. Serve with toasted bread and mustard.

Vegetable and Ham Casserole

(Ready in about 8 hours | Servings 4)

Ingredients

- 1/4 cup extra-virgin olive oil
- 1 parsnip, peeled and chopped
- 1 turnip, peeled and chopped
- 2 cloves garlic, minced
- 1 cup ham, cooked and diced
- 3/4 cup whole milk

- 4 large-sized eggs
- 1/4 teaspoon turmeric
- 1/2 teaspoon rosemary
- 1/4 teaspoon dried thyme
- 1 tablespoon heaping fresh parsley
- Croutons for garnish

Directions

1. In your crock pot, combine together first four ingredients. Top with ham.
2. In a bowl, whisk together milk, eggs, and spices. Pour over the vegetables and ham in the crock pot.
3. Cook on low for 6 to 8 hours. Serve with croutons.

Creamy Oatmeal with Berries

(Ready in about 8 hours | Servings 4)

Ingredients

- 1 cup oats
- 1/2 teaspoon allspice
- 2 cups water
- 1 cup coconut water
- 1 pinch of grated nutmeg
- 1 pinch of ground cinnamon
- 1 pinch of salt
- 1 cup half-and-half cream
- 1/4 cup brown sugar
- Berries of choice, for garnish

Directions

1. Simply put all ingredients together (except berries) into your crock pot, just before going to bed.
2. Set the crock pot on low and cook overnight.
3. Serve with your favourite berries or mixed berries and enjoy warm!

Vegan Steel-Cut Oatmeal

(Ready in about 3 hours | Servings 6)

Ingredients

- 2 bananas, mashed
- 1 cup coconut water
- 4 cups water, divided
- 1 cup steel cut oats
- 1/4 cup dried figs
- 1/4 cup dried cranberries
- 1 teaspoon vanilla extract
- 1/2 teaspoon cardamom
- 1/2 teaspoon ground cinnamon
- Coconut sugar to taste

Directions

1. Purée bananas in your blender; then transfer mashed bananas to a crock pot.
2. Add remaining ingredients.
3. Cook on medium heat setting for 3 hours. Remember to stir every 30 minutes.
4. Serve with additional fruit if desired and enjoy!

Pumpkin Steel Cut Oats

(Ready in about 6 hours | Servings 6)

Ingredients

- Non-stick cooking spray
- 6 cups water
- 1 ½ cups steel-cut oats
- 1/2 cup brown sugar
- 1 (15-ounce) can pumpkin puree
- 1 teaspoon vanilla extract
- 1 teaspoon cardamom
- 1 tablespoon pumpkin pie spice
- 1 teaspoon ground cinnamon

Directions

1. Grease your crock pot with cooking spray.

2. Place all of the ingredients.

3. Cook on low for 6 hours. Divide among six serving bowls, sprinkle with pumpkin seeds and serve.

Mouth Watering French Toast Casserole

(Ready in about 5 hours | Servings 8)

Ingredients

- 2 bread loaves, cut into bite-sized cubes
- 1 teaspoon lemon zest
- 6 large-sized eggs
- 1 ½ cups milk
- 1 teaspoon pure almond extract
- 1 cup half-and-half
- 1/4 teaspoon grated nutmeg
- 1/4 teaspoon ground cloves
- 1 teaspoon ground cinnamon
- 1 cup brown sugar
- 3 tablespoons butter, melted
- 2 cups slivered almonds

Directions

1. Grease a crock pot with non-stick spray or with a melted butter.

2. Preheat the oven to 225 degrees F. Place prepared bread cubes on a cookie sheet and bake for about 30 minutes, or until the bread cubes are dried.

3. Lay the bread cubes on the bottom of your crock pot.

4. Mix together lemon zest, eggs, milk, almond extract, half-and-half, nutmeg, cloves, and cinnamon. Pour this mixture over the bread cubes in the crock pot.

5. In a separate small-sized bowl, combine the brown sugar, butter, and almonds. Stir in your crock pot.

6. Set crock pot to low; cover and cook approximately 5 hours.

7. Serve with fruits and maple syrup if desired.

Tater Tot Breakfast Casserole

(Ready in about 8 hours | Servings 8)

Ingredients

- 1 (30-ounces) package tater tots
- 1 cup bacon
- 1 cup green onions, chopped
- 2 cups sharp cheese, shredded
- 12 eggs
- 1 cup whole milk
- 3 tablespoons all-purpose flour
- 1/4 teaspoon ground black pepper
- 1/4 teaspoon cayenne pepper
- 1 teaspoon kosher salt

Directions

1. In a greased crock pot, place 1/3 of the tater tots, then, 1/3 of the bacon, 1/3 of green onions and finally, add 1/3 of shredded cheeses. Repeat these layers two more times, ending with the cheese.
2. In a large-sized bowl, whisk together the rest of ingredients; add to the crock pot.
3. Cover the crock pot and set on low; then, cook 6 to 8 hours.

Soft and Yummy Buttermilk Bread

(Ready in about 3 hours | Servings 8)

Ingredients

- 1 ½ cups all-purpose flour
- 1 teaspoon baking soda
- 1 teaspoon baking powder
- A pinch of salt
- 4 tablespoons butter, cut into pieces
- A pinch of grated nutmeg
- 3/4 cup buttermilk

Directions

1. In a large-sized mixing bowl, combine all-purpose flour, baking soda, baking powder, and salt; cut in butter until this mixture resembles small crumbs.

2. Stir in grated nutmeg and buttermilk.

3. Knead dough and then pat it into greased springform pan.

4. Place on a rack; cover and cook on high for about 2 ½ hours. Serve with milk.

Delicious Herb Bread

(Ready in about 3 hours | Servings 8)

Ingredients

- 1 ½ cups all-purpose flour
- 1 teaspoon baking powder
- 1 teaspoon baking soda
- 1 teaspoon dried dill weed
- 1 teaspoon ground black pepper
- 1 tablespoon dried chives
- A pinch of salt
- 4 tablespoons cold margarine, cut into pieces
- 3/4 cup buttermilk

Directions

1. In a mixing bowl, combine first seven ingredients. Then, cut in cold margarine until the mixture resembles small crumbs.

2. Stir in buttermilk and replace the dough on the floured surface.

3. Knead your dough for about 3 minutes.

4. Place on a rack and bake on high for about 2 hours. Serve warm and enjoy with cheese.

Cranberry-Raisin Bran Bread

(Ready in about 3 hours | Servings 16)

Ingredients

- 1/2 cup whole-wheat flour
- 1 ½ cups all-purpose flour
- 1 teaspoons baking powder
- 1 teaspoon baking soda
- 1 teaspoon pumpkin pie spice
- 1 teaspoon allspice

- 1/4 teaspoon grated nutmeg
- 1/2 teaspoon salt
- 1 ½ cups whole-bran cereal flakes
- 2 cups buttermilk
- 1/4 cup maple syrup
- 3 tablespoons butter, melted
- 2 eggs
- 1/2 cup dried cranberries, coarsely chopped
- 1/2 cup raisins, coarsely chopped
- 1/4 cup pecans, chopped
- 1/4 walnuts, chopped

Directions

1. In a large-sized mixing bowl, combine first nine ingredients until everything is well combined.
2. Next, add buttermilk, maple syrup, butter, eggs; stir to combine.
3. Gently fold in dried cranberries, raisins, pecans and walnuts.
4. Pour prepared dough into greased and floured loaf pan.
5. Bake on high for about 3 hours, or until a toothpick (or a knife) inserted in centre of your loaf comes out clean.
6. Serve with fruit jam or honey!

Sloppy Joe-Style Burgers

(Ready in about 3 hours | Servings 12)

Ingredients

- 2 pounds lean beef, ground
- 1 yellow onion, finely chopped
- 1 zucchini, chopped
- 1 yellow bell pepper, chopped
- 1 red bell pepper, chopped
- 1 cup button mushrooms, sliced
- 1/2 cup fried bacon, crumbled
- 1 teaspoon garlic powder
- 1/2 teaspoon chili powder
- 3/4 cup tomato paste
- 1 cup reduced-fat cheese, cubed
- 2 bay leaves

- 1 teaspoon sea salt
- 1/4 teaspoon ground black pepper
- 12 burger buns

Directions

1. In a large saucepan or a wok, over medium flame, cook ground beef with onion, zucchini and bell peppers. Cook until ground beef is browned.

2. Add to the slow cooker and then stir in remaining ingredients (except buns).

3. Cook on low for 2 to 3 hours. Serve on burger buns and add pickles if desired.

Nutty Granola with Coconut Oil

(Ready in about 2 hours 30 minutes | Servings 12)

Ingredients

- Cooking spray
- 4 cups rolled oats, old fashioned
- 1 cup almonds, chopped
- 1/2 cup pecans, chopped
- 1/2 teaspoon allspice
- 1 teaspoon cinnamon
- A pinch of salt
- 1/2 cup maple syrup
- 1/2 cup coconut oil, melted
- 1/4 cup brown sugar
- 1 teaspoon pure almond extract

Directions

1. Oil your crock pot with cooking spray. Add the rolled oats and reserve.

2. Add the almonds and pecans.

3. In a mixing bowl, whisk together remaining ingredients.

4. Pour this mixture over the oats and nuts in the crock pot.

5. Cook approximately 2 hours on low, stirring every 30 minutes.

6. Spread prepared granola out on a sheet of aluminium foil and let it cool.

Herbed Chili Cornbread

(Ready in about 2 hours | Servings 8)

Ingredients

- 3/4 cup all-purpose flour
- 1/4 cup cornmeal
- 1 tablespoon sugar
- 1 teaspoon baking soda
- 1 teaspoon baking powder
- 1 teaspoon dried basil
- 1 teaspoon ground cumin
- 1/2 teaspoon dried oregano
- 1/2 teaspoon salt
- 1 large-sized egg, beaten
- 1/2 cup buttermilk
- 1/4 poblano pepper, cooked and minced
- 1/4 cup whole kernel corn

Directions

1. Combine first ten ingredients in a large-sized mixing bowl.
2. Stir in buttermilk, poblano and corn and. Stir well to combine.
3. Transfer the dough to greased and floured baking pan
4. Next, place this baking pan on a rack in your crock pot. Cover; cook on high-heat setting approximately 2 hours.
5. Allow to cool for about 10 minutes before serving time.

Caramel Flavoured Banana Bread

(Ready in about 2 hours | Servings 8)

Ingredients

- 4 tablespoons butter, melted
- 1/4 cup applesauce
- 2 medium-sized eggs
- 1 tablespoon water
- 1 tablespoon milk
- 3/4 cup brown sugar
- 3 ripe bananas, mashed
- 1 ¾ cups all-purpose flour

- 1 teaspoon baking powder
- 1 teaspoon baking soda
- 1/4 teaspoon salt
- 1/4 cup almonds, coarsely chopped

Directions

1. In a bowl, beat butter, applesauce, eggs, water, milk, and brown sugar until creamy and uniform.
2. Add mashed bananas, flour, baking powder, baking soda, and salt. Stir in almonds.
3. Pour batter into suitable loaf pan.
4. Cook on high for about 3 hours until a toothpick (or knife) inserted in centre of your banana bread comes out clean.
5. Remove banana bread from loaf pan and cool to room temperature.

Pumpkin-Almond Bread

(Ready in about 3 hours 30 minutes | Servings 16)

Ingredients

- 1 cup pumpkin, canned
- 4 tablespoons margarine, melted
- 1/2 cup granulated sugar
- 2 medium-sized eggs, beaten
- 1/2 cup milk
- 2 cups all-purpose flour
- 1 teaspoon baking powder
- 1 teaspoon baking soda
- 1/4 teaspoon grated nutmeg
- 1 teaspoon pumpkin pie spice
- A pinch of salt
- 1/2 cup almonds, toasted and chopped

Directions

1. In a large-sized bowl, combine pumpkin with margarine and sugar until well blended; stir in eggs and milk.
2. Add flour, baking powder, baking soda, nutmeg, pumpkin pie spice, and salt; mix in chopped almonds.

3. Spoon batter into loaf pan and place in your crock pot. Cook on high about 3 ½ hours.

4. Allow your pumpkin bread to cool on a wire rack. Serve with honey and enjoy!

Cheesy Rosemary Bread

(Ready in about 2 hours | Servings 8)

Ingredients

- 6 tablespoons butter, room temperature
- 1 cup grated Parmesan cheese
- 1 tablespoon fresh rosemary
- 1 medium-sized loaf bread

Directions

1. Combine butter, Parmesan cheese and fresh rosemary and mix until everything is well blended.

2. Cut loaf bread into 8 slices. Spread both sides of bread slices with rosemary-cheese mixture.

3. Wrap bread slices in an aluminium foil.

4. Place in your crock pot and cook on low-heat setting for 2 hours. Uncover and allow to cool for about 5 minutes.

Vegetarian Sloppy Joes

(Ready in about 3 hours | Servings 8)

Ingredients

- 1 cup mushrooms, thinly sliced
- 1 cup onion, chopped
- 1 red bell pepper, chopped
- 1/4 poblano pepper, minced
- 2 teaspoons minced garlic
- 1 cup tomato catsup
- 1 teaspoon celery seeds
- 1 ½ cup water
- 1/4 cup sugar
- 1 teaspoon kosher salt
- 1/4 ground black pepper
- 8 whole-wheat hamburger buns

Directions

1. Combine mushrooms, onions, bell pepper, poblano pepper, garlic, catsup, celery seeds, water, and sugar.

2. Cover your crock pot with a lid and cook Sloppy Joes on high 2 to 3 hours. Season with salt and pepper.

3. Serve in buns with your favourite salad.

Deluxe Beef Sandwiches

(Ready in about 3 hours | Servings 12)

Ingredients

- 2 pounds lean ground beef
- 1 red bell pepper, chopped
- 1 green bell pepper, chopped
- 1 yellow onion, chopped
- 1 cup mushrooms, thinly sliced
- 2 cloves garlic, minced
- 1/2 cup fried turkey bacon, crumbled
- 3/4 cup tomato paste
- 1 tablespoon tomato catsup
- 2 tablespoons dry red wine
- 1 cup processed cheese, cubed
- Salt and pepper, to taste
- 12 sandwich buns, toasted

Directions

1. Heat a large skillet over medium heat; cook ground beef, bell peppers and onion until meat is browned and onion is translucent. Replace to the crock pot.

2. Add remaining ingredients, except sandwich buns; cook on low-heat setting for about 3 hours.

3. Serve on sandwich buns, garnish with mustard and salad and enjoy.

Best-ever Meat Sandwiches

(Ready in about 3 hours | Servings 12)

Ingredients

- 1 pound mixed beef and pork, ground
- 3/4 cup spring onions, chopped
- 1 clove garlic, minced
- 1 cup tomatoes, diced and drained
- 1 tablespoon Worcestershire sauce
- 1/4 cup packed light brown sugar
- 1 tablespoon mustard
- 1 heaping tablespoon cilantro
- 1 heaping tablespoon fresh parsley
- 1 teaspoon sea salt
- 1/4 teaspoon ground black pepper
- 1/4 teaspoon red pepper, crushed
- 12 sandwich rolls, toasted

Directions

1. In a wide and deep saucepan, over medium-low flame, cook mixed meat, spring onion, and garlic; crumble with a fork; add to the crock pot.
2. Add the rest of ingredients, except sandwich rolls; cook on high 2 to 3 hours.
3. Arrange sandwiches with rolls and serve with some extra ketchup and mustard.

BBQ Chicken Sandwiches

(Ready in about 8 hours | Servings 8)

Ingredients

- 1 pound chicken breasts, boneless and skinless
- 1/2 cup chicken stock
- 1/4 cup BBQ sauce
- 1/4 cup water
- 1 cup catsup
- 2 tablespoons white dry wine
- 1/3 cup yellow mustard
- 1 teaspoon tarragon
- 1 celery stalk, chopped
- 1 large-sized carrot, chopped
- 2 tablespoons brown sugar

- 1/2 cup chopped onion
- 1 clove garlic, minced
- Salt and pepper, to taste
- 8 hamburger buns

Directions

1. In your crock pot, combine all of the ingredients, except hamburger buns.
2. Cover with a lid and cook on low 6 to 8 hours, or overnight. Next, shred cooked chicken, adjust seasoning and serve with buns.

Saucy Pork Sandwiches

(Ready in about 8 hours | Servings 12)

Ingredients

For the Sandwiches:

- 1 pork loin roast, boneless
- 1 teaspoon garlic powder
- 1 teaspoon onion powder
- 1/4 teaspoon ground black pepper
- Sea salt to taste
- 1/2 cup water
- 12 sandwich buns

For the Sauce:

- 1 cup reduced-fat mayonnaise
- 1 clove garlic, minced
- 2 tablespoons lemon juice

Directions

1. Rub pork loin with garlic powder, onion powder, ground black pepper and salt to taste. Pour in water. Place in a crock pot and cook on low-heat setting overnight, or about 8 hours.
2. Remove pork from the crock pot and shred it.
3. Mix all ingredients for the sauce.
4. Spoon cooked pork onto bottoms of sandwich buns. Then spoon prepared sauce and place top of the buns. Enjoy!

Summer Granola with Seeds

(Ready in about 2 hours | Servings 16)

Ingredients

- 6 cups oats, old-fashioned
- 1 cup pumpkin seeds
- 1 cup sunflower kernels
- 1/2 teaspoon kosher salt
- 2 tablespoons orange juice
- 1/2 cup canola oil
- 1 cup maple syrup
- 1/2 cup dried figs, chopped
- 1 cup dried pineapple, chopped

Directions

1. In a crock pot, combine together oats, pumpkin seeds, sunflower kernels, and salt.
2. In a small-sized bowl, whisk orange juice, oil and maple syrup until mixture is blended. Stir this mixture into oat mixture.
3. Cook, covered, on high-heat setting for about 2 hours, stirring every 20 minutes.
4. Remove from the heat and let granola cool. Add dried figs and pineapple and stir well to combine.
5. Place prepared granola on a baking sheets, spreading evenly. Cool completely before storing.

Easy-to-make Date Granola

(Ready in about 3 hours | Servings 6)

Ingredients

- 1/4 cup honey
- 6 tablespoons applesauce
- 1/4 teaspoon cardamom
- 1/4 teaspoon grated nutmeg
- 1/4 teaspoon ground cloves
- 1 teaspoon ground cinnamon
- A pinch of salt
- 1 teaspoon vanilla extract
- 1/2 teaspoon maple extract
- 1 tablespoon hemp seeds

- 3 cups rolled oats
- 1 cup walnuts, toasted and chopped
- 1 cup Medjool dates, pitted and chopped

Directions

1. Put honey, applesauce, cardamom, nutmeg, cloves, cinnamon, salt, vanilla extract and maple extracts into your crock pot. Add hemp seeds and stir well to combine.
2. Stir in rolled oats and walnuts. Stir to combine.
3. Cook on high for 3 hours, venting the lid slightly. Stir occasionally. Allow to cool slightly and then add chopped dates.
4. Pour your granola onto a baking sheet and allow to cool completely before serving in the airtight containers.

Coconut Maple Granola

(Ready in about 3 hours | Servings 6)

Ingredients

- 1/4 cup maple syrup
- 2 tablespoons canola oil
- 1 cup hulled sunflower seeds
- 2 tablespoons chia seeds
- 1/4 teaspoon ground cloves
- 1 teaspoon ground cinnamon
- A pinch of salt
- 1 teaspoon pure vanilla extract
- 1 cup coconut flakes
- 3 cups rolled oats
- 1 cup slivered almonds
- 1 cup dried cherries, chopped

Directions

1. Combine maple syrup, canola oil, sunflower seeds, chia seeds, ground cloves, cinnamon, salt, vanilla extract, coconut flakes and rolled oats in a crock pot.
2. Cook approximately 3 hours, stirring occasionally. Allow granola to cool for about 15 minutes; add almonds and dried cherries. Stir until everything is well incorporated.
3. Spread onto a baking sheet in order to cool completely.

Pulled Pork Sandwiches

(Ready in about 3 hours | Servings 12)

Ingredients

- 1 pork loin roast, boneless
- 1 teaspoon curry powder
- 1 teaspoon cayenne pepper
- 1/2 teaspoon grated ginger
- 1 cup beef broth
- Salt to taste
- 1/4 teaspoon black pepper
- 1 bay leaf
- 48 bread slices

Directions

1. Rub pork loin roast with curry powder and cayenne pepper.
2. Place seasoned pork in your crock pot; add grated ginger and beef broth. Add salt, black pepper and bay leaf.
3. Cook on low for about 3 hours. Cut cooked pork into thin shreds. Taste and adjust the seasonings.
4. Make sandwiches spooning meat with sauce into each bread slice.

Winter Beef Sandwiches

(Ready in about 8 hours | Servings 12)

Ingredients

- 1 medium-sized beef chuck roast, boneless
- 1/2 teaspoon sea salt
- 1/4 teaspoon black pepper
- 1 teaspoon dried basil
- 1 tablespoon fresh sage
- 2 cups beef broth
- 1 cup dry red wine
- 1 clove garlic, minced
- 7-8 peppercorns
- 12 sandwich rolls
- Sauerkraut for garnish
- Chillies for garnish

Directions

1. Season beef chuck roast with sea salt and black pepper and lay in a crock pot.

2. Add basil, sage, beef broth, wine, garlic, and peppercorns. Cover and cook on low approximately 8 hours, or overnight.

3. Serve cooked beef on sandwich rolls with sauerkraut and chillies.

Hearty Sausage Sandwiches

(Ready in about 6 hours | Servings 6)

Ingredients

- 8 links fresh sausages
- 1 cup beef broth
- 4 cups spaghetti sauce
- 1 chili pepper, minced
- 1 red bell pepper, sliced
- 1 green bell pepper, sliced
- 1 cup spring onions, chopped
- 1 heaping tablespoon fresh parsley
- 1 heaping tablespoon fresh cilantro
- 6 cocktail buns, split lengthwise

Directions

1. In a crock pot, place the sausage links, beef broth, spaghetti sauce, chili pepper, bell peppers and spring onions. Add parsley and cilantro. Stir to combine.

2. Cover with a lid; cook on Low for 6 hours. Serve on cocktail rolls and enjoy!

Country Smoked Sausages

(Ready in about 6 hours | Servings 6)

Ingredients

- 1 tablespoon extra-virgin olive oil
- 6 green onions, sliced
- 1 yellow bell pepper, sliced
- 1 red bell pepper, sliced
- 4 garlic cloves, smashed
- 2 pounds smoked sausage

- 1 (28-ounce) can tomatoes, diced
- 1 teaspoon salt
- 1/2 teaspoon ground black pepper
- 1/2 teaspoon red pepper flakes, crushed
- Mustard for garnish

Directions

1. In a large skillet, heat olive oil over medium flame. Sauté onions, bell peppers, garlic and sausages until vegetables are tender and sausages are lightly browned. Transfer to the crock pot.
2. Add tomatoes, salt, black pepper and red pepper.
3. Cook on low approximately 6 hours. Serve with your favourite mustard.

Must-Eat Beef Tacos

(Ready in about 8 hours | Servings 6)

Ingredients

- 1 ½ pounds beef chuck roast, boneless
- 1 large-sized red onion, sliced
- 1 cup beef stock
- 1 (16-ounce) jar taco sauce
- 12 taco shells
- 2 cucumbers, thinly sliced
- 2 ripe tomatoes, sliced

Directions

1. Lay beef chuck roast and sliced onion in a crock pot. Pour in beef stock and taco sauce.
2. Cook on LOW for 8 hours or overnight.
3. In the morning, cut beef into shreds.
4. Fill taco shells with shredded beef; add cucumber and tomato and serve!

Oatmeal with Prunes and Apricots

(Ready in about 8 hours | Servings 4)

Ingredients

- 1 cup steel cut oats
- 4 ½ cups water
- 1/2 teaspoon grated ginger
- 1/2 teaspoon allspice
- 1/2 teaspoon ground cinnamon
- 1/2 teaspoon salt
- 3 tablespoons butter
- 1/2 cup prunes
- 1/2 cup dried apricots
- Maple syrup, to taste

Directions

1. Put all ingredients into a crock pot.
2. Cover and cook on low-heat setting approximately 8 hours.
3. Serve with milk and some extra fruit if desired.

Muesli with Coconut and Peanuts

(Ready in about 2 hours | Servings 12)

Ingredients

- 4 cups rolled oats
- 4 cups water
- 1 teaspoon allspice
- 1/4 teaspoon turmeric
- 1 cup wheat germ
- 1 cup baking natural bran
- 1/2 cup shredded coconut, unsweetened
- 1/2 cup brown sugar
- 4 tablespoons butter, melted
- 1 teaspoon almond extract
- 2 tablespoons pumpkin seeds
- Peanuts for garnish

Directions

1. Add all of the ingredients, except peanuts, to your crock pot.
2. Cover with a lid; cook on high-heat setting approximately 2 hours, stirring twice. Divide among 12 serving bowls, scatter chopped peanuts on top and serve!

Cheese Steak Sandwiches

(Ready in about 8 hours | Servings 8)

Ingredients

- 1 pound round steak, thinly sliced
- 1 cup onions, sliced
- 1 green bell pepper, sliced
- 1 cup beef stock
- 1 clove garlic, minced
- 2 tablespoon red dry wine
- 1 tablespoon Worcestershire sauce
- 1 teaspoon celery seeds
- 1/2 teaspoon salt
- 1/4 teaspoon ground black pepper
- 8 hamburger buns
- 1 cup mozzarella cheese, shredded

Directions

1. Combine all of the ingredients, except buns and cheese, in your crock pot.
2. Cover and cook on low 6 to 8 hours.
3. Make sandwiches with buns, prepared meat mixture and cheese. Serve warm and enjoy!

Beer Brats with Mushrooms and Onion

(Ready in about 8 hours | Servings 8)

Ingredients

- 8 fresh bratwurst
- 2 (12-ounce) 3 bottles beer
- 1 cup mushrooms, sliced
- 2-3 cloves garlic, minced
- 1 red onion, sliced
- 1 red bell pepper, sliced
- 1 teaspoon sea salt
- 1/4 teaspoon ground black pepper
- 1 teaspoon minced poblano pepper
- 8 hot dog buns

Directions

1. Combine all ingredients, except buns, in a crock pot.

2. Cook, covered, on low 6 to 8 hours.

3. Serve cooked bratwurst and veggies in buns. Add mustard, catsup and sour cream if desired.

Yummy Sausage and Sauerkraut Sandwiches

(Ready in about 8 hours | Servings 6)

Ingredients

- 6 fresh sausages of choice
- 1 medium-sized onion, chopped
- 1 cup sauerkraut
- 1 small-sized apple, peeled, cored and thinly sliced
- 1 teaspoon caraway seeds
- 1/2 cup chicken broth
- Salt to taste
- 1/2 teaspoon ground black pepper
- 6 hot dog buns
- Catsup for garnish
- Mustard for garnish

Directions

1. Lay sausages in a crock pot. Then place onion, sauerkraut, apple, caraway seeds, chicken broth, salt and black pepper.

2. Cook, covered, on low 6 to 8 hours.

3. Make sandwiches with buns and serve with catsup and mustard.

Christmas Sausage Casserole

(Ready in about 8 hours | Servings 8)

Ingredients

- Non-stick cooking spray butter flavour
- 1 (26-ounce) package frozen hash brown potatoes, thawed
- 1 zucchini, thinly sliced
- 1 cup whole milk
- 10 eggs, beaten
- 1 teaspoon sea salt

- 1/4 teaspoon crushed red pepper flakes
- 1/4 teaspoon ground black pepper
- 1 teaspoon caraway seeds
- 1 tablespoon ground mustard
- 2 cups sausages
- 2 cups Cheddar cheese, shredded

Directions

1. Grease a crock pot with non-stick cooking spray. Spread hash browns to cover the bottom of the crock pot. Then lay zucchini slices.
2. In a medium-sized bowl, whisk milk, eggs, salt, red pepper, black pepper, caraway seeds, and ground mustard.
3. Heat a cast-iron skillet over medium flame. Next, cook the sausages until they are browned and crumbly, about 6 minutes; discard grease.
4. Lay sausage on zucchini layer, then spread Cheddar cheese. Pour egg-milk mixture over cheese layer.
5. Cook on low for 6 to 8 hours. Serve warm with some extra mustard.

Overnight Sausage Casserole

(Ready in about 8 hours | Servings 12)

Ingredients

- 1 ½ cups spicy sausage
- 1 red onion, chopped
- 2 garlic cloves, smashed
- 1 sweet bell pepper, thinly sliced
- 1 jalapeño pepper
- 1/4 cup fresh parsley
- 1 heaping tablespoon fresh cilantro
- 1 (30-ounce) package hash brown potatoes, shredded and thawed
- 1 1/2 cups sharp cheese, shredded
- 1 cup milk
- 12 eggs
- 1 teaspoon dry mustard
- 1 teaspoon celery seeds
- 1/2 teaspoon salt
- 1/8 teaspoon pepper
- 1/4 teaspoon cayenne pepper

Directions

1. In a non-stick medium skillet, over medium flame, cook sausage; drain and set aside.

2. In a medium-sized bowl, combine onions, garlic, sweet bell pepper, jalapeño pepper, parsley and cilantro. Stir well to combine.

3. Alternate layers. Lay 1/3 of the hash browns, sausage, onion mixture and cheese into the crock pot. In the same way, repeat layers twice.

4. In a separate bowl, beat the rest of ingredients. Pour this mixture into the crock pot by spreading equally.

5. Cover and cook on low approximately 8 hours or overnight. Serve warm.

Sunrise Pork Sandwiches

(Ready in about 8 hours | Servings 12)

Ingredients

- 1 medium-sized pork butt roast
- 1/4 teaspoon black pepper
- 1/4 teaspoon crushed red pepper flakes
- 1 teaspoon sea salt
- 1 teaspoon dried thyme
- 1 tablespoon liquid smoke flavouring
- 12 pretzel buns

Directions

1. Pierce pork with a carving fork for better slow-cooking.

2. Season with spices and then spread liquid smoke over pork butt roast.

3. Lay pork roast into a crock pot.

4. Cover and cook on Low for 8 to 10 hours, turning once or twice.

5. Shred cooked pork roast, adding drippings to moisten. Make sandwiches with pretzel buns and enjoy!

Beer Pulled Pork Sandwiches

(Ready in about 10 hours | Servings 16)

Ingredients

- 1 medium-sized pork butt roast
- 1 large-sized onion, chopped
- 3 cloves garlic, smashed
- 2 carrots, thinly sliced
- 1/2 teaspoon ground black pepper
- 1/2 teaspoon cayenne pepper
- 1 teaspoon sea salt
- 1 teaspoon ground black pepper
- 1 teaspoon cumin powder
- 1 (12 fluid ounce) can beer
- 1 cup barbeque sauce

Directions

1. Pierce pork with a carving fork.
2. Put all of the ingredients, except barbeque sauce, into a crock pot.
3. Set crock pot to high; cook for 1 hour. Then reduce the heat to low and cook 6 to 8 hours longer.
4. Shred the cooked pork and return it to the crock pot. Add barbeque sauce and cook an additional 1 hour.
5. Serve on your favourite hamburger buns and enjoy!

Mom's Apple Crisp

(Ready in about 3 hours | Servings 6)

Ingredients

- 2/3 cup old-fashioned oats
- 2/3 cup brown sugar, packed
- 2/3 cup all-purpose flour
- 1 teaspoon allspice
- 1 teaspoon cinnamon
- 1/2 cup butter
- 5-6 tart apples, cored and sliced

Directions

1. In a medium-sized mixing bowl, combine together first six ingredients. Mix until everything is well blended.

2. Place sliced apples in your crock pot.

3. Sprinkle oat mixture over apples in the crock pot.

4. Cover the crock pot with three paper towels. Set the crock pot to high and cook for about 3 hours.

Vegetarian Quinoa with Spinach

(Ready in about 3 hours | Servings 4)

Ingredients

- 2 tablespoons olive oil
- 3/4 cup spring onions, chopped
- 1 cup spinach
- 2 garlic cloves, minced
- 1 cup quinoa, rinsed
- 2 ½ cups vegetable broth
- 1 cup water
- 1 tablespoon fresh basil
- 1 tablespoon fresh cilantro
- 1/4 teaspoon ground black pepper
- Salt to taste
- 1/3 cup Parmesan cheese

Directions

1. In a saucepan, heat olive oil over medium-high flame. Sauté spring onions, spinach and garlic until tender and fragrant. Transfer to a crock pot.

2. Add remaining ingredients, except the cheese, and cover with a lid.

3. Cook on LOW for about 3 hours.

4. Stir in Parmesan cheese, taste and adjust the seasonings; serve!

Easy Cheesy Quinoa with Veggies

(Ready in about 3 hours | Servings 4)

Ingredients

- 2 tablespoons margarine, melted
- 1 medium-sized onion, chopped
- 1 garlic clove, minced
- 1 cup button mushrooms, sliced
- 1 sweet red bell pepper
- 1 cup quinoa, rinsed
- 2 cups vegetable broth
- 1 ½ cup water
- 1 heaping tablespoon fresh parsley
- 1 heaping tablespoon fresh cilantro
- 1/4 teaspoon crushed red pepper flakes
- A pinch of ground black pepper
- Salt to taste
- 1/3 cup Parmesan cheese

Directions

1. In a medium-sized skillet, heat margarine over medium heat.
2. Sauté onions, garlic, mushrooms and red bell pepper in hot margarine for about 6 minutes or until just tender. Replace to a crock pot.
3. Add the rest of ingredients, except Parmesan cheese; set the crock pot to low and cook for about 3 hours.
4. Add Parmesan cheese and enjoy warm!

Kale Frittata with Sausages

(Ready in about 3 hours | Servings 6)

Ingredients

- Non-stick cooking spray
- 3/4 cup kale
- 1 sweet red bell pepper, sliced
- 1 sweet green pepper, sliced
- 1 medium-sized red onion, sliced
- 8 eggs, beaten
- 1/2 teaspoon ground black pepper
- 1 teaspoon salt
- 1 1/3 cup sausages

Directions

1. Combine all ingredients in a well-greased crock pot.

2. Set the crock pot to low and cook until frittata is set or about 3 hours.

3. You can reheat this frittata in microwave for 60 seconds.

Delicious Weekend Frittata

(Ready in about 3 hours | Servings 6)

Ingredients

- Non-stick cooking spray
- 1 1/3 cup cooked ham
- 1 red bell pepper, sliced
- 1 sweet green bell pepper, sliced
- 1 spring onions, sliced
- 8 eggs, beaten
- 1 tablespoon basil
- 1 heaping tablespoon fresh cilantro
- 1 tablespoon fresh parsley
- 1 teaspoon salt
- 1/4 teaspoon ground black pepper
- 1/4 teaspoon cayenne pepper
- A few drops of tabasco sauce

Directions

1. Grease a crock pot with non-stick cooking spray. Combine all ingredients in the crock pot.

2. Set the crock pot to low and cook your frittata approximately 3 hours.

3. Divide among six serving plates and sprinkle with chopped chives, if desired; garnish with sour cream and serve!

Vegetarian Breakfast Delight

(Ready in about 4 hours | Servings 4)

Ingredients

- 2 tablespoons canola oil
- 1 cup scallions, chopped
- 1 garlic clove, minced
- 2 medium-sized carrots, thinly sliced
- 1 celery stalk, chopped
- 1 cup quinoa, rinsed
- 2 cups vegetable stock
- 1 ½ cup water
- 1 tablespoon fresh cilantro
- A pinch of ground black pepper
- 1/4 teaspoon dried thyme
- 1/4 teaspoon dried dill weed
- Salt to taste
- 1/3 cup Parmesan cheese

Directions

1. In a medium-sized skillet, heat canola oil over medium heat.
2. Sauté scallions, garlic, carrots and celery for about 5 minutes, or until the vegetables are just tender. Transfer the vegetables to a crock pot.
3. Add quinoa, vegetable stock, water, cilantro, black pepper, dried thyme, dill weed and salt to taste.
4. Cover and cook on LOW approximately 4 hours.
5. Scatter Parmesan on top and serve warm!

Protein Rich Bacon Frittata

(Ready in about 4 hours | Servings 6)

Ingredients

- Non-stick cooking spray
- 1 cup scallions, sliced
- 1 1/3 cup bacon
- 1 cup mushrooms, sliced
- 1 poblano pepper, minced
- 10 eggs, beaten

- 1 heaping tablespoon fresh cilantro
- 1 teaspoon salt
- 1/4 teaspoon ground black pepper
- 1/4 teaspoon crushed red pepper flakes

Directions

1. Combine all of the ingredients in greased crock pot.
2. Next, set your crock pot to low; cover and cook the frittata 3 to 4 hours.
3. Cut into six wedges, garnish with mustard and serve!

Chili Mushroom Omelette

(Ready in about 4 hours | Servings 4)

Ingredients

- Non-stick cooking spray
- 1 green onions, sliced
- 2 cloves garlic, minced
- 2 cups mushrooms, sliced
- 1 chilli pepper, minced
- 2 ripe tomatoes, sliced
- 8 eggs, beaten
- 1 tablespoon fresh cilantro
- 1 teaspoon salt
- 1/4 teaspoon ground black pepper
- 1/4 teaspoon cayenne pepper

Directions

1. In your crock pot, place all of the ingredients.
2. Cover with a lid; cook on low 3 to 4 hours.
3. Cut into wedges and serve warm with sour cream and catsup.

Banana Pecan Oatmeal

(Ready in about 8 hours | Servings 4)

Ingredients

- 2 cups water
- 2 ripe bananas
- 1 cup steel-cut oats
- 1/4 cup pecans, coarsely chopped
- 2 cups soy milk
- 1/2 teaspoon cinnamon
- 1 teaspoon pure almond extract
- A pinch of salt
- Honey to taste

Directions

1. Pour water into your crock pot. Use an oven safe bowl (glass casserole dish works here) and place it inside your crock pot.
2. Mash the bananas with a fork or blend them in a blender. Transfer to the oven safe bowl.
3. Add remaining ingredients to the bowl.
4. Cook on low overnight or for 8 hours.
5. Stir well before serving and add toppings of choice. Enjoy!

Hearty Oatmeal with Nuts

(Ready in about 8 hours | Servings 4)

Ingredients

- 1 large-sized ripe banana
- 1 cup steel-cut oats
- 1/4 cup walnuts, coarsely chopped
- 2 tablespoons chia seeds
- 1 tablespoon hemp seeds
- 2 cups milk
- 1/4 teaspoon grated nutmeg
- 1/2 teaspoon cardamom
- 1/2 teaspoon cinnamon
- 1 teaspoon pure vanilla extract
- 2 cups water
- Maple syrup for garnish
- Fresh fruits for garnish

Directions

1. Mash banana with a fork. Add mashed banana to an oven proof dish. Stir in remaining ingredients.

2. Pour water into a crock pot.

3. Place the oven proof dish inside the crock pot. Cook on low heat setting overnight or for 8 hours. Top with maple syrup and fresh fruit.

Tomato Artichoke Frittata

(Ready in about 2 hours | Servings 4)

Ingredients

- Non-stick cooking spray
- 6 large-sized eggs, beaten
- 1 cup chopped artichoke hearts
- 1 medium-sized tomato, chopped
- 1 red bell pepper, chopped
- 1 teaspoon onion powder
- 1 teaspoon garlic powder
- 1/4 teaspoon ground black pepper
- 1/4 teaspoon cayenne pepper
- 1/4 cup Swiss cheese, grated

Directions

1. Coat a crock pot with cooking spray.
2. Add all of the ingredients to the crock pot.
3. Cover with a lid and cook on low-heat setting for about 2 hours.
4. Sprinkle with cheese; let stand for a few minutes until the cheese is melted.

Sausage Mushroom Omelette Casserole

(Ready in about 3 hours | Servings 4)

Ingredients

- 1 pound chicken breast sausage, sliced
- 1 cup scallions, chopped
- 1 cup mushrooms, sliced
- 4 medium-sized eggs

- 1 cup whole milk
- 1 teaspoon sea salt
- 1/4 teaspoon ground black pepper
- 1/2 teaspoon dry mustard
- 1/2 teaspoon granulated garlic
- 1/2 cup Swiss cheese, grated

Directions

1. Arrange sausage in a crock pot. Then, place scallions and mushrooms over the sausages.
2. In a mixing bowl, whisk together eggs, milk, and spices. Whisk to combine.
3. Cook on low-heat setting about 3 hours. Then spread cheese on top and allow to melt.
4. Serve warm with mayonnaise and mustard.

Pumpkin Pie Steel Cut Oats

(Ready in about 8 hours | Servings 4)

Ingredients

- 1 cup steel-cut oats
- 3 cups water
- 1/4 teaspoon ground cinnamon
- 1 cup pumpkin purée
- 1 teaspoon vanilla extract
- A pinch of salt
- 1 tablespoon pumpkin pie spice
- 1/2 cup maple syrup

Directions

1. Combine all ingredients in your crock pot.
2. Cover and cook on low overnight or for 8 hours.
3. Serve warm with raisins or dates, if desired!

Cocoa Steel Cut Oats

(Ready in about 8 hours | Servings 4)

Ingredients

- 3 ½ cups water
- 1 cup steel-cut oats
- 1/4 teaspoon grated nutmeg
- 1/2 teaspoon ground cinnamon
- 3 tablespoons cocoa powder, unsweetened
- A pinch of salt
- 1/2 teaspoon pure vanilla extract
- 1/2 teaspoon pure hazelnut extract

Directions

1. Add all of the ingredients to your crock pot.
2. Cook on low heat settings overnight or for 8 hours.
3. Stir before serving and add natural sweetener, if desired.

Nutty Pumpkin Oatmeal with Cranberries

(Ready in about 9 hours | Servings 4)

Ingredients

- 1 cup steel-cut oats
- 3 cups water
- 1 cup whole milk
- A pinch of salt
- 1 tablespoon pumpkin pie spice
- 1/2 teaspoon cardamom
- 1/4 cup pumpkin purée
- 2 tablespoons honey
- 1/2 cup dried cranberries
- 1/2 cup almonds, coarsely chopped

Directions

1. In a crock pot, place steel-cut oats, water, milk, salt, pumpkin pie spice, cardamom pumpkin purée, and honey.
2. Cook overnight or 8 to 9 hours.
3. Divide among serving bowls; sprinkle with dried cranberries and almonds; serve.

Cocoa Oatmeal with Bananas

(Ready in about 8 hours | Servings 4)

Ingredients

- 3 cups water
- 1 cup milk
- 1 cup steel-cut oats
- 1/2 teaspoon ground cinnamon
- 1 banana, mashed
- 4 tablespoons cocoa powder, unsweetened
- 1/2 teaspoon pure vanilla extract
- 1 banana, sliced
- Chopped pecans for garnish

Directions

1. Pour water and milk into a crock pot. Then place steel-cut oats, cinnamon, mashed banana, cocoa powder, and vanilla.

2. Set your crock pot to low and cook overnight or for 8 hours.

3. Stir before serving time; divide among serving bowls; garnish with banana and pecans and enjoy.

Cheese and Ham Quiche

(Ready in about 2 hours | Servings 4)

Ingredients

- Butter flavour non-stick cooking spray
- 4 slices of whole-wheat bread, toasted
- 2 cups sharp cheese, grated
- 1/2 pound ham, cooked and cut into bite-sized cubes
- 6 large-sized eggs
- 1/2 teaspoon Dijon mustard
- 1 cup heavy cream
- 1/4 teaspoon turmeric powder
- 1 tablespoon fresh parsley, coarsely chopped
- 1/2 teaspoon sea salt
- 1/4 teaspoon crushed red pepper
- 1/4 teaspoon freshly ground black pepper

Directions

1. Generously grease the inside of a crock pot with non-stick cooking spray.

2. Grease each slice of toasted bread with non-stick cooking spray; tear greased bread into pieces; arrange in the crock pot.

3. Spread 1/2 of the sharp cheese over the toast, and then place the cooked ham pieces over the cheese; top with the remaining cheese.

4. In a medium-sized mixing bowl or a measuring cup, beat the eggs together with the rest of ingredients; pour this mixture into the crock pot.

5. Cover and cook on high-heat setting for 2 hours. Serve warm with mayonnaise or sour cream, if desired.

Country Sausage and Cauliflower Breakfast

(Ready in about 6 hours | Servings 8)

Ingredients

- 1 pound sausage
- Non-stick spray
- 1 cup condensed cream of potato soup
- 1 cup whole milk
- 1 teaspoon dry mustard
- Salt to taste
- 1/2 teaspoon freshly ground black pepper
- 1 tablespoon fresh basil or 1 teaspoon dried basil
- 1 (28-ounce) package frozen hash browns, thawed
- 1 cup cauliflower, broken into florets
- 1 cup carrots, sliced
- 1/2 cup Cheddar cheese, shredded

Directions

1. In a cast-iron skillet, brown the sausage; cut into bite-sized chunks.

2. Coat the inside of the crock pot with non-stick spray. Add all ingredients, except Cheddar cheese; gently stir to combine.

3. Cover with a lid and cook for about 6 hours on low. Scatter Cheddar cheese on top. Let sit for 30 minutes before serving.

Broccoli Sausage Casserole

(Ready in about 6 hours | Servings 6)

Ingredients

- 2 tablespoons olive oil
- 3/4 pound sausage
- 1 cup beef broth
- 1 cup milk
- 1 teaspoon dry mustard
- 1/4 teaspoon cayenne pepper
- 1/2 teaspoon black pepper
- 2 pounds frozen hash browns, thawed
- 1 cup broccoli, broken into florets
- 1 cup carrots, sliced
- 1/2 cup Cheddar cheese, shredded

Directions

1. Coat the inside of the crock pot with olive oil.

2. In a medium-sized saucepan, over medium-high heat, cook the sausages until they are no longer pink or about 10 minutes. Transfer the sausage to the greased crock pot.

3. Add in broth, milk, mustard, cayenne pepper, black pepper, hash browns, broccoli and carrot. Cook on low for 6 hours.

4. Next, top with shredded cheese and allow to melt.

5. Serve warm with your favourite mayonnaise and some extra mustard.

Winter Morning Sausage and Vegetables

(Ready in about 6 hours | Servings 6)

Ingredients

- Non-stick spray
- 3/4 pound highly-spiced sausage
- 1 large-sized onion
- 1 sweet green bell pepper
- 1 sweet red bell pepper, chopped
- 1 cup whole milk
- 1 cup vegetable or beef broth
- 1/2 teaspoon chili powder

- 1/2 teaspoon black pepper
- Sea salt to taste
- 2 pounds frozen hash browns, thawed
- 1/2 cup Cheddar cheese, shredded

Directions

1. Oil the inside of your crock pot with non-stick spray.
2. In a medium-sized skillet, cook the sausage about 10 minutes, until it's browned. Replace to the crock pot.
3. Stir in remaining ingredients, except Cheddar cheese.
4. Set the crock pot to low and cook about 6 hours.
5. Scatter Cheddar cheese on top. Serve warm!

Eggs Florentine with Oyster Mushroom

(Ready in about 2 hours | Servings 4)

Ingredients

- Non-stick spray
- 2 cups Monterey Jack cheese, shredded
- 1 cup Swiss chard
- 1 cup oyster mushroom, sliced
- 2-3 garlic cloves, smashed
- 1 small onion, peeled and diced
- 5 large-sized eggs
- 1 cup light cream
- Salt to taste
- 1/4 teaspoon ground black pepper

Directions

1. Treat the inside of the crock pot with non-stick spray. Spread 1 cup of the Monterey Jack cheese over the bottom of the crock pot.
2. Then lay the spinach on top of the cheese.
3. Next, add the oyster mushroom in a layer. Top the mushroom layer with the garlic and onion.

4. In a measuring cup or a mixing bowl, beat the eggs with remaining ingredients. Pour this mixture over the layers in the crock pot.

5. Top with the remaining 1 cup of cheese.

6. Set your crock pot to high, cover with a lid and cook for 2 hours.

Cheese and Swiss chard Casserole

(Ready in about 4 hours | Servings 4)

Ingredients

- Butter flavour non-stick cooking spray
- 4 large-sized eggs
- 1 cup cottage cheese
- 3 tablespoons all-purpose flour
- 1 tablespoon fresh cilantro
- 1/2 teaspoon sea salt
- 1/4 teaspoon freshly ground black pepper
- 1/2 teaspoon dried thyme
- 1/2 teaspoon baking soda
- 2 tablespoons butter, melted
- 1 cup sharp cheese, grated
- 1 cup scallions, finely chopped
- 1 cup Swiss chard

Directions

1. Coat a heatproof casserole dish with cooking spray. Pour 2 cups of water into the crock pot.

2. Add the eggs and whisk them until frothy. Next, stir in the cottage cheese.

3. Add the flour, cilantro, sea salt, black pepper, thyme, baking soda, and butter. Mix well until everything is well incorporated.

4. Next, stir in remaining ingredients; adjust the seasonings.

5. Place the heatproof casserole dish onto the cooking rack in the crock pot; cover with a suitable lid and cook on low-heat setting approximately 4 hours.

6. Let cool to room temperature before serving time and enjoy!

Nutty Banana Frittata

(Ready in about 18 hours | Servings 6)

Ingredients

- 1 tablespoon canola oil
- 1 loaf bread, cut into cubes
- 1 cup cream cheese
- 2 ripe bananas
- 1 cup almonds, coarsely chopped
- 10 large eggs
- 1/4 cup maple syrup
- 1 cup half-and-half
- A pinch of salt

Directions

1. Grease the inside of your crock pot with canola oil.
2. Place 1/2 of bread cubes in the bottom of the crock pot. Then, evenly spread 1/2 of the cream cheese.
3. Arrange the slices of 1 banana over the cream cheese. Then scatter 1/2 of the chopped almonds.
4. Repeat the layers one more time.
5. In a mixing bowl or a measuring cup, whisk the eggs together with maple syrup, half-and-half and salt; pour over the layers in the crock pot.
6. Set in a refrigerator at least 12 hours. After that, cover and cook on low for 6 hours. Serve with some extra bananas if desired.

Yummy Spiced Pumpkin Frittata

(Ready in about 6 hours | Servings 6)

Ingredients

- 2 tablespoons coconut oil, melted
- 1 loaf bread, cut into small cubes
- 1 cup cream cheese
- 1 cup pumpkin, shredded
- 2 bananas, sliced
- 1 cup walnuts, coarsely chopped

- 8 eggs
- 1 cup half-and-half
- 2 tablespoons raw honey
- 1/2 teaspoon ground cinnamon
- 1/4 teaspoon grated cardamom
- 1/2 teaspoon allspice
- 1 teaspoon of pumpkin spice
- Powdered sugar for garnish

Directions

1. Coat the inside of a crock pot with coconut oil.
2. Place 1/2 of bread in the crock pot. Then, place 1/2 of the cream cheese.
3. Next, evenly spread 1/2 of shredded pumpkin. Lay the slices of 1 banana over the pumpkin. Scatter 1/2 of the chopped walnuts over the bananas.
4. Repeat the layers one more time.
5. In a medium-sized mixing bowl, whisk the eggs with the rest of ingredients, except powdered sugar. Pour this mixture over the layers in your crock pot.
6. Cook covered for 6 hours on low-heat setting. Dust your frittata with powdered sugar and serve!

Spiced Porridge for Busy Mornings

(Ready in about 8 hours | Servings 8)

Ingredients

- 2 cups steel-cut oats
- 6 cups water
- 2 cups milk
- 1 tablespoon pure orange juice
- 1 cup dried apricots, chopped
- 1 cup dates, chopped
- 1 cup raisins, chopped
- 1/2 teaspoon ginger
- 1 teaspoon ground cinnamon
- 1/8 teaspoon cloves
- 1/4 cup maple syrup
- 1/2 vanilla bean

Directions

1. Combine all of the ingredients in a crock pot.

2. Set the crock pot to low and leave overnight.

3. In the morning, stir prepared porridge, scraping the sides and bottom. Serve with jam or leftover eggnog, if desired.

Family Mid-Winter Porridge

(Ready in about 9 hours | Servings 8)

Ingredients

- 7 cups water
- 2 cups steel-cut Irish oats
- 1 teaspoon lemon zest
- 1 cup raisins
- 1 cup dried cranberries
- 1 cup dried cherries
- 1 tablespoon shredded coconut
- 1/2 teaspoon ginger
- 1 teaspoon allspice
- 1/8 teaspoon grated nutmeg
- 1/4 cup honey
- 1/2 vanilla bean

Directions

1. Place all ingredients in a crock pot; set crock pot to low.

2. Cook overnight or 8 to 9 hours.

3. Tomorrow, stir the porridge and divide among eight serving bowls. Serve with a dollop of whipped cream and roasted nuts, if desired.

Amazing Apple Oatmeal with Prunes

(Ready in about 7 hours | Servings 8)

Ingredients

- 2 cups steel-cut oats
- 1 cup apple juice

- 5 cups water
- 1/2 cup dried apples
- 1/4 cup dried cranberries
- 1/4 cup prunes
- 1/4 cup maple syrup
- 1 teaspoon allspice
- A pinch of salt

Directions

1. Add all ingredients to a crock pot.
2. Set a crock pot to low; cook the oatmeal for about 7 hours.
3. Serve warm topped with heavy cream if desired.

Tropical Overnight Oatmeal

(Ready in about 8 hours | Servings 8)

Ingredients

- 2 cups steel-cut Irish oats
- 4 cups water
- 1 cup apple juice
- 1 tablespoon fresh orange juice
- 1/2 cup dried papaya
- 1/2 cup dried pineapple
- 1/4 cup dried mango
- 1/4 cup maple syrup
- 2 tablespoon coconut flakes
- A pinch of salt

Directions

1. Combine all of the ingredients in your crock pot.
2. Cover with a suitable lid; leave the oatmeal overnight or 7 to 8 hours.
3. Serve with milk or a dollop of whipped cream. Enjoy!

PART TWO: LUNCH

Cream of Broccoli and Cauliflower Soup

(Ready in about 4 hours | Servings 6)

Ingredients

- 1 cup water
- 2 cups reduced-sodium chicken broth
- 1 pound cauliflower, broken into florets
- 1 pound broccoli, broken into florets
- 1 yellow onion, finely chopped
- 3 cloves garlic, minced
- 1 heaping tablespoon fresh basil
- 1 heaping tablespoon fresh parsley
- 1/2 cup 2% reduced-fat milk
- Salt to taste
- 1/4 teaspoon white pepper
- 1/4 teaspoon black pepper
- Croutons of choice

Directions

1. Place water, broth, cauliflower, broccoli, onion, garlic, basil and parsley in your crock pot.
2. Cook on high 3 to 4 hours.
3. Transfer the soup to the food processor; add milk and spices and blend until uniform and smooth. Taste and adjust the seasonings; serve with croutons.

Family Broccoli-Spinach Soup

(Ready in about 4 hours | Servings 6)

Ingredients

- 2 cups water
- 2 cups reduced-sodium vegetable broth
- 1 pound broccoli, broken into florets
- 1 cup green onions, chopped
- 3 cloves garlic, minced

- 1 heaping tablespoon fresh cilantro
- 1 heaping tablespoon fresh parsley
- 2 cups spinach
- Salt to taste
- 1/4 teaspoon black pepper

Directions

1. Combine together water, vegetable broth, broccoli, green onions, garlic, cilantro and parsley in a crock pot.
2. Cook on high 3 hours. Add spinach and spices and cook for 20 minutes longer.
3. Pour the soup into the food processor; process until smooth.
4. Serve chilled or at room temperature. Garnish with a dollop of sour cream and enjoy!

Delicious Cream of Asparagus Soup

(Ready in about 4 hours | Servings 6)

Ingredients

- 2 cups vegetable stock
- 1 cups water
- 2 pounds asparagus, reserving the tips for garnish
- 1 onion, finely chopped
- 1 teaspoon lemon zest
- 2 cloves garlic, minced
- 1 teaspoon dried marjoram
- 1 heaping tablespoon fresh parsley
- 1/2 cup whole milk
- 1/4 teaspoon white pepper
- Salt to taste

Directions

1. Place stock, water, asparagus, onion, lemon zest, garlic, marjoram and parsley in a crock pot.
2. Cook on high-heat setting for 3 to 4 hours.
3. Meanwhile, steam asparagus tips until crisp-tender.

4. Pour the soup into a food processor; add milk, salt and white pepper and blend until smooth.

5. Garnish with steamed asparagus tips and serve at room temperature. You can also set your soup in a refrigerator and garnish it chilled.

Creamy Cauliflower Potato Chowder

(Ready in about 4 hours | Servings 6)

Ingredients

- 3 cups stock
- 1 cup carrot, chopped
- 3 ½ cups potatoes, diced
- 3 cups cauliflower, chopped
- 4 small-sized leeks, white parts only, chopped
- 1 cup milk
- 2 tablespoons cornstarch
- 1 teaspoon dried basil
- Salt to taste
- Black pepper to taste

Directions

1. Combine first five ingredients in a crock pot; set the crock pot to high and 3 to 4 hours.

2. Stir in remaining ingredients and cook 2 to 3 minutes longer or until thickened.

3. Blend the soup in a food processor or a blender until desired consistency is reached.

4. Adjust the seasonings and serve with sour cream.

Potato Cauliflower Bisque

(Ready in about 5 hours | Servings 6)

Ingredients

- 3 cups chicken broth
- 1 stalk celery, chopped
- 1 large-sized carrot, chopped
- 1/2 large head cauliflower, coarsely chopped
- 1 ½ cups potatoes, chopped

- 1 cup shallots, chopped
- 1 tablespoon dried basil
- 1 teaspoon dried thyme
- 1/2 teaspoon sea salt
- 1/4 teaspoon black pepper
- 1 cup milk

Directions

1. Combine all ingredients, except milk, in a crock pot; cover with a lid and set the crock pot to high
2. Cook for 4 to 5 hours.
3. Pour bisque into a food processor or a blender together with milk. Mix until smooth.
4. Adjust the seasonings; sprinkle with chopped fresh parsley and serve at room temperature or chilled.

Hot Cabbage Soup

(Ready in about 4 hours | Servings 8)

Ingredients

- 3 cups cabbage, shredded green
- 2 quarts reduced-fat beef broth
- 1 celery stalk, chopped
- 1 large-sized carrot, chopped
- 1 sweet red bell pepper, sliced
- 1 sweet yellow bell pepper, chopped
- 1 large-sized onion, chopped
- 1 clove garlic, minced
- 1 tablespoon vegetable oil
- 1 teaspoon ginger, minced
- 2 tablespoons soy sauce
- A few drops of tabasco sauce
- 1 tablespoon brown sugar
- 2 tablespoons cornstarch

Directions

1. Combine cabbage, broth, vegetables, oil and ginger in a crock pot; cover and cook on high-heat setting for 3 to 4 hours.
2. Stir in combined remaining ingredients and cook 5 more minutes. Serve warm and enjoy.

Sour Carrot Soup with Yogurt

(Ready in about 4 hours | Servings 6)

Ingredients

- 3 cups reduced-sodium chicken broth
- 2 cups canned tomatoes, undrained and diced
- 1 pound carrots, thickly sliced
- 1 cup leeks, chopped
- 2 cloves garlic, minced
- 1 teaspoon dried dill weed
- 1 tablespoon apple cider vinegar
- Salt to taste
- 1/4 teaspoon white pepper
- 1/4 teaspoon ground black pepper
- Plain yogurt for garnish

Directions

1. Combine first six ingredients in your crock pot; cover with a suitable lid and cook on high 3 to 4 hours.
2. Next, mix soup in a food processor until smooth; add the rest of ingredients, except the yogurt, and stir well to combine.
3. Stir before serving; garnish with a dollop of yogurt.

Dilled Celery Potato Soup

(Ready in about 4 hours | Servings 6)

Ingredients

- 2 cups canned tomatoes, undrained and diced
- 3 cups vegetable broth
- 1/2 pound celery, chopped
- 1/2 pound potatoes, peeled and diced
- 1 cup scallions, finely chopped
- 1 ½ teaspoon dried dill weed
- 1 tablespoon lemon juice
- Salt to taste
- 1/4 teaspoon white pepper
- 1/4 teaspoon ground black pepper
- Plain yogurt for garnish

Directions

1. Combine tomatoes, broth, celery, potato, scallions and dill weed in your crock pot; cover, set the crock pot to high and cook approximately 4 hours.

2. Then, purée prepared soup in a blender or a food processor until smooth;

3. Add combined remaining ingredients, except the yogurt; stir well until everything is well combined.

4. Garnish with a dollop of yogurt and serve chilled or at room temperature.

Cheesy Cream of Vegetable Soup

(Ready in about 4 hours | Servings 6)

Ingredients

- 1 small head cauliflower
- 1 medium-sized carrot, chopped
- 3 ½ chicken broth
- 2 large-sized Idaho potato, peeled, cubed
- 1/2 cup leeks, chopped
- 2 cloves garlic, minced
- 1 tablespoon soy sauce
- 1/2 cup 2% reduced-fat milk
- 3/4 cup reduced-fat Cheddar cheese, shredded
- 1/4 teaspoon ground nutmeg
- Salt to taste
- Ground black pepper to taste
- Chopped chives, as garnish

Directions

1. Combine first six ingredients in a crock pot; cook on high-heat setting 3 to 4 hours.

2. Purée 1/2 of prepared soup in a blender or a food processor until smooth and creamy; return to the crock pot.

3. Stir in combined soy sauce and milk, and continue cooking, stirring 2 to 3 minutes. Stir well to combine. Add Cheddar cheese, nutmeg, salt and black pepper to taste.

4. Divide among six serving bowls, sprinkle with chopped chives and serve!

Creamy Fennel Soup with Walnuts

(Ready in about 4 hours | Servings 6)

Ingredients

- 3 ½ chicken broth
- 1 ½ cups fennel bulbs
- 1/2 cup celery, chopped
- 1 medium-sized carrot, chopped
- 2 large-sized Idaho potato, peeled, cubed
- 1/2 cup scallions, chopped
- 2 cloves garlic, minced
- 1 tablespoon soy sauce
- 1 tablespoon apple cider vinegar
- 1/2 cup 2% reduced-fat milk
- Salt to taste
- Ground black pepper to taste
- Chopped toasted walnuts, as garnish

Directions

1. In a crock pot, combine first seven ingredients. Cook on high approximately 4 hours.
2. Place prepared soup in a food processor and blend until a smooth consistency is reached.
3. Add remaining ingredients, except chopped walnuts, and continue cooking 5 more minutes.
4. Divide among serving bowls; scatter walnuts on top and serve.

Cream of Turnip Soup

(Ready in about 4 hours | Servings 6)

Ingredients

- 3 ½ vegetable stock
- 1 ½ cups turnips, chopped
- 2 medium-sized carrots, chopped
- 1 large-sized potato, peeled, cubed
- 1/2 cup onions, chopped
- 2 cloves garlic, minced
- 1 tablespoon tamari sauce
- 1/2 cup whole milk
- 1/4 teaspoon ground white pepper
- 1 teaspoon dried thyme

- Salt to taste
- Ground black pepper to taste
- ¾ cup reduced-fat Swiss cheese, shredded
- Toasted bread cubes, as garnish

Directions

1. Pour vegetable stock into a crock pot. Add turnips, carrots, potato, onions, and garlic. Set the crock pot to high; cook for about 4 hours.

2. Pour the soup into a food processor and blend until your desired consistency is reached.

3. Return to the crock pot; add tamari sauce, milk, white pepper, thyme, salt, and black pepper. Cook an additional 5 minutes.

4. Top with Swiss cheese. Garnish with toasted bread cubes and serve.

Fragrant Garlic Soup with Bread

(Ready in about 4 hours | Servings 4)

Ingredients

- 8 cloves garlic, minced
- 1 quart vegetable stock
- 1/2 teaspoon dried oregano leaves
- 1/2 teaspoon celery seeds
- Salt to taste
- Black pepper to taste
- 2 tablespoons olive oil
- 4 slices of bread
- Chopped chives, as garnish

Directions

1. Combine garlic, vegetable stock, dried oregano leaves and celery seeds in a crock pot; cover and cook on high 4 hours.

2. Season with salt and black pepper.

3. In a heavy skillet, heat olive oil over medium heat. Fry the slices of bread, 2 to 3 minutes on each side, until golden.

4. Place slices of bread in soup bowls; ladle garlic soup over them and sprinkle with chopped chives. Enjoy!

Avocado and Potato Chowder

(Ready in about 5 hours | Servings 4)

Ingredients

- 1 ½ cups chicken broth
- 3 cups potatoes, peeled and diced
- 1 cup corn kernels
- 1 cup smoked turkey breast, cubed
- 1 teaspoon dried thyme leaves
- Juice of 1 fresh lime
- 1 cup avocado, cubed
- 1 teaspoon sea salt
- 1/2 ground black pepper

Directions

1. Combine chicken broth, potatoes, corn kernels, turkey breasts and thyme in a crock pot.
2. Cover and cook on high 4 to 5 hours.
3. Stir in lime, avocado, salt and black pepper. Serve.

Cheesy Veggie Sausage Chowder

(Ready in about 5 hours | Servings 6)

Ingredients

- 1 cup smoked sausage, sliced
- 2 cups reduced-sodium beef broth
- 2 ½ cups cream-style corn
- 1 onion, chopped
- 1 ½ cups plum tomatoes, diced
- 1 sweet red bell pepper, chopped
- 2 cups whole milk
- 2 tablespoons cornstarch
- 3/4 cup Swiss cheese
- Salt to taste
- 1/4 teaspoon black pepper
- 1/4 teaspoon cayenne pepper

Directions

1. Combine first six ingredients in your crock pot; cover with a lid.

2. Cook on high approximately 5 hours.

3. Add milk and cornstarch, stirring about 3 minutes.

4. Add in Swiss cheese; season with salt, black pepper and cayenne pepper; serve.

Cold Weather Potato Chowder

(Ready in about 5 hours | Servings 4)

Ingredients

- 2 cups potatoes, cubed
- 2 cups kernel corn
- 1 medium onion, chopped
- 1 cup water
- 1 cup chicken broth
- 1/2 cup celery, sliced
- 1 teaspoon dried basil leaves
- 1/2 teaspoon dried dill weed
- 1 ½ cups milk
- Salt to taste
- 1/4 teaspoon white pepper

Directions

1. Combine potatoes, corn, onion, water, broth, celery, basil and dill weed in a crock pot.

2. Cover and cook on high 4 to 5 hours.

3. Stir in remaining ingredients and serve warm or at room temperature.

Hearty Bean Chowder

(Ready in about 6 hours | Servings 8)

Ingredients

- 2 cups water
- 2 cups beef broth
- 15 ½ ounces canned beans, rinsed and drained
- 1 sweet red bell pepper
- 1 bay leaf
- 2 large sized onions, chopped
- 2 cloves garlic, minced

- 1/2 teaspoon chili powder
- 1/4 cup dry sherry
- Salt and ground black pepper, to taste
- Blue cheese for garnish

Directions

1. In a crock pot, place water, beef broth, canned beans, red bell pepper, bay leaf, onion, garlic, and chili powder.
2. Cook covered on high-heat setting for 5 to 6 hours
3. Add dry sherry during last 15 minutes; season with salt and pepper, taste and adjust the seasonings.
4. Serve with blue cheese and enjoy!

Great Northern Bean Soup

(Ready in about 6 hours | Servings 8)

Ingredients

- 2 cups chicken broth
- 2 cups water
- 2 cups Great Northern beans, rinsed and drained
- 1 large-sized carrot, slices
- 2 cups leeks, finely chopped
- 2-3 garlic cloves, minced
- 1 teaspoon dried basil
- 1 teaspoon dried thyme
- 1 teaspoon celery seeds
- 1 tablespoon apple cider vinegar
- 1/2 teaspoon salt
- 1/2 teaspoon ground black pepper

Directions

1. In a crock pot, combine chicken broth, water, beans, carrot, leeks, garlic, basil, thyme and celery seeds.
2. Cover with a lid; cook on high 5 to 6 hours, adding apple cider vinegar during last 15 minutes. Add salt and ground black pepper; serve warm.

Potato Cauliflower Chowder

(Ready in about 4 hours | Servings 6)

Ingredients

- 3 cups reduced-sodium chicken broth
- 3 ½ cups potatoes, peeled and cubed
- 1 cup scallions, chopped
- 1/2 head cauliflower
- 1/2 cup celery, thinly sliced
- 1/4–1/2 teaspoon celery seeds
- 1 cup whole milk
- 2 tablespoons cornstarch
- Salt and white pepper, to taste
- 1/4 teaspoon red pepper flakes, crushed
- Ground nutmeg, as garnish

Directions

1. Combine all ingredients, except whole milk, cornstarch, salt, white pepper, red pepper and nutmeg, in a crock pot.
2. Cover and cook on high approximately 4 hours.
3. Stir in combined remaining ingredients, except nutmeg, during last 20 minutes.
4. Divide among six soup bowls; serve sprinkled with ground nutmeg!

Mom's Chicken Chili

(Ready in about 8 hours | Servings 6)

Ingredients

- 1 pound chicken breast, boneless and skinless
- 1 cup leeks, finely chopped
- 2 plum tomatoes, diced
- 1 can (15-ounce) beans, rinsed and drained
- 2 cloves garlic, minced
- 1 teaspoon chili powder
- 1/2 teaspoon allspice
- 1 strip orange zest
- Salt and black pepper, to taste
- Chopped fresh parsley, as garnish
- Chopped coriander leaves, as garnish

Directions

1. Cut the chicken into small chunks.
2. In your crock pot, combine all ingredients, except parsley and coriander.
3. Cover and cook on low for about 8 hours.
4. Serve over rice. Sprinkle with parsley and coriander. Enjoy!

Yummy Spicy Mushroom Chili

(Ready in about 8 hours | Servings 6)

Ingredients

- 1 pound chicken breast, cubed
- 2 cups reduced-sodium chicken broth
- 1 cup water
- 2 cups canned kidney beans, rinsed and drained
- 2 large-sized red onions
- 1 sweet red bell pepper, chopped
- 1 cup mushrooms, sliced
- 1 teaspoon gingerroot, minced
- 1 teaspoon jalapeño chili, minced
- 1 teaspoon ground cumin
- 2 bay leaves
- 1/2 teaspoon sea salt
- 1/2 teaspoon ground black pepper
- 1/2 teaspoon cayenne pepper

Directions

1. Add all of the ingredients to a crock pot.
2. Then, cook covered on low-heat setting for 6 to 8 hours.
3. Taste, adjust the seasonings and serve

Chicken and Potatoes with Gravy

(Ready in about 6 hours | Servings 4)

Ingredients

- 3/4 cup chicken breasts, boneless and skinless
- 4 medium-sized potatoes, peeled and diced
- 1 medium-sized yellow onion, sliced
- 1 ½ cup cream of mushroom
- 1 ½ cup cream of chicken soup
- 1/4 teaspoon white pepper
- 1/4 teaspoon black pepper

Directions

1. Arrange all ingredients in your crock pot.
2. Cover and cook on low for about 6 hours or until the meat is cooked through.
3. Serve with a dollop of sour cream and your favorite tossed salad.

Cheesy Saucy Chicken and Veggies

(Ready in about 6 hours | Servings 4)

Ingredients

- 2 cups chicken stock
- 4 medium-sized chicken breasts, boneless, skinless
- 1 pound green beans
- 1 sweet red bell peppers
- 1 onion, cut into wedges
- 3 medium-sized potatoes, peeled and diced
- 3 cloves garlic, minced
- 1/2 teaspoon dried marjoram
- 1/4 teaspoon freshly ground black pepper
- 1/2 cup cream cheese, cut into cubes
- 1 teaspoon Dijon mustard
- 2 tablespoons balsamic vinegar

Directions

1. Simply arrange all ingredients, except cheese, mustard and balsamic vinegar, in a crock pot.

2. Cover and cook on low for 5 to 6 hours.

3. Remove chicken and veggies from the crock pot and keep them warm.

4. To make the sauce, add the cheese, mustard and vinegar to the broth in the crock pot. Stir until everything is well incorporated and cheese is melted.

5. Divide the chicken and vegetables among four soup bowls.

6. Ladle the sauce over the chicken and veggies. Serve warm.

Hot Chicken with Potatoes

(Ready in about 5 hours | Servings 4)

Ingredients

- Non-stick cooking spray
- 1/2 cup potatoes
- 1 cup leftover cooked chicken, cubed
- 2 bay leaves
- 3-4 peppercorns
- 2 cups chicken stock
- 2 cups water
- 2 tablespoons dry white wine
- Ground black pepper, to taste
- 1 teaspoon chili powder

Directions

1. Coat your crock pot with non-stick spray.
2. Place all ingredients in the greased crock pot.
3. Cover and cook on low for 5 hours.

Chicken Paprikash with Noodles

(Ready in about 8 hours | Servings 8)

Ingredients

- 2 tablespoons olive oil
- 1 large-sized onion, peeled and diced
- 2 cloves garlic, minced
- 3 pounds chicken thighs, boneless and skinless

- 2 bay leaves
- 1 teaspoon sea salt
- 1/2 teaspoon ground black pepper, to taste
- 1 tablespoon paprika
- 1/2 cup chicken broth
- 1/4 cup dry white wine
- 1 cup cream cheese
- Egg noodles, cooked

Directions

1. In a heavy skillet, heat olive oil over medium heat. Sauté onions and garlic until just tender.
2. Cut the chicken thighs into small pieces. Add the chicken to the skillet, and stir fry for 5 to 6 minutes. Replace to the crock pot.
3. Add in bay leaves, sea salt, black pepper, paprika, chicken broth and white wine; cover and cook on low approximately 8 hours.
4. Stir in cream cheese and serve over cooked noodles.

Orange Turkey Breasts

(Ready in about 8 hours | Servings 8)

Ingredients

- Non-stick cooking spray
- 3 pounds turkey breasts, boneless and skinless
- 1 medium-sized onion, chopped
- 1/2 cup orange juice
- 1 tablespoon orange marmalade
- 1 tablespoon balsamic vinegar
- 1 tablespoon Worcestershire sauce
- 1 teaspoon mustard
- 1/2 teaspoon kosher salt
- 1/4 teaspoon ground black pepper

Directions

1. Treat your crock pot with non-stick cooking spray. Cut the turkey into small pieces. Transfer to the crock pot and add onion.

2. In a measuring cup or a mixing bowl, combine together the orange juice, marmalade, balsamic vinegar, Worcestershire sauce, mustard, salt and black pepper. Pour into the crock pot.

3. Cover with a lid; cook on low approximately 8 hours.

4. Serve over scalloped potatoes.

Teriyaki Chicken with Basmati Rice

(Ready in about 8 hours | Servings 8)

Ingredients

- 2 pounds chicken, boneless and cut into strips
- 1 cup green peas
- 1 sweet red bell pepper, chopped
- 1 sweet yellow pepper, chopped
- 1 cup scallions
- 1/2 cup chicken stock
- 1 cup teriyaki sauce
- Sea salt to taste
- 1/4 teaspoon ground black pepper

Directions

1. Add all ingredients to the crock pot. Stir to combine.

2. Cover and cook on low for about 6 hours.

3. Serve over basmati rice.

Moist & Tender Chicken with Caramelized Onion

(Ready in about 6 hours | Servings 4)

Ingredients

- 2 tablespoons butter
- 1 large-sized onion, chopped
- 1 teaspoon sugar
- 2 cloves garlic, minced
- 1 tablespoons curry powder
- 1 cup water

- 3/4 teaspoon chicken bouillon concentrate
- 8 chicken thighs, skinless
- Cooked long-grain white rice, as garnish

Directions

1. In a small-sized skillet, melt the butter over medium heat. Add onions and cook for 10 minutes, stirring occasionally.
2. Then, turn the heat to medium-high; add sugar and cook an additional 10 minutes or until the onions become golden brown. Transfer to the crock pot.
3. Add remaining ingredients, except cooked rice; cook covered for about 6 hours.
4. Divide among four serving plates and serve over long-grain white rice.

Curried Chicken with Almonds

(Ready in about 6 hours | Servings 4)

Ingredients

- 1 tablespoon olive oil
- 1 cup leeks, chopped
- 2 cloves garlic, minced
- 1 ½ tablespoons curry powder
- 1 cup almond milk
- 1/2 cup water
- 8 chicken thighs, skinless
- 1 1/2 cups celery, sliced diagonally
- 1 cup slivered almonds, toasted

Directions

1. In a heavy skillet, heat olive oil; sauté leeks until just tender. Transfer to the crock pot.
2. Add the rest of ingredients, except slivered almonds.
3. Cover with a suitable lid and cook for about 6 hours.
4. Scatter the toasted almonds on top and serve warm!

Amazing Chicken in Milk

(Ready in about 8 hours | Servings 4)

Ingredients

- Non-stick cooking spray
- 1 cup chicken soup
- 1 green bell pepper, sliced
- 1 red bell pepper, sliced
- 1 carrot, thinly sliced
- 1/2 cup milk
- 1 cup chicken breasts, boneless and skinless
- 1 ½ cups water

Directions

1. Coat a crock pot with nonstick spray.
2. Add the rest of ingredients.
3. Cover with a lid; set the crock pot to low and cook for 8 hours.

Spiced Turkey with Sauerkraut

(Ready in about 8 hours | Servings 6)

Ingredients

- 1 pound carrots, thinly sliced
- 1 stalk celery, finely chopped
- 1 cup leeks, chopped
- 2 cloves garlic, peeled and minced
- 1 large-sized turkey breast, boneless
- 2 pounds sauerkraut, rinsed and drained
- 6 medium-sized red potatoes, washed and pierced
- 2 cups beer
- 1/2 teaspoon dried sage
- 1/2 teaspoon dried rosemary
- Salt to taste
- 1/2 teaspoon ground black pepper

Directions

1. In a crock pot, arrange all of the ingredients.
2. Set the crock pot to low; cook covered about 8 hours.
3. Then, taste for seasoning and adjust if necessary; serve.

Cranberry Turkey Breasts

(Ready in about 8 hours | Servings 8)

Ingredients

- Butter flavor cooking spray
- 1 teaspoon chicken bouillon concentrate
- 2 cups whole cranberry sauce
- 1/4 teaspoon water
- 1 medium-sized boneless turkey breast, quartered

Directions

1. Coat the crock pot with butter flavor cooking spray. Add the rest of ingredients; stir to combine.
2. Cover and cook on low for 8 hours or cook on high for 4 hours. Serve with sour cream.

Turkey with Onion-Garlic Sauce

(Ready in about 8 hours | Servings 8)

Ingredients

- 5 large-sized red onions, thinly sliced
- 4 cloves garlic, minced
- 1/4 cup dry white wine
- 1/2 teaspoon sea salt
- 1/4 teaspoon ground black pepper
- 1/4 teaspoon cayenne pepper
- 4 large-sized turkey thighs, skinless

Directions

1. Lay onions and garlic into the bottom of your crock pot. Pour in wine and sprinkle with salt, black pepper and cayenne pepper.
2. Add turkey thighs. Cover; cook on low heat setting approximately 8 hours.
3. Remove the turkey thighs from the crock pot. Clean flesh from turkey bones.
4. Uncover the crock pot and continue cooking until the liquid has evaporated. Stir occasionally.
5. Return the turkey to the crock pot. Next, nestle the turkey into the mixture in the crock pot. Serve.

Grandma's Cabbage with Beef

(Ready in about 4 hours | Servings 4)

Ingredients

- 1 pound cooked beef, cut into bite-sized chunks
- 1 medium onion, peeled and diced
- 1 cup cabbage, chopped
- 2 medium-sized potatoes, diced
- 2 carrots, peeled and thinly sliced
- 1 stalk celery, chopped
- 1 clove garlic, peeled and minced
- 2 cups beef broth
- 2 cups canned tomatoes, diced
- Salt, to taste
- 1/4 teaspoon ground black pepper

Directions

1. Arrange all ingredients in a crock pot; stir to combine.
2. Set the crock pot on high and cook for 1 hour. Then, turn heat to low and cook for 3 to 4 hours.
3. Taste and adjust the seasonings; serve warm.

Delicious Beef Stroganoff

(Ready in about 4 hours 30 minutes | Servings 4)

Ingredients

- 1 pound cooked beef, shredded
- 1/2 cup sliced mushrooms, drained
- 1 onion, chopped
- 2-3 cloves garlic, minced
- 1/2 cup beef broth
- 1 cup cream of mushroom soup
- 2 tablespoons dry white wine
- 1 cup cream cheese
- 1 bay leaf
- 1/2 teaspoon dried sage
- 1/2 teaspoon dried rosemary

Directions

1. Place all ingredients, except cream cheese, in your crock pot. Cover and cook on low heat setting for 4 hours.

2. Then, cut the cream cheese into small chunks; add to the crock pot. Cover and cook on low for 1/2 hour longer or until the cheese is melted
3. Serve over your favorite egg noodles.

Country Corned Beef Brisket

(Ready in about 8 hours 45 minutes | Servings 12)

Ingredients

- 4 pounds corned beef brisket
- 2 cloves garlic, peeled and minced
- 2 onions, chopped
- 1 cup water
- 1 bay leaf
- 1/2 cup beef stock
- 1 tablespoon paprika
- 1/2 teaspoon freshly grated nutmeg
- 1/2 teaspoon white pepper
- A few drops of liquid smoke

Directions

1. Remove any excess fat from the beef brisket. Transfer the beef brisket to the crock pot.
2. Add remaining ingredients; cover and cook for 8 hours.
3. Preheat the oven to 350 degrees F. Place the beef brisket on a roasting pan; roast for 45 minutes.
4. Serve over scalloped potatoes, if desired.

Vegetable Pot Roast

(Ready in about 8 hours | Servings 6)

Ingredients

- 1 pound carrots
- 3 medium-sized potatoes, quartered
- 2 cloves garlic, peeled and minced
- 2 stalks of celery, diced
- 1 sweet red bell pepper, seeded and diced
- 1 large-sized onion, chopped
- 3 pounds chuck roast, boneless

- 1 teaspoon broth concentrate
- 1/2 teaspoon black pepper
- 1 cup water
- 1 cup tomato juice
- 1 tablespoon soy sauce

Directions

1. Arrange the vegetables in your crock pot.
2. Cut the chuck roast into serving-sized portions. Place the pieces of roast on top of the vegetables.
3. In a mixing bowl, combine together broth concentrate, black pepper, water, tomato juice and soy sauce. Whisk to combine. Add this liquid mixture to the crock pot.
4. Cover and cook on low approximately 8 hours.

Beef Roast with Root Vegetables

(Ready in about 8 hours | Servings 12)

Ingredients

- 4 russet potatoes, quartered
- 1 cup water
- 4 parsnips, quartered
- 3 rutabagas, quartered
- 1 onion, sliced
- 1/2 cup leeks, sliced
- 7 cloves garlic, sliced
- 4 pounds lean top round beef roast
- 1 beef bouillon concentrate
- 1 teaspoon smoked paprika
- 1/2 teaspoon freshly ground black pepper

Directions

1. Simply place all ingredients in your crock pot.
2. Set the crock pot to low and cook for 8 hours.
3. Slice the beef into serving-sized portions and serve with vegetables. Garnish with mustard if desired.

Beef Steak with Mushroom Gravy

(Ready in about 8 hours | Servings 12)

Ingredients

- 2 medium onions, peeled and sliced
- 2 pounds beef round steak, boneless
- 3 cups mushrooms, sliced
- 1 cup turnips, sliced
- 1 (12-ounce) jar beef gravy
- 1 (1-ounce) envelope dry mushroom gravy mix

Directions

1. Lay the onions on the bottom of the crock pot.
2. Trim fat from the beef round steak; then cut the beef into eight pieces.
3. Place the beef on top of the onions, and then place the mushrooms over it. Top with sliced turnips.
4. Mix together beef gravy and mushroom gravy mix.
5. Add this gravy mixture to the crock pot; cover and cook on low for 8 hours. Serve over mashed potatoes if desired.

Juicy Pork with Apple Sauce

(Ready in about 6 hours | Servings 8)

Ingredients

- 1/4 cup light brown sugar
- 1/4 cup Dijon mustard
- 1/2 teaspoon ground black pepper
- 4 pounds pork loin, fat removed
- 1/2 cup dry red wine
- 4 cups applesauce, unsweetened
- 1/2 cup scallions, chopped

Directions

1. In a small-sized bowl or a measuring cup, combine together sugar, mustard, and black pepper. Mix well to combine.

2. Rub mustard mixture into the pork loin.
3. Place the pork loin in the crock pot; add red wine, applesauce and scallions; cover with a lid.
4. Cook on low for 6 hours. Serve with some extra mustard.

Ham with Pineapple

(Ready in about 6 hours | Servings 6)

Ingredients

- 2 pounds ham steak
- 1 pound canned pineapple tidbits, drained, reserve 2 tablespoons of the juice.
- 1 cup leeks, chopped
- 2 cloves garlic, minced
- 3 large-sized potatoes, diced
- 1/2 cup orange marmalade
- 1/4 teaspoon paprika
- 1/4 teaspoon ground black pepper
- 1/2 teaspoon dried basil

Directions

1. Cut the ham into bite-sized pieces. Transfer to the crock pot.
2. Add the rest of ingredients; stir to combine.
3. Cover and cook on low for 6 hours.

Cranberry Pork Roast with Sweet Potatoes

(Ready in about 6 hours | Servings 6)

Ingredients

- 3 pounds pork butt roast
- 2 cups canned cranberries
- 1 medium onion, peeled and diced
- 1/2 cup orange juice
- 2 tablespoons apple cider vinegar
- 1/2 teaspoon five-spice powder
- Sea salt to taste
- 1/2 teaspoon ground black pepper

- 3 large-sized sweet potatoes, peeled and quartered

Directions

1. Place the pork in a crock pot.

2. In a measuring cup, mix together the cranberries, onion, orange juice, apple cider vinegar, five-spice powder, salt and black pepper; mix to combine.

3. Pour cranberry mixture over pork butt roast in the crock pot. Arrange the potatoes around the pork.

4. Cover and cook on low for about 6 hours.

5. Transfer to a serving platter and enjoy!

Sausages with Sauerkraut and Beer

(Ready in about 3 hours 30 minutes | Servings 8)

Ingredients

- 8 precooked sausages
- 2 large-sized onions, sliced
- 2 pounds sauerkraut, rinsed and drained
- 1 (12-ounce) bottle of beer

Directions

1. Add the sausages and onions to a crock pot. Cook on high for 30 minutes.

2. Add the sauerkraut and beer; cover and cook on low for 3 hours.

3. Serve with mustard if desired.

Pork Steaks in Prune Sauce

(Ready in about 6 hours | Servings 6)

Ingredients

- 12 prunes, pitted
- 3 pounds pork steaks, boneless
- 4 medium-sized apples, cored, and quartered
- 3/4 cup apple juice
- 3/4 cup heavy cream
- 1 teaspoon sea salt
- 1/4 teaspoon freshly ground pepper
- 1 tablespoon butter

Directions

1. Add all ingredients to the crock pot. Cover and cook on low for 6 hours or until the meat pulls apart easily.
2. Serve over mashed potatoes.

Spicy Pork Roast with Vegetables

(Ready in about 6 hours | Servings 4)

Ingredients

- 1 tablespoon canola oil
- 1 large-sized onion, sliced
- 1 celery stalk, chopped
- 1 large-sized carrot, peeled and finely diced
- 1 jalapeño pepper, seeded and minced
- 1 teaspoon garlic powder
- Salt, to taste
- 1/2 teaspoon five-spice powder
- 1/4 teaspoon freshly ground black pepper
- 1/2 teaspoon dried oregano
- 1/2 teaspoon dried basil
- 1 (3-pound) pork shoulder or butt roast
- 1 cup vegetable broth

Directions

1. Add the canola oil to the cast-iron skillet. Heat canola oil over medium-high heat and then add vegetables. Sauté the vegetables until they are just tender or about 15 minutes.

2. In a mixing bowl, combine garlic powder, salt, five-spice powder, black pepper, oregano, and basil; stir to mix.

3. Rub this spice mixture into the meat. Add the pork roast to the crock pot; pour in vegetable broth. Cover and cook on low for 6 hours.

4. Shred the pork with two forks. Ladle the sauce over the pork and serve warm.

Country Pork Ribs with Ginger Sauce

(Ready in about 8 hours | Servings 6)

Ingredients

- 4 pounds country pork ribs
- 1 ¼ cup tomato ketchup
- 2 tablespoons rice vinegar
- 2 tablespoons tamari sauce
- 1/4 teaspoon allspice
- 1 large onion, peeled and diced
- 1 clove garlic, peeled and minced
- 2 teaspoons grated ginger
- 1/4 teaspoon red pepper flakes, crushed

Directions

1. Cut the pork ribs into individual serving-size portions.

2. Broil the ribs for 5 minutes on each side or until they are fragrant and browned.

3. To make the sauce: in a crock pot, combine tomato ketchup, rice vinegar, tamari sauce, allspice, onion, garlic, ginger and red pepper.

4. Place the pork ribs in the crock pot, coating the ribs with the sauce.

5. Cover and cook on low for 8 hours or until the ribs are tender.

Pork Roast in Beer

(Ready in about 6 hours | Servings 4)

Ingredients

- 1 medium-sized pork sirloin
- 2 sweet onions, peeled and sliced
- 4 large-sized potatoes, quartered
- 2 cups carrots
- 1 envelope dry onion soup mix
- 1 (12-ounce) bottle of beer
- 5-6 peppercorns

Directions

1. Place the pork sirloin in your crock pot. Arrange onions, potatoes and carrots around the meat.
2. Sprinkle with the soup mix. Pour in beer; then add peppercorns.
3. Cover and cook on low for 6 hours. Divide among four serving plates and serve warm.

Piquant Chicken Chowder

(Ready in about 8 hours | Servings 8)

Ingredients

- 1 quart chicken stock
- 1 pound chicken breast, boneless skinless, cut into cubes
- 3 cups whole kernel corn
- 1/2 cup chopped onion, finely chopped
- 2 cloves garlic, minced
- 1 green bell pepper, thinly sliced
- 1 teaspoon jalapeño chili, minced
- 1/2 teaspoon dried thyme leaves
- 1 teaspoon dried rosemary
- Salt to taste
- 1/4 teaspoon black pepper, ground
- 1 cup 2% reduced-fat milk
- 2 tablespoons cornstarch

Directions

1. Combine all ingredients, except milk and cornstarch, in a crock pot; cover and cook on low approximately 8 hours.

2. Turn heat to high, stir in combined milk and cornstarch, and cook an additional 5 minutes, stirring constantly.

3. Adjust the seasonings and serve with your favorite garlic croutons.

Hot Chicken Chowder with Spinach

(Ready in about 5 hours | Servings 4)

Ingredients

- 1 cup chicken broth
- 1 ½ cup canned tomatoes, diced
- 1 ½ cup garbanzo beans, rinsed and drained
- 12 ounces chicken breast, boneless, skinless and cubed
- 1 medium-sized sweet onion, chopped
- 2 sweet potatoes, diced
- 2 cups packed spinach
- Salt to taste
- 1/4 teaspoon black pepper
- 1/2 teaspoon chili powder

Directions

1. Combine all ingredients, except spinach, in the crock pot; cover and cook on high for about 5 hours,

2. Stir in spinach; adjust the seasonings.

3. Divide among soup bowls and serve.

Shrimp Chowder with Avocado

(Ready in about 5 hours | Servings 4)

Ingredients

- 2 cups water
- 1 envelope dry onion soup mix
- 1 red onion, chopped
- 1 plum tomato, chopped

- 3/4 teaspoon five-spice powder
- 1/8 teaspoon celery seeds
- 1/2 cup long-grain rice
- 1 ½ cups shrimp, peeled and halved crosswise
- 1 avocado, cubed
- Juice of 1 fresh lime
- Salt to taste
- 1/2 teaspoon paprika
- 1/2 teaspoon ground black pepper

Directions

1. In a crock pot, combine water, onion soup mix, onion, tomato, five-spice powder and celery seeds; cover and cook on high 5 hours.
2. Add long-grain rice during last 2 hours of cooking time; add shrimp during last 20 minutes.
3. Stir in the rest of ingredients. Ladle soup into bowls and serve hot.

Shrimp Chowder with Corn and Potato

(Ready in about 5 hours | Servings 4)

Ingredients

- 2 cups whole kernel corn
- 1 cup water
- 2 cups chicken broth
- 1 can (8 ounces) tomato sauce
- 1 large-sized sweet onion, chopped
- 2 cloves garlic, minced
- 3 medium-sized Yukon potatoes, diced
- 1 sweet red bell pepper, sliced
- 1/4 cup dry sherry, optional
- 3/4 teaspoon five-spice powder
- 1/4 teaspoon dry mustard
- 1/4 teaspoon ground caraway seeds
- A few drops Tabasco sauce
- 1/2 cup whole milk
- 1 ½ cups shrimp, peeled and deveined
- Salt to taste
- Black pepper to taste

Directions

1. Combine all of the ingredients, except shrimp and milk, in your crock pot.

2. Cover and cook on high for about 5 hours, adding milk and shrimp during last 20 minutes.

3. Ladle into four soup bowls and enjoy.

Saucy Pork Spare Ribs

(Ready in about 8 hours | Servings 8)

Ingredients

- 4 pounds lean pork spare ribs
- 1 red bell pepper, sliced
- 1 cup scallions, chopped
- 1/2 cup garlic-chili sauce
- 2 tablespoons brown sugar
- 1/4 cup rice vinegar
- 1 tablespoon dry red wine

Directions

1. Place pork spare ribs in your crock pot. Arrange slices of bell pepper around the pork ribs.

2. In a mixing bowl, combine together remaining ingredients; whisk well to combine.

3. Pour this mixture over the ribs. Cook covered for 8 hours.

4. Place pork spare ribs on a serving platter. Pour the sauce into a small serving bowl; drain off fat. Serve.

Pork Ribs in Sweet Sauce

(Ready in about 8 hours | Servings 4)

Ingredients

- 3 pounds pork ribs
- 1 medium-size onion, diced
- 3 cloves garlic, minced
- 1/2 cup maple syrup
- 2 tablespoons tamari sauce
- 3/4 teaspoon five-spice powder
- 1/2 teaspoon ground ginger
- 1/4 teaspoon paprika

- 1/2 teaspoon dried rosemary
- Sea salt to taste
- 1/4 teaspoon freshly ground black pepper

Directions

1. Arrange the pork ribs and onion in the bottom of the crock pot.
2. Next, add remaining ingredients.
3. Cover and cook on low for 8 hours or until the pork is tender enough to pull away from the bone.

Spicy Pork with Canadian Bacon

(Ready in about 6 hours | Servings 4)

Ingredients

- 2 slices of Canadian bacon
- 1 pound pork shoulder, boneless and fat removed
- 1 cup leeks, chopped
- 2 cloves garlic, minced
- 1 cup chicken broth
- 2 cups canned tomatoes, diced
- 1 ½ cups canned beans, rinsed and drained
- 2 stalks celery, thinly sliced
- 3/4 teaspoon Italian seasoning blend
- 1/2 teaspoon dried thyme
- Salt to taste
- Freshly ground black pepper to taste

Directions

1. Cut the bacon into small-sized pieces. Then, fry the bacon in a nonstick skillet over medium-high heat; fry for 2 minutes or until bacon starts to render its fat. Transfer to your crock pot.
2. Add the rest of ingredients
3. Cover and cook on low for 6 hours or until the pork shoulder is tender.

Mom's Soft and Spicy Pork

(Ready in about 6 hours | Servings 4)

Ingredients

- 1 teaspoon olive oil
- 3 pounds pork loin
- 1 cup spring onions, chopped
- 4 cloves garlic, minced
- 1 cups water
- 1/2 cups dry red wine
- 1 envelope dry onion soup mix
- 1/4 cup orange juice
- 1 tablespoon ground cumin
- 1 teaspoon ground cayenne pepper

Directions

1. Heat the oil in a heavy skillet. Then, cook the pork 1 to 2 minutes on each side. Transfer to the crock pot.
2. Next, pour the remaining ingredients over the pork. Cover with a lid and cook on low for 6 hours.
3. Serve over mashed potatoes.

Asian-Style Pork

(Ready in about 9 hours | Servings 6)

Ingredients

- 2 pounds boneless pork loin
- 1/4 cup dry white wine
- 4 cloves garlic
- 1 cup water
- 1 teaspoon honey
- 3/4 teaspoon five-spice powder
- 2 tablespoons dark soy sauce
- 3 whole star anise
- Salt to taste

Directions

1. Heat a nonstick skillet over medium-high flame. Quickly cook the pork on both side. Transfer to the crock pot.
2. Add the rest of ingredients. Gently stir to coat the pork. Cook on low for 8 to 9 hours.
3. Discard the star anise and serve warm.

Festive Glazed Pork

(Ready in about 8 hours | Servings 4)

Ingredients

- 1/4 cup dried cherries
- 2/3 cup water
- 2 tablespoons dry white wine
- 1/4 teaspoon ground black pepper
- 1/4 teaspoon salt
- 1/8 teaspoon ground nutmeg
- 1¼ pounds pork loin

Directions

1. In a small-sized bowl or a measuring cup, whisk the dried cherries, water, wine, pepper, salt, and nutmeg.
2. Place the pork loin in a crock pot. Next, pour the glaze over the meat.
3. Cook on low for 8 hours. Serve warm.

Old-Fashioned Meatloaf

(Ready in about 7 hours | Servings 8)

Ingredients

- 2 pounds mixed ground beef and pork
- 1 egg
- 1 cup beef stock
- Salt to taste
- 1/2 teaspoon black pepper
- 2 cups crushed seasoned croutons
- 1 ½ cups tomato sauce
- 2 tablespoons Worcestershire sauce
- 1 tablespoon balsamic vinegar

Directions

1. In a large-sized bowl, combine together ground meat, egg, beef stock, salt, black pepper, and croutons. Mix well to combine; then, form into a loaf.
2. Lay the meatloaf into the crock pot.

3. In a separate mixing bowl, whisk the tomato sauce, Worcestershire sauce and balsamic vinegar. Pour this mixture over the meatloaf.

4. Cover and cook on low heat setting for 7 hours.

Easy Zesty Meatloaf

(Ready in about 8 hours | Servings 8)

Ingredients

- 1 ½ pound lean ground beef and lean ground pork, mixed
- 1 teaspoon salt
- 1/4 teaspoon cayenne pepper
- Ground black pepper to taste
- 1 onion, finely chopped
- 1 stalk celery, finely chopped
- 2 medium-sized carrots, grated
- 1 large-sized egg
- 1 cup tomato paste
- 1/2 cup quick-cooking oatmeal
- 1/2 cup crackers, crumbled
- Non-stick cooking spray
- 1/3 cup tomato ketchup
- 1 tablespoon mustard

Directions

1. In a large-sized mixing bowl, place together meat, salt, cayenne pepper, black pepper, onion, celery, carrots, egg, tomato paste, oatmeal and crumbled crackers. Mix well to combine. Form the meatloaf and set aside.

2. Treat the crock pot with non-stick cooking spray. Place the meatloaf in the crock pot.

3. In another bowl, mix together tomato ketchup and mustard; spread this mixture over the top of the meatloaf.

4. Cover and cook on low for 7 to 8 hours, until the meatloaf is cooked through.

5. Allow the meatloaf to stand for 30 minutes before slicing and serving.

Poached Salmon with Onion

(Ready in about 1 hour | Servings 4)

Ingredients

- 2 tablespoons butter, melted
- 1 small-sized onion, thinly sliced
- 1 cup water
- 1/2 cup chicken broth
- 4 (6-ounce) salmon fillets
- 1 tablespoon fresh lemon juice
- 1 sprig fresh dill
- Sea salt, to taste
- Ground black pepper to taste
- 1 lemon, quartered, as garnish

Directions

1. Grease the inside of the crock pot with the butter.
2. Place the onion slices in the crock pot; pour in water and chicken broth. Set the crock pot on high and cook for about 30 minutes.
3. Place the salmon fillets on cooked onion. Add in lemon juice and fresh dill. Cover and cook on high 30 minutes longer, until the salmon is opaque. Season with salt and black pepper.
4. Garnish with lemon and enjoy!

Sunday Crab Supreme

(Ready in about 2 hours 30 minutes | Servings 8)

Ingredients

- 2 cups sour cream
- 2 cups mayonnaise
- 1/4 cup dry sherry
- 2 tablespoons fresh lemon juice
- 1/4 cup fresh cilantro, minced
- 2 heaping tablespoons parsley, minced
- 2 pounds crabmeat
- 1/2 teaspoon dried basil
- 1 teaspoon dried rosemary
- Salt to taste
- Ground black pepper, to taste

Directions

1. Put first four ingredients into your crock pot. Whisk to mix; cook on low heat setting for 2 hours.

2. Add in remaining ingredients. Cover and cook on low until the crabmeat is heated through or about 30 minutes.

3. Serve with boiled potatoes, if desired.

Rich Tomato Shrimp Chowder

(Ready in about 5 hours | Servings 6)

Ingredients

- 3 cups whole kernel corn
- 1 cup tomato juice
- 2 cups chicken broth
- 1 cup clam juice
- 2 large-sized red potatoes, peeled and diced
- 1 cup red onion, chopped
- 1 green bell pepper, chopped
- 2 cloves garlic, minced
- 1/4 cup dry sherry, optional
- 1 teaspoon dried basil
- 1/2 teaspoon dried oregano
- 1/4 teaspoon chili powder
- Salt to taste
- 1/2 teaspoon ground black pepper
- 1 ½ cups cooked halved shrimp, peeled and deveined
- 1/2 cup whole milk

Directions

1. Place all ingredients in your crock pot, except shrimp and milk.

2. Cover with a suitable lid and cook on high 4 to 5 hours, adding shrimp and milk during last 15 minutes of cooking time.

3. Adjust seasonings according to your tastes and serve.

Shrimp, Bean and Corn Chowder

(Ready in about 4 hours | Servings 8)

Ingredients

- 1 ½ cups chicken broth
- 2 cups corn
- 2 cans (15 ½ ounces) Great Northern beans, rinsed and drained
- ¼ cup scallions, chopped
- 1/4 teaspoon caraway seeds, ground
- 1/4 teaspoon dry mustard
- 1 cup 2% reduced-fat milk
- 2 tablespoons cornstarch
- Salt to taste
- 1/2 teaspoon red pepper flakes, crushed
- 1/2 teaspoon dried rosemary
- 1 ½ pounds shrimp, peeled and deveined

Directions

1. In your crock pot, combine broth, corn, beans, scallions, caraway seeds and mustard.
2. Cook on high approximately 4 hours.
3. In a medium-sized mixing bowl, whisk together milk, cornstarch, salt, red pepper and rosemary.
4. Add the milk mixture and the shrimp to the crock pot during last 20 minutes of cooking time.
5. Garnish with lemon wedges and sprinkle with some extra red pepper flakes, if desired. Enjoy!

Summer Seafood Treat

(Ready in about 4 hours | Servings 8)

Ingredients

- 1 cup fish stock
- 1/2 cup water
- 1 ½ cup tomatoes, undrained and diced

- 2 large-sized Yukon gold potatoes, diced
- 1 cup spring onions, chopped
- 1 teaspoon garlic powder
- 1/2 teaspoon onion powder
- 1/2 teaspoon dried thyme
- 1 teaspoon dried tarragon leaves
- 1/2 teaspoon cayenne pepper
- 1 cup lobster tail, cooked and cut into small pieces
- 1/2 cup small shrimp, peeled and deveined
- 1 cup whole milk
- Salt to taste
- Black pepper to taste
- Paprika to taste
- Fresh cilantro, as garnish

Directions

1. Pour fish stock and water into your crock pot. Then, add tomatoes, potatoes, onion powder, garlic powder, thyme, tarragon and cayenne pepper.
2. Next, cover and cook on low 4 hours.
3. Add remaining ingredients, except cilantro, during last 10 minutes of cooking time.
4. Sprinkle with chopped fresh cilantro and enjoy your summer chowder!

Lobster Chowder with Vegetables

(Ready in about 4 hours | Servings 8)

Ingredients

- 1/2 cup water
- 1 cup clam juice
- 1/2 cup plum tomatoes, diced
- 1/2 cup tomato juice
- 1 large-sized carrot, chopped
- 1 celery stalk, chopped
- 1 cup spring onions, chopped
- 1 teaspoon garlic powder
- 1/2 teaspoon Italian seasoning mix
- 1/4 teaspoon Ancho Chile, ground
- 1 teaspoon dried tarragon leaves
- 1 cup lobster meat, cooked and cut into small pieces

- 1/2 cup small shrimp, peeled and deveined
- 1 cup whole milk
- Salt to taste
- Black pepper to taste
- Fresh parsley, as garnish
- Lemon wedges, as garnish

Directions

1. Combine water, clam juice, tomatoes, tomato juice, carrot, celery, spring onions, garlic powder, Italian seasoning mix, Ancho Chile and tarragon leaves in a crock pot.
2. Set the crock pot to low and cook your chowder for about 4 hours.
3. Add remaining ingredients, except parsley and lemon wedges; cook 10 minutes longer.
4. Serve garnished with fresh parsley and lemon wedges.

Delicious Scallop and Potato Chowder

(Ready in about 4 hours | Servings 4)

Ingredients

- 1 cup clam juice
- 1/2 cup water
- 1/2 cup dry white wine
- 2 large-sized red potatoes, peeled and cubed
- 1 clove garlic, minced
- 1 pound bay scallops
- 1/2 cup milk (2% reduced-fat)
- 1/2 teaspoon cumin
- Salt to taste
- Red pepper flakes, as garnish

Directions

1. Put first five ingredients into a crock pot; then, cover and cook on high 3 to 4 hours.
2. Process this mixture in a blender until smooth and creamy; return to the crock pot.
3. Stir in the rest of ingredients, except red pepper flakes. Cover and cook on high until scallops are cooked through or about 10 minutes.
4. Divide among soup bowls, sprinkle with red pepper flakes and serve warm.

Italian-Style Seafood Chowder

(Ready in about 4 hours | Servings 8)

Ingredients

- 1 cup tomatoes, diced
- ½ cup fresh tomato juice
- 1 cup fish stock
- 2 medium-sized potatoes, diced
- 1/2 cup sweet red bell pepper, chopped
- 1 yellow onion, chopped
- 1/2 cup dry white wine
- 1 teaspoon dried Italian seasoning
- 1 cup haddock, cubed
- 1/2 cup bay scallops
- 1 teaspoon hot pepper sauce
- Salt, to taste
- Black pepper, to taste
- Sour cream, as garnish

Directions

1. Combine tomatoes with tomato juice, fish stock, potatoes, bell pepper, onion, white wine, and Italian seasonings.
2. Cover and cook on high about 4 hours, adding haddock and bay scallops during last 20 minutes of cooking time.
3. Stir in the sauce, salt, and black pepper. Serve with a dollop of sour cream.

Salmon Chowder with Root Vegetables

(Ready in about 6 hours | Servings 4)

Ingredients

- 3 cups potatoes, peeled and cubed
- 2 medium-sized carrot, thinly sliced
- 1/2 cup scallions, chopped
- 1 cup turnips, chopped
- 1/2 cup rutabaga
- 1 cup water
- 2 cups clam juice
- 1/2 teaspoon dry mustard
- 1/2 teaspoon dried marjoram leaves
- 1 teaspoon celery seeds

- 1 pound salmon steaks, cut into bite-sized chunks
- 1 cup milk
- 2 tablespoons cornstarch
- Salt, to taste
- Black pepper, to taste

Directions

1. In a crock pot, combine potatoes, carrots, scallions, turnips, rutabaga, water, clam juice, dry mustard, marjoram, and celery seeds.

2. Cover and cook on high 6 hours.

3. Purée chowder in a food processor or a blender until smooth and uniform; return to the crock pot. Stir in salmon and cook an additional 15 minutes.

4. Next, stir in combined milk and cornstarch, stirring frequently about 3 minutes. Season with salt and black pepper. Enjoy!

Salmon with Corn and Roasted Pepper

(Ready in about 5 hours | Servings 4)

Ingredients

- 1 cup reduced-sodium chicken broth
- 1 cup whole kernel corn
- 1 cup chickpea
- 2 medium potatoes, peeled and cubed
- 1 roasted red pepper, chopped
- 1 roasted yellow pepper, chopped
- 2 teaspoons minced garlic
- 1/2 teaspoon Ancho Chile, ground
- 1/2 teaspoon Fenugreek Seed, ground
- 1 teaspoon cumin seeds
- 1 teaspoon dried oregano leaves
- 1 ½ cup salmon steaks, cubed
- Salt, to taste
- White pepper, to taste

Directions

1. Combine all ingredients, except salmon, salt, and white pepper, in a crock pot; cover and cook on high 4 to 5 hours

2. Next, add salmon during last 15 minutes of cooking time. Season with salt and white pepper.

Bermuda-Style Whitefish Chowder

(Ready in about 8 hours | Servings 6)

Ingredients

- 2 cups clam juice
- 1 cup water
- 1/4 cup dry white wine
- 1 ½ cups plum tomatoes, undrained and chopped
- 1/3 cup tomato paste
- 2 cloves garlic, smashed
- 1 cup onion, finely chopped
- 1 celery, chopped
- 1 parsnip, chopped
- 2 small smoked pork hocks
- 2 ½ teaspoons soy sauce
- 2 bay leaves
- 1 teaspoon dried marjoram leaves
- 1/2 teaspoon curry powder
- 1/2 teaspoon grated ginger
- 1 pound whitefish fillet, cubed
- Salt, to taste
- White pepper, to taste
- Avocado slices, as garnish

Directions

1. Combine all ingredients, except fish, salt, pepper and avocado, in your crock pot.
2. Cover and cook on low approximately 8 hours, adding whitefish fillets during last 20 minutes of cooking.
3. Discard pork, season with salt and white pepper; serve garnished with slices of avocado.

Creamy Haddock Chowder

(Ready in about 8 hours | Servings 6)

Ingredients

- 2 cups water
- 1 cup chicken stock
- 1/4 cup dry white wine
- 1 tablespoon apple cider vinegar
- 2 tablespoons tomato ketchup
- 3 medium-sized tomatoes, chopped

- 1 cup shallots, finely chopped
- 1 carrot, chopped
- 1 parsnip, chopped
- 2 ½ teaspoons Worcester sauce
- 1 teaspoon rubbed sage
- 1 teaspoon dried parsley flakes
- 1/2 teaspoon ground nutmeg
- 1 pound haddock fillet, cut into bite-sized chunks
- Salt, to taste
- White pepper, to taste

Directions

1. Combine all of the ingredients, except fish fillets, salt, and white pepper, in a crock pot.
2. Cook, covered, about 8 hours, adding fish during last 15 minutes.
3. Season to taste with salt and white pepper.

Cod and Tomato Chowder

(Ready in about 8 hours | Servings 6)

Ingredients

- 3 cups fish stock
- 1/4 cup dry white wine
- 1 cup tomato paste
- 1 cup spring onions, chopped
- 1 Yukon gold potato, diced
- 1 carrot, chopped
- 1 parsnip, chopped
- 1 tablespoon tamari sauce
- 1 teaspoon rubbed sage
- 1 teaspoon dried parsley flakes
- 1/4 teaspoon ground Mace, optional
- 1 pound cod fillet, cut into bite-sized pieces
- Salt, to taste
- Cayenne pepper, to taste
- Fresh parsley, to taste

Directions

1. Combine all of the ingredients, except cod fillets, salt, cayenne pepper and parsley, in your crock pot.
2. Cook, covered, 7 to 8 hours. Add cod fillets, salt, cayenne pepper and fresh parsley; continue cooking 15 more minutes. Serve warm.

Cheesy Monkfish Chowder with Cauliflower

(Ready in about 8 hours | Servings 4)

Ingredients

- 1 can (14 ounces) reduced-sodium chicken broth
- 1 pound Yukon potatoes, peeled and cubed
- 1/2 cup green onions, chopped
- 1 large-sized carrot, chopped
- 1/2 head cauliflower, broken into florets
- 1 pound monkfish, cubed
- Salt, to taste
- Crushed red pepper flakes, to taste
- 3/4 teaspoon hot pepper sauce
- 1/2 cup reduced-fat Cheddar cheese, shredded

Directions

1. Arrange first five ingredients in your crock pot. Set the crock pot to low; cook about 8 hours.
2. Next, process cooked mixture in a food processor until your desired consistency is reached; return to the crock pot.
3. Add remaining ingredients, except the hot sauce and cheese; continue cooking on low heat setting for 15 minutes longer.
4. Add the hot pepper sauce and cheese; allow to sit until Cheddar cheese is melted. Serve warm or at room temperature.

Hearty Flounder Chowder

(Ready in about 6 hours | Servings 4)

Ingredients

- 2 cups clam juice
- 3 medium-sized potatoes, cubed peeled
- 1 cup broccoli florets
- 1 cup green beans
- 1 cup leeks, chopped
- 1 carrot, chopped

- 1 rib celery, chopped
- 1 garlic clove, smashed
- 1/2 teaspoon dried marjoram leaves
- 1/4 teaspoon Mace, ground
- 1/4 teaspoon dry mustard
- 2 cups whole milk
- 8 ounces flounder fillets, skinless and cubed
- 4 ounces crabmeat
- Celery salt to taste
- 1/4 teaspoon white pepper

Directions

1. In a crock pot, place clam juice, potatoes, broccoli, green beans, leeks, carrot, celery, garlic, marjoram, mace, and dry mustard.

2. Set the crock pot to low and then cook approximately 6 hours.

3. Add milk and continue cooking for 30 minutes longer. Increase heat to high; add flounder fillets, crabmeat, celery salt and white pepper during last 15 minutes of cooking time.

4. Divide among soup bowls and serve with croutons, if desired.

Rich Seafood Soup with Bacon

(Ready in about 5 hours | Servings 4)

Ingredients

- 1 ½ cups clam juice
- 1/4 cup dry cherry wine
- 4 large-sized Yukon gold potatoes, peeled and cubed
- 1 large-sized sweet onion, chopped
- 1 rib celery, chopped
- 1 rutabaga, chopped
- 1 cup 2% reduced-fat milk
- 1 pound halibut, cubed
- A few drops of Tabasco sauce
- 3/4 teaspoon rubbed sage
- 1 teaspoon dried parsley flakes
- Salt, to taste
- Paprika to taste
- 2 slices of cooked bacon, crumbled

Directions

1. First of all, put first six ingredients into your crock pot.

2. Next, cook on high 4 to 5 hours. Replace prepared soup to a blender or a food processor; add in milk and blend until everything is well combined; return to the crock pot.

3. Add remaining ingredients, except crumbled bacon. Continue cooking an additional 15 minutes.

4. Divide the soup among four serving bowls, scatter the bacon on top and enjoy!

Refreshing Fish Chowder with Eggs

(Ready in about 8 hours | Servings 6)

Ingredients

- 2 cups water
- 1 teaspoon chicken bouillon concentrate
- 2 large-sized sweet potatoes, diced and peeled
- 1 cup baby carrot, halved
- 1/2 cup leeks, chopped
- 3/4 teaspoon dried dill weed
- 1/2 teaspoon red pepper flakes, crushed
- 2 cups 2% reduced-fat milk, divided
- 1 ½ pounds skinless fish fillets of choice, sliced
- 1 cup cucumber, seeded and chopped
- 1 tablespoon lime juice
- Celery salt to taste
- Chopped chives, as garnish
- Hard-cooked egg slices, as garnish

Directions

1. Combine first seven ingredients in your crock pot; cook on low 6 to 8 hours.

2. Add in milk during last 30 minutes. Stir in fish and cucumber during last 10 minutes of cooking time.

3. Add lime juice and celery salt and stir to combine.

4. Garnish bowls of soup with chives and hard-cooked egg slices.

Spicy Sweet Potato Chili

(Ready in about 8 hours | Servings 6)

Ingredients

- 1 pound chicken breast, boneless and skinless
- 2 cups chicken broth
- 1 tablespoon apple cider vinegar
- 2 cups canned beans, rinsed and drained
- 1 cup spring onions, chopped
- 2 cloves garlic, minced
- 1 cup button mushrooms, sliced
- 1 carrot, thinly sliced
- 2 medium-sized sweet potatoes, peeled and cubed
- 3/4 teaspoon jalapeño chilli
- 1 ½ teaspoon gingerroot
- 1 teaspoon, ground cumin
- 1/2 teaspoon ground coriander
- 1/2 teaspoon allspice
- Salt, to taste
- Ground black pepper, to taste
- Sour cream, as garnish

Directions

1. Combine all of the ingredients, except sour cream, in your crock pot.
2. Cover with a lid and cook on low heat setting 6 to 8 hours.
3. Serve with sour cream and enjoy.

Chili with Turkey and Roasted Pepper

(Ready in about 8 hours | Servings 6)

Ingredients

- 1 pound ground turkey
- 1 ½ cup canned tomatoes, stewed
- 1 can (15 ounces) red beans, rinsed drained
- 1 small-sized jalapeño pepper, minced
- 1 cup red onion, chopped
- 1/2 cup roasted red pepper, coarsely chopped

- 1/2 tablespoon chili powder
- 1/4 teaspoon ground cinnamon
- Celery salt, to taste
- Black pepper, to taste
- Smoked paprika to taste

Directions

1. Heat a non-stick skillet over medium-high flame. Brown turkey for about 5 minutes, crumbling with a fork. Transfer browned ground beef to the crock pot.
2. Add the rest of ingredients; cover with a lid and cook on low heat setting approximately 8 hours.
3. Serve with corn chips, if desired.

Black Bean Chili with Squash

(Ready in about 8 hours | Servings 6)

Ingredients

- 1 pound ground beef
- 2 cups tomato juice
- 1 cup chunky tomato sauce
- 1 cup water
- 1 tablespoon lime
- 1 ½ cups canned black beans, rinsed and drained
- 2 cups scallions, chopped
- 2 cloves garlic, minced
- 1/2 cup celery, cubed
- 2 cups butternut squash
- 1 cup zucchini
- 1 cup mushrooms
- 1 small-sized jalapeño chili, finely chopped
- 1 ½ teaspoons chili powder
- 1 sea salt
- 1/4 teaspoon ground black pepper
- 6 lime wedges

Directions

1. First of all, brown ground beef in non-stick skillet about 8 minutes, crumbling with a fork. Transfer to the crock pot.

2. Stir in remaining ingredients, except lime wedges; set the crock pot to low and cook 6 to 8 hours.

3. Serve garnished with lime wedges.

Turkey and Cannellini Bean Chili

(Ready in about 8 hours | Servings 6)

Ingredients

- 1 pound lean ground beef
- 2 cups tomato sauce
- 2 cups cannellini beans
- 1 cup spring onions, chopped
- 1 clove garlic, minced
- 1 tablespoon chili powder
- 2 teaspoons brown sugar
- 1 teaspoon celery seeds
- 1 teaspoon ground cumin
- Salt, to taste
- Ground black pepper, to taste

Directions

1. Cook ground beef in a cast-iron skillet over medium heat 8 to 10 minutes or until browned.

2. Add remaining ingredients and cook on low 6 to 8 hours.

3. Divide prepared chili among six soup bowls and serve warm with your favorite salad.

Easy Beef and Pork Chili

(Ready in about 8 hours | Servings 6)

Ingredients

- 1 tablespoon olive oil
- 1 pounds lean ground beef
- 1/2 pounds ground pork
- 2 cups pinto beans, rinsed and drained
- 2 cups stewed tomatoes
- 2 cups whole kernel corn
- 1 cup leeks, chopped
- 1/2 cup red bell pepper, chopped

- 2 tablespoons taco seasoning mix
- Salt to taste
- Black pepper to taste
- Paprika to taste
- Reduced-fat sour cream, as garnish
- Biscuits, as garnish

Directions

1. Heat the olive oil in a wide saucepan. Next, cook ground beef and pork about 10 minutes. Crumble with a fork.
2. Add the rest of ingredients, except sour cream and biscuits; cover and cook on low for about 8 hours.
3. Divide among serving bowls, serve with sour cream and biscuits.

Italian-Style Chili

(Ready in about 8 hours | Servings 8)

Ingredients

- 12 ounces lean ground turkey
- 3 cups water
- 1 can (28-ounce) tomatoes, crushed
- 1 red bell pepper, sliced
- 1 yellow bell pepper, sliced
- 1/2 cup onion, chopped
- 3 cloves garlic, minced
- 1 teaspoon ground cumin
- 2 tablespoons chili powder
- 1 dried parsley
- 2 teaspoons dried oregano leaves
- 1 teaspoon allspice
- Salt, to taste
- 1/4 teaspoon black pepper
- 1 pound spaghetti, cooked
- Reduced-fat Cheddar cheese, shredded

Directions

1. In a large non-stick skillet, brown the ground turkey over medium heat, about 5 minutes.
2. Combine turkey with remaining ingredients, except spaghetti and Cheddar cheese, in your crock pot; cook on low 8 hours.
3. Serve with spaghetti and Cheddar cheese.

Family Favourite Chili

(Ready in about 8 hours | Servings 8)

Ingredients

- 1 pound ground beef
- 1 cup onions, chopped
- 1 green bell pepper, chopped
- 1 red bell pepper, chopped
- 1 poblano pepper, minced
- 2 cloves garlic, minced
- 2 teaspoons ground cumin
- 1 teaspoon dried oregano leaves
- 1 teaspoon dried basil leaves
- 1/2 teaspoon grated ginger
- 1 tablespoon cilantro
- 2 cups tomatoes, undrained and diced
- 1 cup water
- 1 can (15 ounces) pinto beans, rinsed and drained
- 1/4 cup tomato ketchup
- 3/4 cup beer
- 1 tablespoon unsweetened cocoa
- Salt, to taste
- Black pepper, to taste
- Paprika, to taste
- Sour cream, as garnish

Directions

1. First of all, cook ground beef in lightly greased saucepan over medium heat. Cook until the beef is browned and cooked through or about 10 minutes.
2. Add beef to the crock pot. Then, add remaining ingredients, except sour cream, to the crock pot; cover with a lid and cook on low about 8 hours.
3. Garnish each bowl of chili with sour cream.

Easy Tenderloin Chili

(Ready in about 6 hours | Servings 4)

Ingredients

- 1 pound pork tenderloin, cubed
- 1 can (15-ounces) reduced-sodium fat-free vegetable broth

- 1 can (15-ounces) beans, rinsed
- 1 pound plum tomatoes, sliced
- 1 large-sized jalapeño chili, minced
- 1 tablespoon chili powder
- 1 teaspoon toasted cumin seeds
- Salt, to taste
- Black pepper, to taste
- Cayenne pepper to taste
- Corn chips, as garnish

Directions

1. Combine all ingredients, except corn chips, in a crock pot.
2. Cook covered on high about 6 hours.
3. Serve with corn chips and enjoy!

Yummy Tomato Bean Soup

(Ready in about 7 hours | Servings 6)

Ingredients

- 1 quart chicken stock
- 2 cans (15-ounce) navy beans, rinsed, drained
- 1 cup cooked bacon, chopped
- 1 pound lamb, cubed
- 1 cup scallions
- 1 rib celery, chopped
- 1 large-sized carrot, chopped
- 1 clove garlic, minced
- 1 teaspoon Italian seasoning mix
- 3 Roma tomatoes, chopped
- Salt, to taste
- Black pepper, to taste
- Cayenne pepper, to taste
- Biscuits, as garnish

Directions

1. Combine all ingredients, except biscuits, in a crock pot.
2. Next, cover and cook on low for about 7 hours.
3. Serve with biscuits and enjoy!

Lamb Chili with Ham

(Ready in about 8 hours | Servings 6)

Ingredients

- 1 quart vegetable stock
- 2 cans (15-ounce) pinto beans, rinsed, drained
- 1 cup partially cooked ham, diced
- 1 pound lamb, cubed
- 1 large-sized red onion, finely chopped
- 2 cloves garlic, minced
- 1 large-sized carrot, chopped
- 1 rib celery, chopped
- 1 teaspoon Italian seasoning mix
- 1 cup tomato sauce
- Salt, to taste
- Black pepper, to taste
- Cayenne pepper, to taste
- Sour cream, as garnish

Directions

4. Place all ingredients, except sour cream, in a crock pot.
5. Set the crock pot to low; cook your chili for 7 to 8 hours.
6. Garnish with a sour cream and serve.

Creamy Vegetable Soup

(Ready in about 4 hours | Servings 4)

Ingredients

- 2 cups vegetable stock
- 2-3 spring onions, chopped
- 3/4 cup mushrooms, thinly sliced
- 1 cup frozen artichoke hearts, thawed and finely chopped
- 1 cup light cream
- 2 tablespoons cornstarch
- Salt, to taste
- Black pepper, to taste
- Red pepper flakes, as garnish

Directions

1. Combine first four ingredients in your crock pot; cover and cook on high heat setting 4 hours.

2. Combine light cream and cornstarch. Add this mixture to the crock pot, stirring 2 to 3 minutes.

3. Season with salt and black pepper. Sprinkle each bowl of soup with red pepper flakes.

Fall Brussels sprouts Soup

(Ready in about 4 hours | Servings 4)

Ingredients

- 1 pound Brussels sprouts, halved
- 1/2 cup sweet onion, chopped
- 1 clove garlic, minced
- 1 teaspoon onion powder
- 1 teaspoon celery seeds
- 1/2 teaspoon dried rosemary leaves
- 1 cup vegetable broth
- 1 cup 2% reduced-fat milk
- Salt, to taste
- Black pepper, to taste
- Ground nutmeg, as garnish

Directions

1. Add Brussels sprouts, sweet onion, garlic, onion powder, celery seeds, rosemary, and vegetable broth to the crock pot; cover and cook on high 3 to 4 hours.

2. Pour the soup in a food processor or a blender. Add 2% reduced-fat milk. Blend until a smooth consistency is reached.

3. Season with salt and black pepper. Divide among four soup bowls and sprinkle lightly with nutmeg; serve.

PART THREE: DINNER

Family Red Chili

(Ready in about 8 hours | Servings 4)

Ingredients

- 8 ounces ground beef sirloin
- 1 can (28-ounces) tomatoes, crushed
- 1 can (15-ounces) red kidney beans, rinsed and drained
- 1 red bell peppers, chopped
- 1 yellow bell pepper, chopped
- 1/2 cup red onion, chopped
- 1 cup large red onion
- 2 tablespoons red wine vinegar
- 1 teaspoon chili powder
- 1/4 teaspoon ground cinnamon
- 2/3 cup mild picante sauce
- Salt, to taste
- Black pepper, to taste

Directions

1. In lightly greased large skillet, brown ground beef over medium flame. Cook about 5 minutes, crumbling with a fork.
2. Transfer cooked beef to a crock pot, then, add remaining ingredients; cover and cook on low 6 to 8 hours. Serve warm with cornmeal crisps, if desired.

Turkey Chili with Kale

(Ready in about 8 hours | Servings 8)

Ingredients

- 1 tablespoon olive oil
- 1 ½ pounds lean ground turkey
- 2 cans (15-ounce) cannellini beans, rinsed and drained
- 1 cup tomato paste
- 1/2 cup red onion, chopped
- 1 bay leaf
- 1/2 teaspoon dried rosemary

- 1 teaspoon ground cumin
- 1/2 teaspoon caraway seeds
- 1 ½ cup kale, coarsely chopped
- 1/4 teaspoon black pepper
- 1/4 teaspoon cayenne pepper
- Celery salt, to taste

Directions

1. Lightly grease a large skillet with olive oil. Cook ground turkey until browned or about 10 minutes.
2. Place cooked meat and remaining ingredients, except kale, in a crock pot; cover and cook on low heat setting approximately 8 hours.
3. Add kale during the last 20 minutes of cooking time.
4. Taste, adjust the seasonings and serve warm.

Piquant Chicken Sausage Chili

(Ready in about 6 hours | Servings 4)

Ingredients

- 4 ounces chicken sausage, sliced
- 2 Roma tomatoes, chopped
- 2 heaping tablespoons tomato ketchup
- 2 cups canned beans
- 1 large-sized red onion, finely chopped
- 1 green bell pepper, chopped
- 1 red bell pepper, chopped
- 1 teaspoon ground cumin
- 1 tablespoon cilantro, chopped
- 1 tablespoon chili powder
- Salt, to taste
- Sour cream, as garnish

Directions

1. In a non-stick skillet, cook sausage until browned or about 6 minutes. Replace to the crock pot.
2. Stir in remaining ingredients, except sour cream; cover and cook on low heat setting about 6 hours.
3. Serve with a dollop of sour cream.

Pepperoni Hot Chili

(Ready in about 8 hours | Servings 8)

Ingredients

- 12 ounces turkey sausage
- 4 ounces pepperoni, sliced
- 1 can (14 1/2 ounces) diced tomatoes, undrained
- 1 ½ cup beef broth
- 1 ½ cup tomato sauce
- 1 teaspoon lemon zest
- 1 cup garbanzo beans
- 1/2 cup canned green chilies, chopped
- 1 large-sized red onion, chopped
- 1 ½ teaspoons dried Italian seasoning
- 2 tablespoons hot chili powder
- 1 tablespoon Worcestershire sauce
- Salt, to taste
- Paprika, to taste
- Hot pepper sauce, optional

Directions

1. Cook sausage and pepperoni in lightly greased saucepan over medium heat. Cook 10 to 12 minutes; transfer to a crock pot.
2. Add the rest of ingredients; cover and cook on low about 8 hours.
3. Divide among serving bowls and serve with cornbread.

Spaghetti with Beans and Asparagus

(Ready in about 3 hours | Servings 4)

Ingredients

- 1 cup vegetable stock
- 1/2 cup green beans
- 1 can (15-ounces) Great Northern beans, rinsed and drained
- 2 medium-sized tomatoes, chopped
- 2 medium-sized carrots, chopped
- 3/4 teaspoon dried rosemary leaves
- 1 pound asparagus, cut into bite-sized pieces
- 1/2 teaspoon celery salt

- 1 teaspoon onion powder
- 1 teaspoon garlic powder
- 8 ounces spaghetti, cooked
- 1/4 cup Parmesan cheese, shredded

Directions

1. In a crock pot, place vegetable stock, green beans, Great Northern beans, tomatoes, carrots, and rosemary.
2. Cook covered for 3 hours, adding asparagus pieces during last 30 minutes of cooking time.
3. Season with celery salt, onion powder and garlic powder; toss with spaghetti and Parmesan cheese. Enjoy!

Easy Spicy Green Beans

(Ready in about 4 hours | Servings 4)

Ingredients

- 1 pound green beans
- 1 can (28-ounce) petite-diced tomatoes
- 1 large-sized red onion, chopped
- 4 cloves garlic, minced
- 1 teaspoon celery seeds
- 1 teaspoon dried basil
- 1 teaspoon dried oregano
- 1 teaspoon sea salt
- 1/4 teaspoon freshly ground black pepper
- 1/4 teaspoon red pepper flakes, crushed

Directions

1. Combine all ingredients in a crock pot.
2. Cook covered on high about 4 hours or until green beans are tender.
3. Taste, adjust the seasonings and divide among serving bowls. Enjoy this easy and healthy dinner with boiled potatoes and favorite seasonal salad!

Favorite Creamy Green Beans

(Ready in about 6 hours | Servings 4)

Ingredients

- 1/2 cup sour cream
- 1/4 cup 2 % reduced-fat milk
- 1 ½ cup canned fat-free cream of mushroom soup
- 1 package (10 ounces) green beans, thawed
- 2 cloves garlic, minced
- 1 carrot, chopped
- 1 celery stalk, chopped
- Salt, to taste
- Cayenne pepper, to taste
- Chopped cashews, as garnish

Directions

1. Mix all of the ingredients, except cashews, in your crock pot.
2. Cover and cook on low heat setting about 6 hours.
3. Scatter chopped cashews on top; serve over macaroni or cooked brown rice.

Steak Roll Ups with Mushrooms

(Ready in about 6 hours | Servings 4)

Ingredients

- 1 pound beef steaks, cut into 4 serving-size portions
- 4 slices of smoked ham
- 1 cup Portobello mushrooms, chopped
- 1/4 cup dill pickle, finely chopped
- 1 large-sized sweet onion, chopped
- 1 teaspoon Dijon mustard
- 1/2 teaspoon dried tarragon
- 1 teaspoon dried basil
- 1/2 teaspoon dried oregano
- 1/2 cup beef broth
- Celery salt, to taste
- Black peppercorns, to taste
- Mayonnaise, as garnish

Directions

1. Top each portion of beef steak with ham slice.

2. In a mixing bowl, combine mushrooms, dill pickle, onion, mustard, tarragon, basil and oregano. Spread this mixture over ham.

3. Next, roll up steaks and secure them with toothpicks; place in the crock pot.

4. Pour in broth, sprinkle with celery salt and peppercorns; cook on low 5 to 6 hours. Garnish with mayonnaise and serve.

Favorite Hot Rouladen

(Ready in about 6 hours | Servings 4)

Ingredients

- 1 pound beef steaks, cut into 4 serving-size portions
- 4 slices of reduced-fat Provolone cheese
- 1 sweet red bell pepper, cut into thin strips
- 1 sweet green bell pepper, cut into thin strips
- 1/4 cup sun-dried, finely chopped
- 1 jalapeño pepper, minced
- 1/2 cup green onions, chopped
- 1 teaspoon mustard
- 1 teaspoon dried basil
- 1/2 teaspoon celery seeds
- Sea salt, to taste
- Ground black pepper, to taste
- 1/2 cup beef broth

Directions

1. Top each portion of beef steak with the slice of cheese. Then, place bell peppers on each slice of steak.

2. In a bowl, combine the rest of ingredients, except beef broth. Spread this mixture over slices of cheese.

3. Then, roll up steaks; secure with toothpicks; place in the bottom of your crock pot.

4. Pour in beef broth; cook covered on low about 6 hours. Serve warm.

Juicy Beef Short Ribs

(Ready in about 8 hours | Servings 4)

Ingredients

- 1/2 cup dry red wine
- 1/2 cup beef broth
- 1 teaspoon mustard
- 4 large-sized carrots, sliced
- 1 large-sized red onion, cut into wedges
- 1 heaping tablespoon cilantro
- 1/2 teaspoon dried tarragon
- 2 pounds beef short ribs

Directions

1. Arrange all ingredients in a crock pot, placing beef short ribs on the top.
2. Cover and cook on low approximately 8 hours.
3. Serve warm with some extra mustard.

Easy Italian-Style Meatloaf

(Ready in about 7 hours | Servings 4)

Ingredients

- 1 ½ pounds lean ground beef
- 1 cup quick-cooking oats
- 1 teaspoon lemon zest
- 1/2 cup milk
- 1 medium-sized egg
- 1/4 cup tomato catsup
- 1/2 cup scallions, chopped
- 1 green bell pepper, chopped
- 1 teaspoon granulated garlic
- 1 teaspoon Italian seasoning
- 1 teaspoon sea salt
- 1/2 teaspoon ground black pepper

Directions

1. Mix all ingredients until everything is well incorporated; place your meatloaf on slow cooker liner in a crock pot.
2. Cover and cook on low 6 to 7 hours.
3. Serve over mashed potatoes and enjoy!

Cheesy Everyday Meatloaf

(Ready in about 6 hours | Servings 4)

Ingredients

- 1/2 pound lean ground pork
- 1/2 pound lean ground beef
- 1/2 cup reduced-fat cream cheese
- 1 cup quick-cooking oats
- 2 tablespoons Worcestershire sauce
- 1 medium-sized egg
- 1/4 cup tomato ketchup
- 1/2 cup onion, chopped
- 1 green bell pepper, chopped
- 1/2 teaspoon ground ginger
- 1 clove garlic, minced
- 1 teaspoon sea salt
- 1/2 teaspoon ground black pepper
- 1/2 cup reduced-fat Cheddar cheese, grated

Directions

1. In a large-sized mixing bowl, combine all of the ingredients, except Cheddar cheese. Shape into a meatloaf.
2. Place the meatloaf on slow cooker liner in a crock pot.
3. Cook on low approximately 6 hours.
4. Scatter grated Cheddar cheese on top and let stand until cheese is melted. Serve.

Curried Peanut Meat Loaf

(Ready in about 6 hours | Servings 4)

Ingredients

- 1 cup quick-cooking oats
- 1 teaspoon grated ginger
- 1/2 cup milk
- 1 egg
- 1/4 cup chutney, chopped
- 1/2 cup onion, chopped
- 1 sweet red bell pepper, chopped
- 1 teaspoon granulated garlic

- 1 teaspoon dried basil
- 1/3 cup chopped peanuts
- 1 teaspoon curry powder
- 1 teaspoon sea salt
- 1/2 teaspoon ground black pepper
- 1 ½ pounds ground beef and pork, mixed

Directions

1. Line a crock pot with a wide strip of aluminium foil.
2. In a large mixing bowl, combine oats, ginger, milk, egg, chutney, onion, bell pepper, garlic, basil, peanuts, curry powder, sea salt and black pepper. Mix well to combine.
3. Stir in ground meat and mix again. Shape the mixture into a round loaf.
4. Place in the crock pot; set crock pot to low and cook 6 hours. Serve warm or at room temperature.

Mom's Spiced Mashed Beans

(Ready in about 8 hours | Servings 10)

Ingredients

- 9 cups water
- 3 cups canned pinto beans, rinsed
- 1 yellow onion, cut into wedges
- 1/2 poblano pepper, seeded and minced
- 2 cloves garlic, minced
- 1 tablespoon Cajun seasoning
- 1 teaspoon fine sea salt
- 1 teaspoon ground black pepper
- 1 teaspoon cayenne pepper

Directions

1. Arrange all of the ingredients in a crock pot.
2. Cook on high heat setting for 8 hours.
3. Strain and reserve the liquid. Mash the beans, adding the reserved liquid as needed. Serve with sausage and your favourite salad.

Kicked Up Cajun Jambalaya

(Ready in about 8 hours | Servings 12)

Ingredients

- 1 (28-ounce) can tomatoes, diced
- 1 pound chicken breast, skinless, boneless and cut into bite-sized pieces
- 1 pound Andouille sausage, sliced
- 1 large-sized onion, chopped
- 1 celery stalk, chopped
- 1 bell pepper, chopped
- 1 cup chopped celery
- 1 cup chicken stock
- 1 teaspoon dried basil leaves
- 1 teaspoon dried oregano
- 1 teaspoon Cajun seasoning
- 1 teaspoon cayenne pepper
- 1 pound frozen cooked shrimp without tails
- 1 cup cooked rice

Directions

1. In a crock pot, place all of the ingredients, except shrimp and cooked rice.
2. Cover and cook 8 hours on low.
3. Stir in the shrimp and cooked rice during the last 30 minutes of cooking time. Enjoy!

Tangy Pork Roast

(Ready in about 8 hours | Servings 8)

Ingredients

- 1 large red onion, sliced
- 2 cloves garlic, minced
- 2 pounds pork loin roast, boneless
- 1 cup water
- 2 tablespoons brown sugar
- 3 tablespoons dry red wine
- 2 tablespoons Worcestershire sauce
- 1/4 cup tomato juice
- 1/2 teaspoon salt
- 1/2 teaspoon black pepper

Directions

1. Arrange the slices of onion and minced garlic over the bottom of a crock pot; place the roast on top.

2. In a measuring cup or a mixing bowl, mix together the rest of ingredients; pour over pork loin roast.

3. Cover and cook on high for 3 to 4 hours or on low for 8 hours. Serve over mashed potatoes.

Hearty Stuffed Cabbage Leaves

(Ready in about 8 hours | Servings 4)

Ingredients

- 8 large-sized cabbage leaves
- 1 pound lean ground beef
- 1/4 cup onion, finely chopped
- 1/4 cup water
- 1 red bell pepper
- 1/4 cup cooked rice
- 3/4 teaspoon salt
- 1/4 teaspoon ground black pepper
- 1 ½ cup tomato sauce
- 1 can (16-ounce) tomatoes, diced

Directions

1. Place cabbage leaves in boiling water and cook until softened; drain.

2. Combine together ground beef and remaining ingredients, except tomato sauce and tomatoes. Stuff cabbage leaves, folding ends and sides over.

3. Stir in tomato sauce and tomatoes; cover and cook on low approximately 8 hours.

4. Serve with a dollop of sour cream.

Milk Braised Pork Loin

(Ready in about 4 hours | Servings 8)

Ingredients

- Ground black pepper, to taste
- Fine cooking salt, to taste
- 1 pork loin roast, boneless
- 1 cup green onions, chopped
- 2 cloves garlic, minced
- 1/2 cup milk
- 1/4 cup dry red wine
- 1 teaspoon dried sage
- 1 teaspoon dried rosemary
- Chives for garnish

Directions

1. Rub black pepper and salt into pork loin roast. Place in a crock pot.
2. Scatter chopped onions and minced garlic on top; then add combined milk and wine. Sprinkle with sage and rosemary.
3. Cover and cook on low about 4 hours.
4. Sprinkle with fresh chives and serve!

Mashed Potatoes with Carrots

(Ready in about 3 hours | Servings 8)

Ingredients

- 5 pounds red potatoes, cut into chunks
- 2 cloves garlic, minced
- 2 carrots, thinly sliced
- 1 cube chicken bouillon
- 1 cup sour cream
- 1 cup cream cheese
- 1/2 cup butter
- 1/2 teaspoon salt
- 1/2 teaspoon ground black pepper

Directions

1. In a large stockpot of boiling water, cook the potatoes, garlic, carrots and chicken bouillon about 15 minutes. Reserve water.

2. Next, mash boiled potatoes with sour cream and cream cheese.

3. Transfer the mashed potato to the crock pot; cover the crock pot with a lid, cook on low for about 3 hours.

4. Stir in butter; sprinkle with salt and black pepper; serve.

Holiday Cooked Ham

(Ready in about 8 hours | Servings 24)

Ingredients

- 1 cured, bone-in picnic ham
- 2 cups packed brown sugar
- 1/4 teaspoon ground cloves
- 2 tablespoons balsamic vinegar

Directions

1. Spread brown sugar and ground cloves on the bottom of the crock pot.

2. Place the ham in the crock pot and then add balsamic vinegar.

3. Cover and cook on low approximately 8 hours.

Family Favourite Apple Butter

(Ready in about 10 hours | Servings 24)

Ingredients

- 5 pounds apples, peeled, cored and chopped
- 4 cups brown sugar
- 1/2 teaspoon grated nutmeg
- 1 tablespoon ground cinnamon
- 1/2 teaspoon ground cloves
- A pinch of salt

Directions

1. Place the chopped apples in your crock pot.

2. In a medium-sized bowl, mix remaining ingredients until everything is well combined.

3. Pour this mixture over the apples in the crock pot and stir to combine.

4. Cover and cook on high for 1 hour. Turn heat to low and then cook about 9 hours. Stir with a whisk and refrigerate.

Italian-style Chicken with Broccoli

(Ready in about 9 hours | Servings 6)

Ingredients

- 3 chicken breasts, skinless and boneless
- 1 cup Italian-style salad dressing
- 1 ½ cups cream of chicken soup
- 1 cup chicken stock
- 1 cup cream cheese
- 1 teaspoon dried oregano
- 1/2 teaspoon dried basil
- Celery salt, to taste
- Ground black pepper, to taste
- Cayenne pepper, to taste

Directions

1. In a crock pot, combine the chicken breasts with Italian-style dressing.

2. Cover, set the crock pot to low and cook for 8 hours.

3. Shred the chicken meat and return to the crock pot. In a medium-sized mixing bowl, mix remaining ingredients.

4. Pour over the shredded chicken in the crock pot; add broccoli. Turn the heat to low and continue cooking for about 1 hour.

Pork Shoulder with Noodles

(Ready in about 8 hours | Servings 6)

Ingredients

- 1 pork shoulder roast, boneless
- 1 cup red onion, chopped
- 1 cup chicken broth
- 1/4 cup dry cherry

- 1 teaspoon garlic powder
- 1 teaspoon celery seeds
- 1/2 teaspoon cumin seeds
- Sea salt, to taste
- Ground black pepper, to taste
- 2 tablespoons cornstarch
- 1/3 cup cold water
- 6 cups cooked noodles, warm

Directions

1. Place first seven ingredients in a crock pot; cover and cook on low 8 hours.
2. Remove pork shoulder and shred. Season with sea salt and black pepper.
3. Turn the crock pot to high and cook 10 more minutes. Stir in combined cornstarch and cold water, stirring often 2 to 3 minutes.
4. Return shredded pork to the crock pot and toss; serve over cooked noodles and enjoy.

Teriyaki Pork with Tortillas

(Ready in about 8 hours | Servings 6)

Ingredients

- 1 cup vegetable stock
- 1/4 cup dry red wine
- 1 pork shoulder roast, boneless
- 1 package (1.06 ounces) teriyaki marinade mix
- 2 cloves garlic, minced
- 1 cup onion, chopped
- 1 teaspoon dried rosemary
- 1/2 teaspoon cumin seeds
- Sea salt, to taste
- Ground black pepper, to taste
- Red pepper flakes, crushed
- 6 flour tortillas

Directions

1. Add all of the ingredients, except tortillas, to the crock pot.
2. Cook on low heat setting approximately 8 hours or until the pork is falling-apart tender.
3. Next, cut cooked pork into shreds. Roll up in warm tortillas and enjoy!

Pork Chops with Creamy Sauce

(Ready in about 5 hours | Servings 4)

Ingredients

- 4 loin pork chops, boneless
- Salt to taste
- Freshly ground black pepper, to taste
- 1/2 cup leeks, thinly sliced
- 1 small rib celery, sliced
- 1 can (10 ounces) cream of celery soup
- 1/2 cup 2% reduced fat milk
- Cornbread, as garnish

Directions

1. Sprinkle pork with salt and freshly ground black pepper; add to the crock pot.
2. Place leeks and sliced celery on top.
3. Combine cream of celery soup with milk; whisk to combine. Pour the mixture into the crock pot.
4. Cover the crock pot with a lid and cook on low 4 to 5 hours. Serve with cornbread.

Pork Chops with Apricot and Hoisin Sauce

(Ready in about 3 hours | Servings 4)

Ingredients

- 6 pork chops, boneless
- 1/2 teaspoon seasoned salt
- 1/2 teaspoon ground black pepper
- 1/2 teaspoon paprika
- 1/4 cup vegetable broth
- 1/2 cup apricot preserves
- 3 tablespoons hoisin sauce
- 1 tablespoon cornstarch

Directions

1. Sprinkle meat with salt, pepper and paprika; place in a crock pot; pour in vegetable broth.
2. Cover and cook on low heat setting about 3 hours; reserve pork chops.

3. To make the sauce, turn heat to high and cook 10 more minutes; add the rest of ingredients into the broth, stirring 2 to 3 minutes.

4. Serve warm over steamed vegetables.

Pork Chops with Honey and Mustard

(Ready in about 4 hours | Servings 4)

Ingredients

- 4 loin pork chops, boneless
- 1/4 cup leeks, chopped
- 1/2 cup chicken broth
- 1/2 cup dry white wine
- 1 tablespoon cornstarch
- 2 tablespoons honey
- 2 tablespoons mustard
- 1 teaspoon grated ginger
- Salt, to taste
- Black pepper, to taste

Directions

1. Combine pork chops, leeks, chicken broth and white wine in a crock pot.

2. Cover and cook on low about 3 to 4 hours.

3. Remove pork chops from the crock pot and keep warm.

4. Add cornstarch, honey, mustard, ginger, salt and black pepper; continue cooking about 5 minutes. Serve warm.

Smoked Pork with Prunes

(Ready in about 8 hours | Servings 8)

Ingredients

- 2 pounds pork loin, boneless and cubed
- 1 cup prunes, pitted
- 1 ½ cups vegetable broth
- 1/2 cup dry white wine
- 1 teaspoon lemon juice
- Salt, to taste

- Black pepper, to taste
- Smoked paprika, to taste
- 2 tablespoons corn starch
- 1/4 cup cold water
- Liquid smoke, to taste
- 4 cups cooked couscous, warm

Directions

1. Place all of the ingredients, except corn starch, water, liquid smoke and couscous, in a crock pot.
2. Cover and cook on low approximately 8 hours. Next, turn heat to high; cook about 10 minutes.
3. In a bowl, combine corn starch with cold water. Add this mixture and liquid smoke to the crock pot and stir constantly 2 to 3 minutes. Serve with couscous.

Sweet Orange Smoked Ham

(Ready in about 3 hours | Servings 10)

Ingredients

- 3 pounds smoked ham, boneless
- 1/3 cup orange juice
- 1/4 cup honey
- 1 teaspoon allspice
- 1/2 teaspoon ground cinnamon
- 1 1/2 tablespoons corn starch
- 1/4 cup cold water
- 2 tablespoons dry sherry

Directions

1. Put all of the ingredients, except corn starch, water and sherry, into a crock pot.
2. Cover and cook on low until ham is tender or about 3 hours. Transfer prepared ham to a serving platter.
3. Measure 1 cup broth into skillet; heat to boiling; whisk in combined remaining ingredients about 1 minute.
4. Serve ham with sauce and enjoy!

Sherry Chicken with Mashed Potatoes

(Ready in about 4 hours | Servings 4)

Ingredients

For the Sherry Chicken:

- 1/4 cup dry sherry
- 1 cup raisins
- 4 medium-sized chicken breast
- 1 tart cooking apple, peeled and chopped
- 1 sweet onion, sliced
- 1 cup chicken broth
- Salt and pepper, to taste

For the mashed Potatoes:

- 2 pounds Idaho potatoes, peeled and cooked
- 1/4 sour cream
- 1/3 cup whole milk
- 2 tablespoons butter
- 1 teaspoon sea salt
- 1/4 teaspoon black pepper
- 1/4 teaspoon cayenne pepper

Directions

1. In a crock pot, place all of the ingredients for the sherry chicken; cover and cook on high until chicken breasts are tender or 3 to 4 hours.
2. Meanwhile, beat potatoes, adding sour cream, milk, and butter; beat until smooth and uniform.
3. Season with spices and serve on the side with sherry chicken.

Kicked Up Chicken with Zucchini

(Ready in about 4 hours | Servings 6)

Ingredients

- 3 medium-sized chicken breasts, halved
- 1 cup almond milk
- 1/4 cup water
- 1/4 cup lemon juice
- 2 cloves garlic, minced
- 1 medium-sized onion, chopped
- Salt, to taste

- Red pepper, to taste
- 1 teaspoon ground ginger
- 1 teaspoon ground cumin
- 1 pound zucchini, sliced
- 1 tablespoon cornflour
- 2 tablespoons water
- 1/3 cup fresh parsley, chopped
- 4 cups rice, cooked

Directions

1. Place all ingredients, except zucchini, cornflour, water, parsley and rice, in your crock pot.
2. Cover and cook on low heat setting about 4 hours, adding zucchini during last 30 minutes of cooking time. Reserve chicken breasts.
3. Turn heat to high and continue cooking 10 minutes; stir in combined cornflour and water, stirring about 3 minutes.
4. Sprinkle with parsley; serve over rice.

Festive Cornish Hens

(Ready in about 6 hours | Servings 4)

Ingredients

- 2 frozen Cornish hens, thawed
- 1/2 teaspoon sea salt
- 1/4 teaspoon ground black pepper
- 1/2 teaspoon cayenne pepper
- 1 clove garlic, minced
- 1/3 cup chicken broth
- 2 tablespoons cornflour
- 1/4 cup water

Directions

1. Sprinkle Cornish hens with salt, black pepper and cayenne pepper; add minced garlic and place in a crock pot. Pour in chicken broth.
2. Cover and cook on low 6 hours. Remove Cornish hens and reserve.
3. Stir in combined cornflour and water, stirring 2 to 3 minutes; serve.

Salmon with Caper Sauce

(Ready in about 45 minutes | Servings 4)

Ingredients

- 1/2 cup dry white wine
- 1/2 cup water
- 1 yellow onion, thin sliced
- 1/2 teaspoon salt
- 1/4 teaspoon black pepper
- 4 salmon steaks

- 2 tablespoons butter
- 3 tablespoons flour
- 1 cup chicken broth
- 2 teaspoons lemon juice
- 3 tablespoons capers

Directions

1. Combine wine, water, onion, salt and black pepper in a crock pot; cover and cook on high 20 minutes.
2. Add salmon steaks; cover and cook on high until salmon is tender or about 20 minutes.
3. To make the sauce, in a small skillet, melt butter over medium flame. Stir in flour and cook for 1 minute.
4. Pour in chicken broth and lemon juice; whisk for 1 to 2 minutes. Add capers; serve the sauce with salmon.

Herbed Salmon Loaf with Sauce

(Ready in about 5 hours | Servings 4)

Ingredients

For the Salmon Meatloaf:

- 1 cup fresh bread crumbs
- 1 can (7 ½ ounce) salmon, drained

- 1/4 cup scallions, chopped
- 1/3 cup whole milk
- 1 egg

- 1 tablespoon fresh lemon juice
- 1 teaspoon dried rosemary
- 1 teaspoon ground coriander
- 1/2 teaspoon fenugreek
- 1 teaspoon mustard seed
- 1/2 teaspoon salt
- 1/4 teaspoon white pepper

For the Sauce:
- 1/2 cup cucumber, chopped
- 1/2 cup reduced-fat plain yogurt
- 1/2 teaspoon dill weed
- Salt, to taste

Directions

1. Line your crock pot with a foil.
2. Mix all ingredients for the salmon meatloaf until everything is well incorporated; form into loaf and place in the crock pot.
3. Cover with a suitable lid and cook on low heat setting 5 hours.
4. Combine all of the ingredients for the sauce; whisk to combine.
5. Serve your meatloaf with prepared sauce.

Lazy Man Mac and Cheese

(Ready in about 4 hours | Servings 4)

Ingredients

- Non-stick cooking spray-butter flavour
- 16 ounces macaroni of choice
- 1/2 cup butter, melted
- 1 (12-ounce) can evaporated milk
- 1 cup milk
- 4 cups Colby jack cheese, grated

Directions

1. Lightly grease a crock pot with cooking spray.
2. First of all, cook your favourite macaroni according to package directions; rinse and drain; transfer to the crock pot.
3. Add the rest of ingredients and stir well. Cook on low heat setting 3 to 4 hours. Enjoy!

Mediterranean Chicken with Zucchini

(Ready in about 8 hours | Servings 4)

Ingredients

- 4 medium-sized chicken breasts, skinless
- 2 cups petite-diced tomatoes
- 1 stock cube
- 1/2 cup dry white wine
- 1/2 cup water
- 1 medium zucchini, sliced
- 1 large-sized onion, chopped
- 1/3 cup fennel bulb, chopped
- 1 teaspoon ground cumin
- 1 teaspoon dried basil leaves
- 1 bay leaf
- A pinch of black pepper
- 1/4 cup olives, pitted and sliced
- 1 teaspoon lemon juice
- 3 cups cooked rice

Directions

1. Place all ingredients, except olives, lemon juice and cooked rice, in a crock pot; cover and cook on low about 8 hours, adding pitted olives during last 30 minutes of cooking time.

2. Add lemon juice; discard bay leaf. Serve over cooked rice and enjoy.

Mediterranean Stuffed Spaghetti Squash

(Ready in about 8 hours | Servings 4)

Ingredients

- 1 medium-sized spaghetti squash, halved lengthwise and seeded
- 2 Roma tomatoes, diced
- 2 cans (6-ounces) tuna in water, drained and flaked
- 1 teaspoon dried basil leaves
- 1 teaspoon dried oregano leaves
- 1/2 teaspoon dried thyme
- Salt, to taste
- Black pepper, to taste
- Cayenne pepper, to taste
- 1/2 cup water
- 1/4 cup Pecorino Romano, grated

Directions

1. Place squash halves on a plate.

2. In a measuring cup or a mixing bowl, combine all of the ingredients, except water and Pecorino Romano. Spoon this mixture into squash halves and place in the crock pot.

3. Add water to the crock pot; cover and cook 6 to 8 hours on low.

4. Sprinkle with Pecorino Romano and serve.

Everyday Tomato Casserole

(Ready in about 3 hours | Servings 6)

Ingredients

- 8 ounces macaroni, cooked
- 1 can (16-ounce) petite-diced tomatoes, drained
- 1/2 cup leeks, chopped
- 1 cup whole milk
- 1 cup water
- 1 tablespoon cornflour
- 3 eggs, lightly beaten
- 1/2 cup sharp cheese, grated
- 1/2 teaspoon ground cinnamon
- Salt, to taste
- Paprika, as garnish

Directions

1. Combine macaroni, tomatoes and leeks in a crock pot.

2. In a bowl, mix remaining ingredients, except paprika; pour over macaroni in the crock pot.

3. Cook on low about 3 hours or until custard is set; divide among serving plates and sprinkle with paprika.

Four Cheese Macaroni Casserole

(Ready in about 3 hours | Servings 8)

Ingredients

- Non-stick cooking spray-butter flavour
- 3 cups whole milk
- 1/3 cup all-purpose flour
- 1 cup Colby-Jack, crumbled
- 1 cup reduced-fat mozzarella, shredded
- 1 cup Cheddar cheese, shredded
- 1 pound macaroni, cooked al dente
- 1/2 cup Parmesan cheese

Directions

1. Treat a crock pot with cooking spray.
2. In a large mixing bowl, combine milk and flour until smooth; add the rest of ingredients, except macaroni and Parmesan cheese.
3. Stir in macaroni and sprinkle with Parmesan cheese.
4. Cover and cook on low 3 hours.

Creamy Vegetable Noodle Casserole

(Ready in about 5 hours | Servings 6)

Ingredients

- 1 cup 2% reduced-fat milk
- 1 ½ cups cream of mushroom soup
- 2 tablespoons mayonnaise, reduced-fat
- 1 cup processed cheese, shredded
- 1 green bell pepper
- 1 large-sized carrot, chopped
- 1/3 celery stalk, chopped
- 1/3 cup onion, chopped
- 1/4 teaspoon sea salt
- 1/4 teaspoon ground black pepper
- 6 ounces noodles, cooked al dente
- 1/2 cup chickpea
- 1 tablespoon butter
- 1/3 cup fresh bread crumbs
- 1/3 cup pine nuts, chopped

Directions

1. In a crock pot, combine first ten ingredients.

2. Stir in cooked noodles; cover with a suitable lid and cook on low 5 hours. Add chickpeas during last 30 minutes of cooking time.

3. In a cast-iron skillet, melt butter over medium heat; cook bread crumbs and pine nuts about 5 minutes. Sprinkle on prepared casserole and serve!

Old-Fashioned Pasta Bolognese

(Ready in about 7 hours | Servings 6)

Ingredients

- 1/2 pound ground pork
- 1/2 pound ground beef
- 1/4 cup onion, chopped
- 3 cloves garlic, minced
- 1/4 cup carrot, chopped
- 1 1/2 teaspoons dried Italian seasoning
- 1 can (8-ounces) tomato sauce, undrained,
- 1 large-sized tomato, diced
- 1/4 cup dry red wine
- 1 teaspoon sea salt
- 1/4 teaspoon pepper
- 1/4 teaspoon cayenne pepper
- 12 ounces spaghetti, cooked

Directions

1. In a non-stick heavy skillet, brown ground meat over medium heat for 8 minutes; crumble with a fork.

2. Add remaining ingredients, except spaghetti, to the crock pot. Cover and cook on low 6 to 7 hours.

3. Ladle prepared sauce over spaghetti and serve warm.

Mexican Traditional Enchiladas

(Ready in about 1 hour 15 minutes | Servings 6)

Ingredients

- 1 pound mixed ground beef and pork
- 3 slices of Canadian bacon, chopped
- 1 ¼ cups water
- 1 (1-ounce) package taco seasoning mix
- 1 cup chunky salsa
- 2 cups chicken stock
- Sea salt, to taste
- 4 cups Mexican cheese blend, shredded
- 10 corn tortillas, quartered

Directions

1. In a wide saucepan, cook ground meat and bacon over medium heat. Cook until they are browned or about 10 minutes.
2. In a medium-sized mixing bowl, combine together water, taco seasoning mix, salsa, chicken stock, salt and 2 cups of cheese.
3. Arrange a layer of tortillas on the bottom of a crock pot. Add a layer of the ground beef, and then spoon a layer of the salsa mixture over that.
4. Repeat the layers one more time, ending with the layer of tortillas. Top with remaining 2 cups of cheese.
5. Cover with a lid; cook on high for 1 hour.

Stuffed Chicken Breasts

(Ready in about 3 hours | Servings 4)

Ingredients

- 1/2 cup sharp cheese, shredded
- 1 red bell pepper, chopped
- 1 green bell pepper, chopped
- 1 yellow bell pepper, chopped
- 2 heaping tablespoons fresh parsley, chopped
- 1/4 cup cilantro, minced
- 1/4 cup tomatoes, diced

- 1/2 teaspoon chili powder
- 1/2 teaspoon celery salt
- 4 small-sized chicken breast, boneless and pounded to 1/4 inch thickness

Directions

1. In a bowl, mix together all of the ingredients, except chicken.
2. Spread this mixture on the chicken breast. Roll up chicken breasts tightly and secure them with toothpicks or the skewers.
3. Arrange the chicken rolls in the crock pot. Cover and cook 3 hours on high.

Pasta with Tomato Sauce

(Ready in about 7 hours | Servings 6)

Ingredients

- 4 large-sized tomatoes, chopped
- 1 large-sized yellow onion, finely chopped
- 2 cloves garlic, minced
- 1/2 cup dry red wine
- 2 tablespoons tomato ketchup
- 1 tablespoon brown sugar
- 1 teaspoon dried oregano leaves
- 1 teaspoon celery seeds
- 1 teaspoon dried thyme leaves
- 1/8 teaspoon paprika
- 1/4 teaspoon kosher salt
- 12 ounces pasta, cooked and warm

Directions

1. Combine all of the ingredients, except pasta, in your crock pot.
2. Cover and cook 7 hours on low.
3. Ladle sauce over pasta and enjoy.

Farfalle with Mushroom Sauce

(Ready in about 8 hours | Servings 6)

Ingredients

- 1 onion, finely chopped
- 2 cloves garlic, minced
- 1 medium-sized plum tomatoes, chopped
- 1 ½ cups cream of mushroom soup
- 2 tablespoons tomato ketchup
- 1 tablespoon brown sugar
- 1 teaspoon dried oregano leaves
- 1 cup mushrooms, thinly sliced
- 1 teaspoon dried basil leaves
- 1/4 teaspoon kosher salt
- 1/4 teaspoon ground black pepper
- 12 ounces Farfalle, cooked and warm

Directions

1. In a crock pot, place all ingredients, except farfalle.
2. Cover with a lid and cook about 8 hours on low.
3. Ladle mushroom sauce over Farfalle and serve.

Northern Italian Risi Bisi

(Ready in about 1 hour 30 minutes | Servings 4)

Ingredients

- 1 cup water
- 2 cups vegetable stock
- 1/2 cup green onions, finely chopped
- 2 cloves garlic, minced
- 1 ½ cups rice
- 1 teaspoon dried oregano leaves
- 1 tablespoon dried basil leaves
- Ground black pepper, to taste
- Cayenne pepper, to taste
- 8 ounces green peas, trimmed
- 1 teaspoon fresh lemon juice
- 1/2 cup Parmesan cheese, grated

Directions

1. In a crock pot, arrange all ingredients, except green peas, lemon juice and cheese.

2. Cover and cook on high heat setting about 1 ¼ hours or until the liquid is almost absorbed. Add green peas in the last 15 minutes of cooking time.

3. Stir in lemon juice and cheese; divide among serving plates and serve.

Pecorino and Green Pea Risotto

(Ready in about 1 hour 30 minutes | Servings 4)

Ingredients

- 2 cups vegetable stock
- 1 cup tomato juice
- 1/2 cup shallots, finely chopped
- 2 cloves garlic, minced
- 1 ½ cups cooked chicken, cubed
- 1 ½ cups rice
- 1 teaspoon dried Italian seasoning
- Salt, to taste
- Ground black pepper, to taste
- Paprika, to taste
- 8 ounces green peas, trimmed
- 1/2 cup Pecorino cheese, grated

Directions

1. In your crock pot, place all ingredients, except green peas and Pecorino cheese.

2. Cover; cook on high about 1 hour 30 minutes, adding green peas during last 15 minutes of cooking time.

3. Add cheese and serve warm.

Risotto with Zucchini and Yellow Squash

(Ready in about 1 hour 25 minutes | Servings 4)

Ingredients

- 3 cups vegetable broth
- 1 medium-sized onion, chopped

- 2 cloves garlic, minced
- 1 cup sliced cremini mushrooms
- 1 teaspoon dried rosemary
- 1 ½ cups short-grain rice
- 1 cup each zucchini, cubed
- 3/4 cup summer yellow squash, cubed
- 1 sweet potato, peeled cubed
- 1/4 cup Pecorino cheese, grated
- 1/2 teaspoon sea salt
- 1/2 teaspoon ground black pepper
- 1/2 teaspoon cayenne pepper

Directions

1. Combine all ingredients, except cheese, in your crock pot.
2. Cover and cook on high about 1 ¼ hours or until rice is al dente.
3. Stir in cheese; divide among four serving plates and enjoy.

Egg Pie with Mushrooms

(Ready in about 4 hours | Servings 4)

Ingredients

- 4 large-sized eggs
- 1/4 cup all-purpose flour
- 1/2 teaspoon baking soda
- 1/4 teaspoon salt
- 1/8 teaspoon freshly ground black pepper
- 2 cups Colby Jack cheese, shredded
- 1 cup reduced-fat cottage cheese
- 1 Chipotle pepper, minced
- 1 cup mushrooms, sliced
- 1/2 teaspoon dried rosemary
- 1/2 teaspoon dried basil leaves

Directions

1. In a large bowl, beat the eggs until foamy; mix in flour, baking soda, salt, and ground black pepper. Stir in remaining ingredients.
2. Pour the mixture into oiled crock pot; cover and cook about 4 hours on low.
3. Divide among four serving plates and enjoy!

Aromatic Apple Risotto

(Ready in about 9 hours | Servings 6)

Ingredients

- 1/4 cup butter, melted
- 1 ½ cups Arborio rice
- 3 apples, cored and sliced
- 1/4 teaspoon freshly ground nutmeg
- 1/4 teaspoon ground cloves
- 1 teaspoon ground cinnamon
- 1/3 cup brown sugar
- A pinch of salt
- 1 cup apple juice
- 2 cups whole milk
- 1 cup water

Directions

1. Add the butter and rice to the crock pot.
2. Then, add the rest of ingredients; stir to combine.
3. Cover and cook 9 hours on low. Serve with dried fruit, if desired.

Delicious Savory Soufflé

(Ready in about 3 hours | Servings 8)

Ingredients

- 8 slices of bread
- 8 ounces Cheddar cheese, shredded
- 8 ounces mozzarella cheese, shredded
- Non-stick cooking spray
- 2 cups fat-free evaporated milk
- 4 eggs
- 1/4 teaspoon allspice

Directions

1. Tear the bread into pieces and reserve.
2. Combine the cheeses and reserve.

3. Grease your crock pot with non-stick cooking spray. Then, add bread and cheese. Stir to combine.

4. In a measuring cup or a mixing bowl, whisk the milk, eggs, and allspice. Pour over the bread and cheese in the crock pot. Cook 2 to 3 hours on low.

5. Serve sprinkled with pitted and chopped olives, if desired.

Spaghetti with Asparagus and Beans

(Ready in about 3 hours | Servings 8)

Ingredients

- 1 can (15-ounce) Great Northern beans, rinsed and drained
- 3/4 cup vegetable stock
- 2 tomatoes, chopped plum
- 1 carrot, chopped
- 1 teaspoon dried basil leaves
- 1 teaspoon dried rosemary leaves
- Salt and pepper, to taste
- 1 pound asparagus, sliced
- 8 ounces spaghetti, cooked
- 1/2 cup Parmesan cheese, shredded

Directions

1. Combine all ingredients, except asparagus, spaghetti and cheese, in your crock pot.

2. Cook on low about 3 hours, adding asparagus during last 30 minutes of cooking time.

3. Adjust seasonings to your taste, then, add spaghetti and Parmesan cheese; serve.

Easy Yummy Green Beans

(Ready in about 4 hours | Servings 8)

Ingredients

- 1 pound green beans
- 4 large-sized tomatoes, chopped
- 1/2 cup shallots, chopped
- 3 cloves garlic, minced
- 1 teaspoon dried basil leaves
- 1 teaspoon dried rosemary

- 1/2 teaspoon celery salt
- 1/4 teaspoon black pepper
- 1/4 teaspoon cayenne pepper

Directions

1. Combine all ingredients in your crock pot.
2. Cover with a lid; then, cook on high about 4 hours or until beans are tender.
3. Serve with poultry entrée.

Vegan Mediterranean Treat

(Ready in about 2 hours | Servings 8)

Ingredients

- 2 cups green beans
- 1/4 cup onion, finely chopped
- 2 cloves garlic, minced
- 1 large-sized red bell pepper, chopped
- 1 large-sized carrot, chopped
- 1 teaspoon ginger root, ground
- 1/2 cup water
- 1 cup canned black beans, drained
- 1 tablespoon rice wine vinegar
- 2 teaspoons tamari sauce
- 1/2 teaspoon sea salt
- 1/4 teaspoon ground black pepper

Directions

1. In your crock pot, combine green beans, onion, garlic, bell pepper, carrot, ginger root, and water; cover with a lid and set the crock pot to high.
2. Cook about 1 ½ hours; drain. Add remaining ingredients and cook 30 minutes longer. Taste, adjust the seasonings and serve.

Hot Baked Beans

(Ready in about 6 hours | Servings 8)

Ingredients

- 1 cup chopped onion
- 2 cans (15-ounce) pinto beans, rinsed and drained
- 1 serrano pepper, chopped
- 1 jalapeño chili, finely chopped
- 1 cup whole kernel corn
- 1 cup cherry tomatoes, halved
- 2 tablespoons sugar
- 1/2 teaspoon dried thyme leaves
- 1 bay leaf
- 1/2 teaspoon sea salt
- 1/4 teaspoon white pepper
- 1/2 cup Pecorino cheese, grated
- 1/4 cup fresh parsley, finely chopped

Directions

1. Combine all ingredients, except cheese and parsley, in your crock pot.
2. Cover and cook on low 5 to 6 hours.
3. Sprinkle with cheese and parsley and serve!

Baked and Herbed Cannellini Beans

(Ready in about 6 hours | Servings 6)

Ingredients

- 1 cup vegetable broth
- 3 cans (15-ounces) cannellini beans
- 1/2 cup leeks, chopped
- 2-3 cloves garlic, minced
- 1 celery stalk, chopped
- 1 sweet red bell pepper, chopped
- 1 teaspoon dried sage
- 2 bay leaves
- 6 sun-dried tomatoes, softened and sliced
- 1/2 teaspoon paprika
- 1/2 teaspoon sea salt
- 1/4 teaspoon freshly ground black pepper

Directions

1. Put all of the ingredients into your crock pot.

2. Cover and cook 5 to 6 hours on low. Serve with sausage and your favorite salad, if desired.

Delicious Sweet-Spiced Beans

(Ready in about 6 hours | Servings 10)

Ingredients

- 1 ½ cups leeks, chopped
- 4 cans (15-ounce) Great Northern beans, rinsed and drained
- 2 tablespoons gingerroot, finely chopped
- 3 cloves garlic, minced
- 1 tablespoon sugar
- 1 cup tomato paste
- 1 teaspoon mustard seeds
- 1 teaspoon dried thyme leaves
- 1 teaspoon dried sage leaves
- 1/4 teaspoon nutmeg, grated
- 2 bay leaves
- Black pepper, to taste
- 5-6 peppercorns
- 1/2 cup gingersnap crumbs, coarsely ground

Directions

1. Combine all ingredients, except gingersnap crumbs, in a crock pot.

2. Cover the crock pot with a lid and cook 6 hours on low, adding gingersnap crumbs during last hour.

3. Discard bay leaves and serve warm.

Easy Honey Beets with Raisins

(Ready in about 2 hours 30 minutes | Servings 6)

Ingredients

- 2 cups hot water
- 1 ½ pounds medium beets
- 1 large-sized red onion, finely chopped
- 2 cloves garlic, minced
- 1/4 cup raisins
- 3 heaping tablespoons pine nuts, toasted
- 1/4 cup honey
- 3 tablespoons red wine vinegar
- 1 tablespoon olive oil
- Salt and pepper, to taste

Directions

1. In a crock pot, place hot water and beets; cover and cook on high approximately 2 hours; drain.
2. Next, peel beets and cut into small pieces. Return to the crock pot; add remaining ingredients.
3. Cook for 30 minutes longer. Serve with poultry entrée and enjoy!

Glazed Brussels Sprouts with Pearl Onions

(Ready in about 2 hours 10 minutes | Servings 6)

Ingredients

- 8 ounces frozen pearl onions, thawed
- 8 ounces small Brussels sprouts
- 1 1/2 cups hot water
- 1/4 teaspoon ground black pepper
- 1/4 teaspoon cayenne pepper
- 1/2 teaspoon sea salt
- 1 tablespoon margarine
- 1/4 cup brown sugar

Directions

1. Combine pearl onions, Brussels sprouts and hot water in a crock pot.

2. Cover with a lid and cook on high about 2 hours or until the vegetables are tender; drain. Season with black pepper, cayenne pepper, and sea salt.

3. Add margarine and sugar and cook 10 more minutes. Serve warm and enjoy.

Herbed Potato-Carrot Purée

(Ready in about 3 hours 30 minutes | Servings 8)

Ingredients

- 2 cups potato, peeled cubed
- 2 pounds carrots, sliced
- 1 cup water
- 2 tablespoons butter
- 1/4 cup milk, warm
- 1/2 teaspoon dried rosemary
- 1/2 teaspoon allspice
- 1/2 teaspoon celery seeds
- 1 teaspoon dried basil
- 1 teaspoon dried oregano
- 1/2 teaspoon salt
- 1/2 teaspoon red pepper flakes, crushed

Directions

1. Place potatoes, carrots and water in your crock pot; cover with a lid and cook 3 hours on high. Drain well.

2. Purée cooked potato and carrots in a food processor until creamy and uniform; return to the crock pot. Uncover and cook on high about 30 minutes; stir occasionally.

3. Beat butter and milk into mashed potatoes and carrots. Make a creamy consistency. Season with spices and serve.

Winter Cabbage with Bacon

(Ready in about 4 hours | Servings 6)

Ingredients

- 1 head cabbage, thinly sliced
- 3/4 cup leeks, chopped
- 2 medium-sized carrots, chopped
- 1 sweet red bell pepper, thinly sliced
- 2 cloves garlic, minced
- 1/2 teaspoon anise seeds
- 1/4 cup canned beef broth
- 1/4 cup dry white wine
- Salt, to taste
- 1/2 teaspoon ground black pepper
- 2 slices of diced bacon, cooked crisp and drained

Directions

1. Combine all ingredients, except bacon, in your crock pot.
2. Cover and cook on high about 4 hours or until cabbage is tender.
3. Add bacon, adjust the seasonings to taste, and enjoy!

Vegetarian Creamed Cabbage

(Ready in about 4 hours 10 minutes | Servings 6)

Ingredients

- 1 large-sized head cabbage, thinly sliced
- 3/4 cup red or yellow onion, chopped
- 2 medium-sized carrots, chopped
- 1 sweet bell pepper, thinly sliced
- 2 cloves garlic, minced
- 1/2 teaspoon caraway seeds
- 1/2 teaspoon celery seeds
- 1 cup canned vegetable stock
- Salt, to taste
- Ground black pepper, to taste
- Cayenne pepper, to taste
- 1/2 cup reduced-fat sour cream
- 1 tablespoon cornflour

Directions

1. In your crock pot, place all ingredients, except sour cream and cornflour.

2. Cover with a lid and cook 4 hours on high.

3. Stir in combined sour cream and cornflour and continue cooking 10 minutes longer. Serve warm.

Amazing Orange-Glazed Carrots

(Ready in about 3 hours 10 minutes | Servings 4)

Ingredients

- 1 pound baby carrots
- 3/4 cup orange juice
- 1 tablespoon butter
- 1/2 cup brown sugar, packed light
- 1/2 teaspoon allspice
- 1/4 teaspoon ground mace
- 1/2 teaspoon sea salt
- 1/2 teaspoon white pepper
- 2 tablespoons cornflour
- 1/4 cup water

Directions

1. In a crock pot, place all ingredients, except cornflour and water; cover and cook on high about 3 hours or until carrots are crisp-tender.

2. In a small mixing bowl, combine cornflour and water; add to the crock pot. Stir 2 to 3 minutes.

3. Divide among four serving plates and serve with meat or fish entrée, if desired.

Mediterranean Creamy Cabbage

(Ready in about 4 hours 10 minutes | Servings 6)

Ingredients

- 1 large-sized head Savoy cabbage, sliced
- 3/4 cup red or yellow onion, chopped
- 1 celery rib, chopped

- 1 green bell pepper, thinly sliced
- 1 yellow bell pepper, thinly sliced
- 2 cloves garlic, minced
- 1 teaspoon celery seeds
- 1 cup canned vegetable stock
- Salt, to taste
- Ground black pepper, to taste
- Paprika, to taste
- Grating of nutmeg
- 1 cup spinach, torn into pieces
- 1/2 cup plain Greek yogurt
- 1 tablespoon corn starch

Directions

1. In a crock pot, arrange all of the ingredients, except spinach, yogurt and corn starch.
2. Cook covered for 4 hours, adding the spinach during last 30 minutes of cooking time and sprinkling with some extra spices, if desired.
3. Add combined yogurt and corn starch, stirring about 10 minutes. Serve warm and enjoy!

Orange-Glazed Sweet Potatoes

(Ready in about 3 hours 5 minutes | Servings 4)

Ingredients

- 1 pound sweet potatoes
- 3/4 cup orange juice
- 1 tablespoon margarine
- 1/2 cup brown sugar
- 1/2 teaspoon grated nutmeg
- 1/4 teaspoon ground mace
- 1/4 teaspoon ground cloves
- 1/2 teaspoon ground cinnamon
- 1/2 teaspoon kosher salt
- 1/2 teaspoon white pepper
- 2 tablespoons cornflour
- 1/4 cup water

Directions

1. Place all ingredients, except cornflour and water, in a crock pot.
2. Cover and cook on high about 3 hours or until sweet potatoes are crisp-tender.
3. Add combined cornflour and water, stirring constantly 3 to 4 minutes. Serve with your favorite meat entrée.

Delicious Family Corn Flan

(Ready in about 3 hours | Servings 6)

Ingredients

- 1 teaspoon sugar
- 1 cup milk
- 3 eggs, lightly beaten
- 1 ½ cup creamed corn
- 1 cup kernel corn
- 1/2 teaspoon allspice
- 1/2 teaspoon salt
- 1/4 teaspoon white pepper

Directions

1. Mix all of the ingredients together. Place in a soufflé dish.
2. Place this soufflé dish on a rack in the crock pot.
3. Cover and cook on low about 3 hours.

Spicy Corn Pudding

(Ready in about 3 hours | Servings 6)

Ingredients

- Non-stick cooking spray
- 3 medium-sized eggs
- 1 cup whole milk
- 1/2 cup frozen whole kernel corn, thawed
- 2 tablespoons all-purpose flour
- 1/2 teaspoon ground cumin
- 1 teaspoon fine sea salt
- 1/4 teaspoon red pepper flakes, crushed
- 1/4 teaspoon black pepper
- 1/2 cup creamed corn
- 2 cups reduced-fat sharp cheese, shredded
- 1 chipotle pepper, minced

Directions

1. Treat the inside of your crock pot with non-stick cooking spray.

2. Purée eggs, milk, whole-kernel corn, all-purpose flour, cumin, salt, red pepper flakes and black pepper in your food processor or a blender until uniform and smooth.

3. Pour the mixture into the oiled crock pot. Add the rest of the ingredients.

4. Cover and cook about 3 hours on low.

Pork Shoulder with Hot Sauce

(Ready in about 12 hours | Servings 10)

Ingredients

- 1 pork shoulder roast
- 1/2 teaspoon ground black pepper
- 1/2 teaspoon cayenne pepper
- 1 teaspoon fine sea salt
- 1 tablespoon fresh orange juice
- 1 cup balsamic vinegar
- 2 tablespoons brown sugar
- 1 tablespoon Tabasco sauce

Directions

1. On the bottom of your crock pot, place the pork. Season with black pepper, cayenne pepper, and sea salt. Pour in orange juice and balsamic vinegar.

2. Cover and cook 12 hours on low.

3. Remove the pork from the crock pot; discard any bones.

4. To make the sauce, save 2 cups of liquid. Add sugar and tabasco sauce to the reserved liquid.

5. Shred the pork and return to the crock pot. Pour the sauce over the pork.

6. Keep warm before serving time.

Leek and Garlic Custard

(Ready in about 3 hours | Servings 6)

Ingredients

- 2 tablespoons extra-virgin olive oil
- 4 leeks (white parts only), sliced

- 2 cloves garlic, minced
- 1/2 teaspoon allspice
- 2 eggs, lightly beaten
- 1 cup whole milk
- 1/8 teaspoon ground nutmeg
- 1/2 teaspoon sea salt
- 1/4 teaspoon ground black pepper
- 1/4 teaspoon red pepper flakes, crushed
- 1/2 cup Swiss cheese, shredded

Directions

1. In a small cast-iron skillet, heat olive oil over medium-high. Sauté leeks and garlic about 8 minutes.
2. Add sautéed leeks and garlic to a suitable soufflé dish; add remaining ingredients; place on a rack in your crock pot.
3. Cover and cook on low 3 to 3 ½ hours or until custard is set.
4. Let stand for 10 minutes before slicing and serving. This custard can be a delicious dinner and it also will complement your favorite entrée.

Stuffed Vidalia Onions

(Ready in about 4 hours | Servings 6)

Ingredients

- 4 medium-sized Vidalia onions, peeled
- 1/2 cup bread crumbs
- 1/2 cup Queso fresco cheese, Crumbled
- 4 sun-dried tomatoes, chopped
- 1/4 cup water chestnut
- 2 cloves garlic, minced
- 1/2 teaspoon dried basil leaves
- 1/4 teaspoon salt
- 1/4 teaspoon black pepper
- 1 egg white
- 1/2 cup warm chicken stock

Directions

1. Boil Vidalia onions in water about 10 minutes; drain.

2. Cut Vidalia onions into halves and remove centres. You can reserve centres for another use.

3. In a mixing bowl, mix together remaining ingredients, except chicken stock; fill onion halves with prepared mixture.

4. Add stuffed onions to the crock pot; pour in chicken stock.

5. Cook covered on high about 4 hours.

Fruit and Nut Candied Yams

(Ready in about 4 hours | Servings 8)

Ingredients

- 2 pounds yams, peeled and thinly sliced
- 1/4 cup currants
- 1/4 cup toasted pecans, chopped
- 2/3 cup packed light brown sugar
- A pinch of salt
- 1/2 teaspoon allspice
- 1/4 teaspoon ground black pepper
- 2 tablespoons cold butter
- 1/2 cup water
- 2 tablespoons cornflour

Directions

1. Arrange yams in your crock pot, sprinkling with currants, pecans, brown sugar, salt, allspice and pepper and dotting with cold butter. Repeat the layers until you run out of ingredients.

2. Combine water and cornflour; pour into a crock pot.

3. Cover and cook on low 3 hours; then turn heat to high and cook 1 hour longer. Enjoy!

Maple Honey Ribs

(Ready in about 5 hours | Servings 6)

Ingredients

- 3 pounds pork ribs
- 1 cup canned vegetable broth

- 1/2 cup water
- 1/4 cup honey
- 3 tablespoons mustard
- 1/4 cup barbeque sauce
- 1/4 cup tamari sauce
- 1/4 cup pure maple syrup

Directions

1. In the crock, mix together all ingredients, except pork ribs.
2. Slice ribs apart; place the pork ribs in the crock pot.
3. Cover and cook 5 hours on high or until the pork falls from the bones. Serve warm with hot tomato sauce and some extra mustard, if desired.

Yam Loaf for Winter Holidays

(Ready in about 3 hours | Servings 6)

Ingredients

- 1 ¼ cups yams, peeled and coarsely grated
- 1/3 cup shallots, finely chopped
- 2 tart apples, shredded
- 1/4 cup golden raisins
- 1/8 teaspoon ground nutmeg
- 1/4 teaspoon ground cloves
- 1/4 teaspoon ground cinnamon
- 1/4 cup all-purpose flour
- 1/4 cup fresh orange juice
- A pinch of salt
- 1/4 teaspoon white pepper
- 1 large-sized egg

Directions

1. Mix all ingredients, except egg; adjust the seasonings to taste. Mix in egg.
2. Put the mixture into greased loaf pan; place the loaf pan on rack in your crock pot. Cover with aluminium foil.
3. Pour 2 inches hot water into the crock pot; cover and cook on high about 3 hours.
4. Let stand on wire rack at least 5 minutes; invert onto serving plates and serve.

Squash and Sweet Potato Pudding

(Ready in about 3 hours 30 minutes | Servings 6)

Ingredients

- Canola oil
- 1 cup Hubbard squash
- 1 cup carrots, sliced
- 4 medium-sized sweet potatoes, peeled and cubed
- 1/4 cup orange juice
- 2 tablespoons butter
- 1/4 cup packed light brown sugar
- 1/4 teaspoon cloves
- A pinch of salt
- 3 eggs, lightly beaten
- 1 cup miniature marshmallows

Directions

1. Oil the inside of the crock pot with canola oil.
2. Add squash, carrots, and sweet potatoes; cover and cook on high about 3 hours.
3. Remove vegetables from the crock pot; mash with remaining ingredients, except marshmallows.
4. Return mashed vegetables to the crock pot; cover and cook on high 30 minutes longer. Scatter the marshmallows on top and serve.

Rich and Creamy Potato Gratin

(Ready in about 3 hours 30 minutes | Servings 8)

Ingredients

- 2 pounds potatoes, peeled and sliced
- 1/4 cup green onion, sliced
- 1/2 teaspoon salt
- 1/4 teaspoon ground black pepper
- 2 tablespoons butter
- 3 tablespoons shallots, finely chopped
- 3 tablespoons all-purpose flour
- 1 cup milk
- 2 ounces reduced-fat processed cheese, cubed
- 1 cup Cheddar cheese, shredded

- 1/2 teaspoon dried basil leaves
- 1/2 teaspoon dried oregano leaves
- 1/2 teaspoon paprika

Directions

1. Layer half of the sliced potatoes and green onions in the bottom of your crock pot; sprinkle with salt and ground black pepper.
2. To make the sauce, melt butter in a small skillet; add shallots and flour and cook about 2 minutes. Gradually whisk in milk, stirring until thickened or 2 to 3 minutes.
3. Then, turn the heat to low; add remaining ingredients. Stir until everything is well combined and melted.
4. Pour half of this cheese sauce over layers in the crock pot. Repeat layers, ending with cheese sauce.
5. Cover and cook on high about 3 ½ hours. Serve warm and enjoy!

Creamy Potatoes with Smoked Ham

(Ready in about 4 hours | Servings 8)

Ingredients

- 2 pounds potatoes, sliced
- 12 ounces smoked ham, cubed
- 1 cup canned cream of mushroom soup
- 1 teaspoon dried basil leaves
- 1 cup milk
- 1 ½ cups Monterey Jack cheese
- Sea salt, to taste
- 1/4 teaspoon black pepper, freshly ground
- 1/4 teaspoon cayenne pepper
- Smoked paprika, to taste

Directions

1. Place potatoes and smoked ham in the bottom of the crock pot.
2. In a large-sized mixing bowl, combine the rest of ingredients; pour into the crock pot.
3. Cover and cook on high approximately 4 hours. Enjoy!

Creamed Root Vegetables

(Ready in about 5 hours | Servings 6)

Ingredients

- 4 small potatoes, sliced
- 1 medium-sized fennel bulb, sliced
- 1 turnips, sliced
- 1 large-sized carrot, sliced
- 2 medium parsnips, sliced
- 3 small leeks (white parts only), sliced
- 2 cloves garlic, minced
- 1/2 teaspoon dried basil leaves
- Salt, to taste
- 1/4 teaspoon ground black pepper
- 1/4 teaspoon paprika
- 1 cup chicken broth
- 1/2 cup half-and-half
- 1 cup sour cream
- 2 tablespoons cornflour

Directions

1. Combine all ingredients, except sour cream and cornflour, in your crock pot.
2. Cover and cook on high about 5 hours or until the vegetables are tender.
3. Add combined sour cream and cornflour, and continue cooking, stirring 2 to 3 minutes. Serve.

Mushroom and Zucchini Soufflé

(Ready in about 4 hours | Servings 8)

Ingredients

- 4 medium-sized eggs
- 3/4 cup whole milk
- 1/4 cup all-purpose flour
- 1 cup mushrooms, sliced
- 1 pound zucchini, chopped
- 2 tablespoons parsley, coarsely chopped
- 1 clove garlic, minced
- 1/2 teaspoon dried basil leaves
- 1/2 teaspoon dried oregano leaves

- 1/2 teaspoon dried rosemary
- 1 teaspoon salt
- 1/4 teaspoon ground black pepper
- 1/4 teaspoon cayenne pepper
- 1/2 cup Parmesan cheese, grated

Directions

1. In a mixing bowl, beat eggs, milk, and all-purpose flour until smooth.
2. Next, add remaining ingredients, except 1/4 cup Parmesan cheese.
3. Pour this mixture into casserole; sprinkle with remaining 1/4 cup of Parmesan cheese.
4. Place casserole dish on a rack in the crock pot; cover and cook 4 hours on high. Serve warm.

Cheesy Spinach and Noodle Delight

(Ready in about 4 hours | Servings 8)

Ingredients

- 1/2 cup reduced-fat cream cheese
- 1 cup cottage cheese
- 3 large eggs, lightly beaten
- 1 cup whole milk
- 1/2 cup currants
- 1/2 teaspoon allspice
- 2 cups spinach
- 1/2 cup egg noodles, cooked al dente
- 1/2 teaspoon salt
- 1/2 teaspoon ground black pepper
- 1/2 teaspoon red pepper flakes, crushed
- Parmesan cheese, as garnish

Directions

1. In a medium-sized bowl, combine cream cheese and cottage cheese; whisk eggs and add to the cheese mixture.
2. Stir in remaining ingredients, except Parmesan cheese; spoon into a soufflé dish.
3. Sprinkle with Parmesan cheese; place soufflé dish on a rack in the crock pot.
4. Cover and cook on low about 4 hours or until set.

Savory Bread Pudding

(Ready in about 5 hours | Servings 8)

Ingredients

- Non-stick cooking spray
- 8 ounces bread, cubed
- 1 teaspoon dried basil leaves
- 1/2 teaspoon mustard seeds
- 2 tablespoons butter, melted
- 1 celery rib, thinly sliced
- 1 large-sized carrots, sliced
- 8 ounces mushrooms, thinly sliced
- 1 cup shallots, finely chopped
- 1 clove garlic, minced
- 1 cup light cream
- 1 cup whole milk
- 4 eggs, lightly beaten
- 1/2 teaspoon salt
- 1/4 teaspoon ground black pepper
- 1/4 cup Provolone cheese, shredded

Directions

1. Spray bread cubes with non-stick cooking spray; sprinkle with basil and mustard seeds and toss.
2. Bake on a cookie sheet at 375 degrees F about 15 minutes or until golden brown.
3. Heat butter in a heavy skillet. Sauté celery, carrots, mushrooms, shallots and garlic about 8 minutes.
4. In a large bowl, mix the rest of ingredients, except Provolone cheese; add greased bread cubes and sautéed vegetables.
5. Spoon into greased crock pot; scatter shredded Provolone cheese on top and refrigerate overnight. Cook covered on high approximately 5 hours.

Corn and Potatoes with Shrimp

(Ready in about 2 hours | Servings 8)

Ingredients

- 4 ears corn, halved
- 2 pounds red potatoes, peeled and quartered

- 1/4 cup shrimp boil seasoning
- 1 tablespoon celery seeds
- 1 teaspoon dried basil leaves
- 4 leeks, thinly sliced
- Water, as needed
- 1 ½ pounds medium shrimp

Directions

1. Place all ingredients, except shrimp, in a crock pot.
2. Cook for 2 to 2 ½ hours on high.
3. Add the shrimp; continue to cook for 20 minutes or until the shrimp is thoroughly cooked. Serve warm.

Rich and Healthy Summer Paella

(Ready in about 6 hours | Servings 12)

Ingredients

- 1 tablespoon extra-virgin olive oil
- 2 medium-sized onions, sliced
- 3 cloves garlic, minced
- 1 pound spicy sausage
- 2 pounds tomatoes, chopped
- 2 cups chicken stock
- 2 cups clam juice
- 1 cup dry vermouth
- 2 ½ cups rice, uncooked
- 1/2 teaspoon ground cumin
- 1/2 teaspoon caraway seeds
- 1 teaspoon saffron
- Sea salt, to taste
- 1/4 teaspoon ground black pepper
- 2 tablespoons olive oil
- 1 pound fish, cubed
- 1 pound shrimp
- 1 pound fresh mussels
- 1 green pepper, minced
- 1 cup fresh green peas

Directions

1. Heat olive oil in a heavy skillet over medium heat; then, sauté the onions, garlic and sausage until sausage is browned and crumbled. Drain and transfer to the crock pot.

2. Stir in tomatoes, chicken stock, clam juice, vermouth, rice, cumin, caraway seeds, saffron, salt and black pepper; cover and cook on low for 6 hours.

3. In the same skillet, heat 2 tablespoons of oil; sauté the fish and shrimp. Transfer to the crock pot. Add remaining ingredients and cook until cooked through. Serve warm.

Rabbit in Coconut Sauce

(Ready in about 6 hours | Servings 8)

Ingredients

- 1 cup coconut milk
- 1 cup water
- 3 medium-sized tomatoes, diced
- 2 leeks, chopped
- 1 teaspoon salt
- 1 bay leaf
- 1/2 teaspoon ground black pepper
- 1/2 teaspoon red pepper flakes, crushed
- 3 pounds rabbit meat, cut into serving-sized pieces

Directions

1. In a crock pot, combine all of the ingredients.
2. Cover with a lid and heat on low for 5 to 6 hours.
3. Serve over noodles or cooked rice.

Vegetarian Potato and Eggplant Moussaka

(Ready in about 7 hours | Servings 8)

Ingredients

- 1 cup dry brown lentils, rinsed and drained
- 3 medium-sized potatoes, peeled and sliced
- 1 cup water
- 1 bouillon cube
- 1 celery rib, diced fine
- 1 medium-sized onion, sliced
- 3 cloves garlic, minced

- 1/2 teaspoon salt
- 1/4 teaspoon freshly ground black pepper
- 1/4 teaspoon ground cinnamon
- 1 teaspoon Italian seasonings
- 1 cup carrots, sliced
- 1 medium-sized eggplant, diced
- 1 cup tomatoes, diced
- 1 cup cream cheese, softened
- 2 large eggs

Directions

1. In your crock pot, layer ingredients as follows: lentils, potatoes, water, bouillon cube, celery, onions, garlic, salt, pepper, cinnamon, Italian seasonings, carrots and eggplant.
2. Cover and heat on low for 6 hours.
3. Stir in diced tomatoes, cream cheese and eggs. Cover and cook on low one more hour.

Curried Chicken Thighs with Potatoes

(Ready in about 8 hours | Servings 8)

Ingredients

- 1 tablespoon curry powder
- 1 teaspoon ground cloves
- 1 teaspoon ground nutmeg
- 1 teaspoon ground ginger
- 2 pounds chicken thighs, boneless, skinless cubed
- 1 teaspoon olive oil
- 1 medium-sized yellow onion, chopped
- 2 cloves garlic, chopped
- 1 chili pepper, minced
- 1 ½ pounds red skin potatoes, cubed
- 1 cup coconut milk

Directions

1. In a medium-sized mixing bowl, whisk the curry powder, cloves, nutmeg, and ginger. Cut the chicken thighs into bite-sized pieces. Add the chicken to the bowl; toss to coat evenly.

2. Heat olive oil in a skillet; sauté seasoned chicken pieces until they start to brown. Add to the crock pot.

3. Add the rest of the ingredients. Stir to combine. Cook approximately 8 hours on low heat setting.

Yummy Evening Pear Clafoutis

(Ready in about 3 hours | Servings 4)

Ingredients

- 2 pears, cored
- 1/2 cup rice flour
- 1/2 cup arrowroot starch
- 1 teaspoon baking soda
- 1 teaspoon baking powder
- 1/2 teaspoon xanthan gum
- A pinch of salt
- 1/4 cup sugar
- 1 teaspoon cloves
- 1/2 teaspoon grated nutmeg
- 1 teaspoon ground cinnamon
- 2 tablespoons vegetable shortening, melted
- 2 eggs
- 1 cup milk
- Maple syrup for garnish

Directions

1. Cut the pears into chunks and transfer them to the crock pot.

2. In a large-sized mixing bowl, whisk together the rice flour, arrowroot starch, baking soda, baking powder, xanthan gum, salt, sugar, cloves, nutmeg and cinnamon.

3. To make the batter, create a well in the centre of the dry ingredients; add shortening, eggs, and milk. Stir well to combine.

4. Pour batter over pear chunks in the crock pot. Vent a lid of the crock pot with a chopstick.

5. Cook on high for 3 hours. Serve with maple syrup.

Evening Risotto with Apples

(Ready in about 9 hours | Servings 6)

Ingredients

- 1/4 cup butter, melted
- 1 ½ cups Carnaroli rice
- 3 apples, peeled, cored, and sliced
- 1/4 teaspoon ground cloves
- 1 teaspoon ground cinnamon
- 1/4 teaspoon kosher salt
- 1/3 cup brown sugar
- 1 cup water
- 2 cups whole milk
- 1 cup apple juice

Directions

1. Add the butter and rice to your crock pot; stir to coat.
2. Add the rest of ingredients; stir well to combine.
3. Cover with a lid and cook on low for 9 hours. Serve warm.

Cheese and Bread Casserole

(Ready in about 3 hours | Servings 8)

Ingredients

- 1 tablespoon butter, melted
- 8 ounces Gruyère cheese, shredded
- 8 ounces cream cheese, shredded
- 8 slices bread
- 2 cups milk
- 4 eggs
- Salt, to taste
- 1/2 teaspoon dried basil
- 1/4 teaspoon paprika
- Chopped fresh chives, as garnish

Directions

1. Treat a crock pot with butter.
2. In a mixing bowl, combine the cheeses; reserve.

3. Tear the slices of bread into pieces; transfer to the crock pot. Place cheese mixture on the bread layer. Alternate layers, ending with the bread.

4. In a small-sized mixing bowl, whisk remaining ingredients, except chives. Pour over the layers in the crock pot.

5. Set the crock pot to low and cook for 3 hours. Serve garnished with fresh chives and enjoy!

French-Style Sandwiches

(Ready in about 2 hours | Servings 12)

Ingredients

- 1 cup leeks, chopped
- 1 beef bottom round roast
- 1 cup water
- 1/2 cup dry red wine
- 1 envelope au jus gravy mix
- Salt, to taste
- 1/4 teaspoon freshly ground black pepper
- 1/4 teaspoon red pepper flakes, crushed
- French bread

Directions

1. Line bottom of the crock pot with the leeks.
2. Add roast to the crock pot on top of the leeks.
3. Next, add remaining ingredients, except bread; vent a lid and cook on low for 2 hours.
4. Cut the roast into thin slices. Serve on French bread. Use the sauce for dipping.

Bratwurst and Sauerkraut Pitas

(Ready in about 2 hours 30 minutes | Servings 6)

Ingredients

- 2 tablespoons olive oil
- 2 pounds sauerkraut, drained
- 1 large-sized apple, cored and chopped
- 1 teaspoon ground cumin

- 1 teaspoon celery seeds
- 6 bratwursts
- 1/2 cup dry white wine
- 2 bay leaves
- 5-6 black peppercorns
- 1 tablespoon mustard
- 6 pita loaves

Directions

1. Heat olive oil in a heavy skillet over medium heat. Sauté the sauerkraut and apple until the sauerkraut is soft and the liquids are reduced. Add cumin and celery seeds and gently stir to combine.

2. In a separate non-stick skillet, brown the bratwurst on all sides over medium heat; drain. Pour in white wine; add bay leaves and peppercorns; cook an additional 10 minutes.

3. To make the sandwiches: roll bratwursts and sauerkraut into the pita loaves. Add mustard and wrap the sandwiches in aluminium foil. Pour water to coat the bottom of the crock pot.

4. Place the sandwiches in the crock pot. Heat on a high setting for about 2 hours.

Romantic Winter Dinner

(Ready in about 2 hours 20 minutes | Servings 6)

Ingredients

- 6 spicy sausages
- 6 long sourdough rolls
- 2 tablespoons mustard
- 2 tablespoons tomato ketchup
- 6 pickles, sliced

Directions

1. Heat a non-stick skillet over medium flame. Then, sauté the sausages until thoroughly cooked and browned; drain.

2. Next, cut off the tips of the sourdough rolls. Make sandwiches with sausage and mustard.

3. Next, wrap the sandwiches in a foil; arrange on a trivet in the crock pot. Then, you need to pour lukewarm water around the base of the trivet.

4. Cover with a lid and heat on a high setting for 2 hours. Serve with ketchup and pickles.

PART FOUR: FAST SNACKS

Delicious Cashew Snacks

(Ready in about 2 hours 30 minutes | Servings 24)

Ingredients

- 6 cups cashews
- 3 tablespoons butter, melted
- 1 tablespoon brown sugar
- A pinch of salt
- 2 tablespoons dried thyme
- 3 tablespoons dried rosemary leaves
- 3/4 teaspoon paprika
- 1/2 teaspoon onion powder
- 1/2 teaspoon garlic powder

Directions

1. Heat your crock pot on high for 15 minutes; then add cashews. Drizzle melted butter over cashews.
2. Sprinkle cashews with combined spices and toss.
3. Cover with a lid and cook on low about 2 hours, stirring every hour.
4. Next, uncover and cook 30 minutes longer, stirring occasionally.
5. Serve cool or at room temperature.

Curried Honey Cashews

(Ready in about 2 hours 30 minutes | Servings 24)

Ingredients

- 3 cups cashews, whole
- 1 tablespoon sea salt
- 1 tablespoon honey
- 1 teaspoon red pepper flakes, crushed
- 2 tablespoons curry powder
- 2 tablespoons water
- 1 teaspoon olive oil

Directions

1. Set a crock pot to high and add cashews.

2. Add remaining ingredients and toss to combine.

3. Cook on low heat setting about 2 hours, stirring every hour. Uncover and cook an additional 30 minutes, stirring occasionally. Serve.

Party Pepper Almonds

(Ready in about 2 hours 30 minutes | Servings 24)

Ingredients

- 6 cups whole almonds
- 4 tablespoons margarine, melted
- 1/2 teaspoon turmeric
- 1 teaspoon garlic powder
- 1 teaspoon ground black or red peppercorns
- 1 teaspoon ground green peppercorns

Directions

1. Heat a crock pot on high for 15 minutes; then, add almonds.

2. Drizzle melted margarine over almonds and toss to combine; sprinkle with turmeric, garlic powder, and peppercorns; toss again. Turn heat to low; cook covered 2 hours; stir every 30 minutes.

3. Next, increase heat to high; uncover and cook 30 minutes longer, stirring every 15 minutes.

4. You can store the snack in a sealed container for up to 3 weeks.

Curried Party Mix

(Ready in about 2 hours 30 minutes | Servings 24)

Ingredients

- 1 cup walnuts
- 1 cup almonds
- 1 cup peanuts
- 1 cup hulled sunflower seeds
- 4 tablespoons margarine, melted
- 2 tablespoons sugar

- 1 tablespoon curry powder
- 1 teaspoon garlic powder
- 1 teaspoon ground allspice

Directions

1. Set the crock pot to high for 15 minutes; add nuts and seeds.

2. Drizzle margarine and toss to coat;

3. Add combined remaining ingredients. Cover and cook on low heat setting for about 2 hours; stir every 20 minutes.

4. Turn heat to high; remove a lid and cook 30 minutes longer, stirring after 15 minutes.

5. You can store this snack in a sealed container for up to 3 weeks.

Spiced Soy Nuts and Pumpkin Seeds

(Ready in about 2 hours 30 minutes | Servings 24)

Ingredients

- 4 tablespoons butter, melted
- 5 cups roasted soy nuts
- 1 cup hulled pumpkin seeds
- 2 tablespoons sugar
- 1 tablespoon turmeric powder
- 1 tablespoon basil
- 1 teaspoon red pepper flakes
- Sea salt, to taste

Directions

1. Heat a crock pot on high for 15 minutes.

2. Drizzle butter over soy nuts and pumpkin seeds; toss to coat.

3. Sprinkle with combined remaining ingredients, cover and cook on low 2 hours, stirring every 15 minutes.

4. Next increase heat to high; uncover and cook 30 minutes, stirring after 15 minutes.

Crunchy Colourful Mix

(Ready in about 2 hours | Servings 10)

Ingredients

- 1/2 cup roasted peanuts
- 1 cup sesame sticks
- 3 cups rice cereal squares
- 1/2 cup wasabi peas
- 2 tablespoons butter, melted
- 1 tablespoon soy sauce
- 1 teaspoon paprika
- 1 tablespoon curry powder
- Sugar, to taste
- Sea salt, to taste

Directions

1. Heat the crock pot on high for 15 minutes; add peanuts, sesame sticks, rice cereal, and wasabi peas.
2. Drizzle mixture with combined butter and soy sauce and toss.
3. Next, sprinkle the mixture with paprika, curry powder, sugar and salt; toss again.
4. Cook on high 1 ½ hours, stirring every 30 minutes. Serve warm or at room temperature.

Indian-Style Dipping Sauce

(Ready in about 2 hours | Servings 10)

Ingredients

- 1 pound cream cheese
- 2 cups sharp cheese, shredded
- 2-3 cloves garlic, minced
- 1/2 cup chopped mango chutney, divided
- 1/3 cup sweet onion, finely chopped
- 1/4 cup Sultanas
- 1–2 teaspoons curry powder
- Veggie stick, as garnish

Directions

1. Place cream cheese and sharp cheese in a crock pot; cover and cook about 30 minutes.

2. Then, add remaining ingredients, except veggie sticks; cover and cook 1 to 1 ½ hours.

3. Serve with favorite veggie stick and enjoy!

Party Favorite Artichoke Dip

(Ready in about 1 hour 30 minutes | Servings 16)

Ingredients

- 1/2 cup cream cheese, room temperature
- 1/2 cup sharp cheese, grated
- 2 cups canned artichoke hearts, drained and chopped
- 1/2 cup mayonnaise
- 1 teaspoon lemon juice
- 1-2 green onions, sliced
- 1/2 teaspoon sea salt
- 1 teaspoon cayenne pepper
- Dippers: bread sticks

Directions

1. Melt cheese in a crock pot about 30 minutes.

2. Stir in remaining ingredients, except dippers; cover and cook 1 to 1 ½ hours.

3. Serve with dippers such as bread sticks and enjoy!

Artichoke Spinach Dip

(Ready in about 1 hour 30 minutes | Servings 16)

Ingredients

- 1/2 cup Pecorino Romano, grated
- 1/2 cup cream cheese, room temperature
- 1/2 cup shrimp, chopped
- 2 cups canned artichoke hearts, drained and chopped
- 1/4 cup roasted red pepper, chopped
- 1/2 cup sour cream
- 2 tablespoons mayonnaise
- 1 teaspoon lemon juice
- 1/2 cup scallions, sliced

- 1/2 teaspoon sea salt
- 1 teaspoon cayenne pepper
- Dippers: crackers

Directions

1. Place cheese in a crock pot and cook about 30 minutes.
2. Then, add remaining ingredients, except crackers; cook approximately 1 hour.
3. Serve with crackers.

Cheese Pepperoni Dip

(Ready in about 2 hours | Servings 10)

Ingredients

- 1 cup cream cheese
- 1/2 cup scallions, chopped
- 1 ½ cups Swiss cheese, shredded
- 1/2 cup pepperoni, chopped
- 1 teaspoon mustard seeds
- 1/4 teaspoon paprika
- 3/4 cup whole milk
- Chopped fresh chives for garnish
- Dippers: bread sticks

Directions

1. Place cheeses in the crock pot and cook about 30 minutes.
2. Stir in remaining ingredients, except chives and dippers.
3. Cover and cook about 1 ½ hours. Sprinkle with chopped chives and serve with bread sticks.

Cereal Mix with Peanuts

(Ready in about 3 hours | Servings 12)

Ingredients

- 5 cups corn cereal
- 4 cups rice cereal

- 2 cups pretzels
- 1 cup breakfast cereal of choice
- 1 cup peanuts
- 1/3 cup butter, melted
- A pinch of black pepper
- 1 teaspoon garlic powder
- 1/2 teaspoon allspice
- 1 tablespoon seasoned salt
- 1/4 cup Worcestershire sauce

Directions

1. In your crock pot, place corn cereal, rice cereal, pretzels, breakfast cereal and peanuts.
2. To make the sauce: In a middle-sized mixing bowl or a measuring cup, combine remaining ingredients. Mix well to combine.
3. Drizzle the sauce over the top of the cereal-nut mixture. Toss to combine.
4. Cover with a lid; slow cook on low for 3 hours, stirring every 1 hour. You can store this amazing snack in a sealed container for up to 3 weeks.

Crispy Hot Chicken Taquitos

(Ready in about 8 hours 15 minutes | Servings 8)

Ingredients

- 1 ½ cups cream cheese
- 1/2 cup water
- 4 medium-sized chicken breasts
- 3 jalapeños, roughly chopped
- 1/2 teaspoon onion powder
- 1/2 teaspoon garlic powder
- 1 teaspoon salt
- 16 taco-sized flour tortillas
- 1 ½ cups Monterey jack, shredded
- 1/2 cup Mexican blend cheese
- Green goddess dressing to taste

Directions

1. Add cream cheese, water, chicken, jalapeños, onion powder, garlic powder and salt to a crock pot. Cover and cook on low for 8 hours.

2. Meanwhile, preheat the oven to 425 degrees F; oil a cookie sheet with non-stick cooking spray.

3. Cut cooked chicken into shreds with shredder claws or two forks. Remove to the crock pot. Stir to combine.

4. Next, heat flour tortillas in the microwave to soften them up.

5. Place cheese on each tortilla. Top with 3 tablespoons of chicken mixture.

6. Roll stuffed tortillas into log-shape taquitos. Bake taquitos in preheated oven for 15 minutes. Serve with green goddess dressing and enjoy!

Mom's Cocktail Party Mix

(Ready in about 3 hours | Servings 12)

Ingredients

- 9 cups rice cereal
- 1 cup almonds
- 1 cup pine nuts
- 1 cup peanuts
- 1/3 cup margarine, melted
- Cayenne pepper, to taste
- Black pepper, to taste
- 1/2 teaspoon onion powder
- 1/2 teaspoon garlic powder
- 1/2 teaspoon grated nutmeg
- 1 tablespoon seasoned salt
- 1/4 cup Worcestershire sauce
- 2 tablespoons tamari sauce

Directions

1. In a crock pot, place rice cereal, almonds, pine nuts and peanuts.

2. To make the sauce, in a mixing bowl, combine the rest of the ingredients. Whisk well to combine.

3. Drizzle the sauce over the top of the mixture in the crock pot. Toss to coat well.

4. Then, slow cook for 3 hours on low, stirring every 1 hour. Keep in a cool dry place for up to 3 weeks.

Candied Cashews and Walnuts

(Ready in about 3 hours | Servings 10)

Ingredients

- 2 cups cashews
- 2 cups walnuts
- 1 ½ cup sugar
- 1 tablespoon ground cinnamon
- 1 egg white
- 1 teaspoon pure almond extract
- 1/4 cup water

Directions

1. Place cashews and walnuts into a crock pot prepared with non-stick cooking spray.
2. In a bowl, mix together sugar and cinnamon. Sprinkle over nuts.
3. In another mixing bowl, beat egg white with almond extract until they become frothy.
4. Cook covered 3 hours on low, stirring every 15-20 minutes. Pour water into the crock pot during last 20 minutes.
5. Spread candied nuts out on a parchment paper to cool for 20 minutes.

Sugar-Glazed Pine Nuts and Pecans

(Ready in about 3 hours | Servings 10)

Ingredients

- Butter-flavored cooking spray
- 2 cups pine nuts
- 2 cups pecan halves
- 3/4 teaspoon five-spice powder
- 1 cup sugar
- 1/2 cup powdered sugar
- 1 teaspoon ground cinnamon
- 1 egg white
- 1 teaspoon vanilla
- 1/4 cup water

Directions

1. Place pine nuts and pecans into a crock pot prepared with non-stick cooking spray.

2. In a bowl, mix five-spice powder, sugar, powdered sugar and cinnamon. Sprinkle this mixture over nuts in the crock pot.

3. In a separate mixing bowl, beat egg white with vanilla until they become frothy.

4. Cook 3 hours on low, stirring every 20 minutes. Pour water into the crock pot during last 20 minutes of cooking time.

5. Spread pine nuts and pecans out on a cookie sheet to cool for 20 minutes.

Granola and Fruit Mix

(Ready in about 1 hour 30 minutes | Servings 16)

Ingredients

- 3 cups granola
- 2 cups mini pretzel twists
- 1/2 cup sesame sticks, broken into halves
- 2 cups blueberries, coarsely chopped
- 1 cup cranberries, coarsely chopped
- Butter-flavored cooking spray
- 1/2 teaspoon ground nutmeg
- 1 teaspoon ground cinnamon
- 1 teaspoon brown sugar

Directions

1. Heat your crock pot on high 15 minutes; add granola, pretzel, sesame sticks, blueberries and cranberries.

2. Spray mixture generously with butter-flavored cooking spray and toss; sprinkle with nutmeg, cinnamon and sugar, and toss to coat.

3. Cook on high 1 ½ hours, stirring every 30 minutes.

Kicked-Up Hot Party Mix

(Ready in about 1 hour 30 minutes | Servings 16)

Ingredients

- 2 cups crackers
- 4 cups baked pita chips
- 1/2 cup almonds
- 1 cup dried pineapple chunks
- Hot red pepper sauce, to taste
- Butter-flavored cooking spray
- 1 teaspoon chili powder
- 1 teaspoon smoked paprika
- 1 teaspoon dried oregano leaves
- 1 teaspoon dried sage leaves
- A pinch of ground black pepper

Directions

1. Set a crock pot to high for 15 minutes; add crackers, pita chips, almonds, dried pineapple chunks and red pepper sauce. Generously grease the mixture with the cooking spray; toss to coat
2. Sprinkle with combined herbs and spices. Toss to coat evenly.
3. Remove a lid from the crock pot; cook on high 1 ½ hours, stirring every 20 minutes.

Cereal and Nut Snack Mix

(Ready in about 1 hour 30 minutes | Servings 16)

Ingredients

- 2 cups oat cereal
- 3 cups rice cereal
- 1 cup sesame sticks
- 1 ½ cups pretzels goldfish
- 1 cup walnuts, halved
- 1 cup almonds
- 1 cup pecans
- 1/2 cup pumpkin seeds
- 1 teaspoon sea salt
- 1/2 teaspoon garlic powder
- 1/4 cup butter, melted
- 3 tablespoons Worcestershire sauce
- 1 teaspoon hot pepper sauce

Directions

1. Set a crock pot to high for about 15 minutes. Add oat cereal, rice cereal, sesame sticks, pretzels, walnuts, almonds, pecans and pumpkin seeds.

2. Drizzle remaining ingredients over mixture in the crock pot.

3. Cook on high 1 ½ hours, stirring every 30 minutes.

Summer Pizza Dipping Sauce

(Ready in about 1 hour 30 minutes | Servings 12)

Ingredients

- 2 cups mozzarella cheese, shredded
- 1 pound processed cheese, cubed
- 1/3 cup ripe olives, sliced
- 1 ½ cups pizza sauce
- 1 tablespoon Italian seasoning mix
- 1 cup salami, chopped
- Dippers: tortilla chips

Directions

1. Place mozzarella cheese and processed cheese in a crock pot. Cover and cook for about 30 minutes or until cheese is melted.

2. Stir in remaining ingredients, except tortilla chips.

3. Cover with a lid and cook 1 ½ hours. Serve with tortilla chips.

Italian Style Cheese Dip

(Ready in about 1 hour 30 minutes | Servings 12)

Ingredients

- 1 ½ cups cream cheese
- 2 cups mozzarella cheese, shredded
- 1/3 cup roasted pepper, chopped
- 1 cup pizza sauce
- 1/2 cup tomato juice
- 1 teaspoon dried oregano leaves

- 1 teaspoon dried basil leaves
- 1 cup pepperoni, chopped
- 1/3 cup cilantro, chopped
- Dippers: celery sticks

Directions

1. Place cheese in a crock pot. Cover with a lid and cook about 30 minutes.
2. Stir in remaining ingredients, except celery sticks.
3. Cover with a lid and cook 1 ½ hours. Serve with celery sticks.

Sauerkraut Beef Dip

(Ready in about 2 hours | Servings 24)

Ingredients

- 1 cup reduced-fat sharp cheese, shredded
- 1 ½ cups cream cheese
- 1 ½ cups sauerkraut, rinsed and drained
- 1 cup lean corned beef, chopped
- 1/4 cup Thousand Island dressing
- 1 tablespoon caraway seeds
- Kosher salt, to taste
- Vegetable sticks, as garnish

Directions

1. Place sharp cheese and cream cheese in a crock pot.
2. Cover and cook approximately 30 minutes.
3. Mix in remaining ingredients, except vegetable sticks; cover and cook 1 ½ hours.
4. Serve with vegetable sticks.

Warm Dried Beef Dip

(Ready in about 2 hours | Servings 24)

Ingredients

- 1 ½ cup cream cheese
- 1 cup reduced-fat mayonnaise
- 1/2 cup green onions, chopped
- 2-3 cloves garlic, minced
- 4 ½ ounces dried beef, chopped
- 1 teaspoon seasoned salt

Directions

1. Put the cream cheese into a crock pot; cook covered until cream cheese is melted, about 30 minutes.
2. Next, add remaining ingredients and cook 1 to 1 ½ hours or until heated through.
3. Serve with bread sticks or garlic crackers.

Roasted Pepper and Garlic Dip

(Ready in about 1 hour 30 minutes | Servings 24)

Ingredients

- 1/2 goat cheese
- 1 ½ pound reduced-fat cream cheese, room temperature
- 1/2 cup roasted pepper, chopped
- 3 tablespoons roasted garlic, minced
- 1/4 teaspoon ground black pepper
- 1 teaspoon smoked paprika
- 1/4 teaspoon sea salt
- 3/4 cup milk

Directions

1. Arrange all of the ingredients into your crock pot.
2. Cover the crock pot with a lid; cook 1 to 1 ½ hours.
3. Serve with your favorite dippers.

Hot Cheese Bean Dip

(Ready in about 2 hours 20 minutes | Servings 12)

Ingredients

- 1 pound processed cheese food, cubed
- 1 (14-ounce) can diced tomatoes with green chile peppers, drained
- 2 medium-sized cooked chicken breast, shredded
- 1/3 cup sour cream
- 1/4 cup scallions, chopped
- 1 large-sized poblano pepper, minced
- A pinch of black pepper (optional)
- 1 cup canned beans, rinsed and drained

Directions

1. Place all of the ingredients, except beans, into a crock pot.
2. Cook about 2 hours on high, stirring occasionally.
3. Stir in the drained beans and cook 20 more minutes. Serve with corn tortilla chips.

Yummy Chili Dipping sauce

(Ready in about 2 hours | Servings 12)

Ingredients

- 2 small-sized roasted jalapeño pepper, coarsely chopped
- 1 cup shredded reduced-fat sharp cheese
- 2 cups reduced-fat processed cheese, shredded
- 1/3 cup plum tomatoes, chopped
- 2-3 cloves garlic
- 1/2 cup green onions, chopped
- 1/2 teaspoon dried basil leaves
- 1/2 teaspoon dried oregano leaves
- 3 tablespoons milk

Directions

1. Place cheeses in your crock pot; cover and cook until cheeses are melted or about 30 minutes.

2. Add the rest of the ingredients.
3. Cover and cook until heated through or about 1 ½ hours.

Three-Cheese Bean Appetizer

(Ready in about 1 hour 30 minutes | Servings 16)

Ingredients

- 1 cup Provolone cheese, cubed
- 1 cup cream cheese, room temperature
- 1/2 cup sharp blue cheese, grated
- 1/2 cup mayonnaise
- 1 cup canned kidney beans, drained and rinsed
- 1 can green chilies, diced
- 1 teaspoon Tabasco sauce
- 2-3 cloves garlic, minced

Directions

1. Mix all ingredients in your crock pot.
2. Cover and cook 1 to 1 ½ hours on high.
3. Serve with your favorite dippers and enjoy!

Mexican Queso Fundido

(Ready in about 2 hours | Servings 16)

Ingredients

- 1 ½ cups sharp cheese shredded
- 1 cup reduced-fat processed cheese, cubed
- 1/2 roasted red pepper, chopped
- 2/3 cup milk
- 1 cup chorizo sausage, chopped
- 2 teaspoons pickled jalapeño chilies
- 16 corn tortillas, warm
- Chopped cilantro, as garnish
- Chopped chives, as garnish

Directions

1. Place cheeses in a crock pot; cook on high until cheeses are melted, about 30 minutes.

2. Add remaining ingredients, except tortillas, cilantro and chives; cover and cook about 1 ½ hours.

3. Divide prepared mixture among tortillas. Sprinkle with chopped cilantro and chives and roll up. Enjoy!

Easy Seafood Dipping Sauce

(Ready in about 2 hours | Servings 8)

Ingredients

- 1 cup sharp cheese, cubed
- 1 cup cream cheese
- 3/4 cup whole milk
- 1 cup cooked shrimp, chopped
- 1 cup cooked crab, chopped
- 1 teaspoon red pepper flakes
- 1/2 teaspoon ground black pepper

Directions

1. Place cheeses in a crock pot; cover with a lid; set the crock pot to low and cook about 30 minutes.

2. Add the rest of the ingredients; cover and cook 1 ½ hours.

3. Serve with bread sticks, crackers or veggie sticks.

Delicious Salmon Dipping Sauce

(Ready in about 2 hours | Servings 16)

Ingredients

- 1 cup cream cheese, at room temperature
- 1 cup mayonnaise
- 1 teaspoon Dijon mustard
- 1 can (14-ounce) artichoke hearts, drained and chopped

- 1 ½ cups canned salmon
- 1 tablespoon lemon
- 1/2 cup Monterey Jack cheese, diced
- 4 dashes hot pepper sauce
- Lemon wedges, as garnish

Directions

1. Arrange all ingredients in your crock pot.
2. Cover and slow cook 2 hours on high heat setting.
3. Garnish with lemon wedges; serve with dippers such as sweet bell pepper strips or steamed asparagus spears.

Romantic Cheese Fondue

(Ready in about 1 hour | Servings 12)

Ingredients

- 2 cups Swiss cheese, shredded
- 1 tablespoon all-purpose flour
- 1 cup cream cheese, room temperature
- 3 tablespoons milk
- 3/4 cup apple juice
- 1/2 teaspoon allspice
- 1/2 teaspoon paprika
- 1-2 cloves garlic, minced

Directions

1. Toss Swiss cheese with flour.
2. Combine Swiss cheese, cream cheese, milk, apple juice, allspice, paprika and garlic in your crock pot.
3. Cook covered 1 to 1 ½ hours. Serve with bread sticks or sweet bell pepper strips and enjoy.

Honey Party Wings

(Ready in about 7 hours | Servings 10)

Ingredients

- 3 pounds chicken wings
- 1/4 cup tamari sauce
- 1/4 cup honey
- 1/2 teaspoon celery salt
- 1/2 teaspoon ground black pepper
- 2 tablespoons chili sauce
- 1/2 teaspoon onion powder
- 1/2 teaspoon garlic powder

Directions

1. Place the wings into a crock pot.
2. In a small-sized bowl, whisk the rest of the ingredients. Pour this sauce over the wings; toss to coat well.
3. Cook for 7 hours on low.

Party-Pleasing Fondue

(Ready in about 4 hours | Servings 12)

Ingredients

- 2 cloves garlic, cut into halves
- 2 cups milk
- 1 cup sparkling white grape juice
- A few drops Tabasco sauce
- 1/4 cup all-purpose flour
- 1 teaspoon onion powder
- 1 teaspoon mustard seeds
- 1/2 teaspoon paprika
- 4 cups sharp cheese, cubed
- 4 cups semi-soft cheese, cubed

Directions

1. Rub the inside of the crock pot with the garlic.
2. Add the milk, sparkling grape juice, and Tabasco sauce to the crock pot.

3. Add remaining ingredients to a large zip-closure bag. Then, shake to mix well. Transfer to the crock pot.

4. Cover and cook on low until heated through or for 4 hours.

5. Serve with roasted asparagus spears or pickle slices.

Red Currant Jelly Meatballs

(Ready in about 6 hours | Servings 8)

Ingredients

- 2 tablespoons olive oil
- 2 pounds precooked meatballs, frozen
- 1 cup red currant jelly
- 1 (12-ounce) jar chili sauce

Directions

1. Add the olive oil to the bag of meatballs; toss to coat as good as you can. Transfer to the crock pot. Cover and cook for 4 hours on high.

2. In a measuring cup or a mixing bowl, mix the chili sauce with the red currant jelly. Pour over the meatballs in the crock pot.

3. Cover and cook on low for 2 hours.

Jalapeño Corn and Cheese Dip

(Ready in about 2 hours | Servings 6)

Ingredients

- 4 slices bacon, diced
- 6 cups canned whole kernel corn, drained
- 2 jalapeños, seeded and diced
- 1 cup Swiss cheese, shredded
- 1/2 cup sour cream
- 1 cup cream cheese, cubed
- 1/4 cup grated Parmesan cheese
- 1/2 teaspoon ground black pepper
- Salt to taste
- 1 heaping tablespoon cilantro, chopped

Directions

1. Brown bacon in a cast-iron skillet about 8 minutes. Drain and set aside.
2. Place kernel corn, jalapeños, Swiss cheese, sour cream, cream cheese and Parmesan into a crock pot.
3. Season with black pepper and salt. Cover and cook on low heat setting for 2 hours. Sprinkle with chopped cilantro.
4. Serve with bell pepper strips or celery sticks.

Picante Bean Dipping Sauce

(Ready in about 2 hours | Servings 12)

Ingredients

- 1 cup picante sauce
- 4 cups of refried beans
- 2 cups Cheddar cheese, shredded
- 1/4 fresh parsley, chopped
- 1/2 cup shallots, chopped

Directions

1. Place all of the ingredients in your crock pot.
2. Cook covered on low for 2 hours.
3. Serve with pickle slices or baby carrots.

Saucy Tomato Meatballs

(Ready in about 4 hours | Servings 8)

Ingredients

- 2 pounds veal, coarsely ground
- 1 clove garlic, crushed
- 1/4 pound Mozzarella cheese, grated
- 3 eggs, lightly beaten
- 1 tablespoon cayenne pepper
- 1/2 ground black pepper

- 1 teaspoon salt
- 1 teaspoon dried oregano leaves
- 1 cup bread crumbs
- 1/2 cup whole milk
- 2 tablespoons olive oil
- 2 tomatoes, diced
- 1 cup tomato juice

Directions

1. In a large-sized mixing bowl, combine all ingredients, except tomatoes and tomato juice.
2. Shape the mixture into ¾-inch balls.
3. Heat olive oil in a saucepan over medium-high heat. Sauté the meatballs for about 10 minutes.
4. Arrange sautéed meatballs in the crock pot.
5. Pour the tomatoes and tomato juice over the meatballs in the crock pot.
6. Cover and slow cook for 3 to 4 hours. Transfer to a serving platter and serve with skewers!

Turkey Meatballs with Paprika Sauce

(Ready in about 6 hours | Servings 6)

Ingredients

- 12 frozen turkey meatballs, defrosted
- 1 teaspoon olive oil
- 1/2 cup green onions, chopped
- 2-3 cloves garlic, minced
- 1 celery rib, chopped
- 1 carrot, diced
- 4 cups canned tomatoes, crushed
- 2 tablespoons tomato paste
- 1/2 teaspoon kosher salt
- 1/2 teaspoon ground black pepper
- 1 teaspoon dried oregano leaves
- 1 teaspoon dried thyme leaves
- 1 teaspoon paprika

Directions

1. Place the meatballs in the crock pot.

2. To make the sauce: Heat olive oil in a large non-stick pan. Sauté the onions, garlic, celery and carrot until the vegetables start to soften.

3. Add the rest of the ingredients and continue cooking over medium-low heat until most of the liquid has evaporated.

4. Pour prepared sauce over the meatballs in the crock pot. Slow cook about 6 hours on low.

5. Serve with mini pumpernickel.

Beer-Braised Meatballs

(Ready in about 7 hours | Servings 10)

Ingredients

- 2 medium-sized yellow onions, finely chopped
- 1 (16-ounce) package frozen meatballs
- 1 (12-ounce) can nonalcoholic beer
- 1 cup tomato paste
- 1/2 cup chili sauce
- Salt, to taste
- Ground black pepper, to taste
- 1 teaspoon dried tarragon
- 1/4 cup pickle relish

Directions

1. Arrange onions in a crock pot; add meatballs.

2. In a mixing bowl or a measuring cup, combine remaining ingredients; pour into the crock pot.

3. Cover and cook on low for about 7 hours. Serve mini pumpernickel and mustard, if desired.

Saucy Cocktail Franks

(Ready in about 4 hours | Servings 8)

Ingredients

- 1/4 cup tomato sauce
- 2 tablespoons apple juice
- 2/3 cup apricot preserves
- 2 tablespoons apple cider vinegar
- 3 cloves garlic, minced
- 1 shallot, chopped
- 1/3 cup chicken stock
- 2 tablespoons soy sauce
- 1/4 teaspoon cayenne pepper
- 1/4 teaspoon black pepper
- 2 pounds mini cocktail frankfurters

Directions

1. In a crock pot, combine all ingredients, except franks; mix well to combine. Then, add franks.
2. Cover and cook on high for 3 to 4 hours.
3. Serve with toothpicks, garnished with mustard.

Best Cocktail Sausages

(Ready in about 7 hours | Servings 8)

Ingredients

- 1 cup sweet chilli sauce
- 2 tablespoons apple cider vinegar
- 3 cloves garlic, minced
- 1 shallot, chopped
- 1 cup vegetable stock
- 1/2 cup cranberry sauce
- 2 tablespoons tamari sauce
- 1/4 teaspoon cayenne pepper
- 1/4 teaspoon black pepper
- 1 ½ pounds mini cocktail sausages

Directions

4. In your crock pot, arrange all ingredients. Stir to combine.
5. Cover and cook 7 hours on high.
6. Serve with cocktail sticks and enjoy.

Yummy Cereal Snack Mix

(Ready in about 3 hours | Servings 20)

Ingredients

- 2 tablespoons margarine, melted
- 1/2 teaspoon onion powder
- 1 teaspoon garlic powder
- 1 teaspoon paprika
- 1 teaspoon Italian seasoning mix
- 1 teaspoon chili powder
- 1 tablespoon soy sauce
- 2 cups corn cereal squares
- 2 cups crispy wheat cereal squares
- 1 cup pretzels
- 1/2 cup roasted almonds
- 1/2 cup roasted walnuts

Directions

1. Place all ingredients into your crock pot, Stir well to combine.
2. Cook on low for 2 to 3 hours, stirring every 30 minutes.
3. Spread onto a baking sheet and allow to cool. Then, store in an airtight container.

Easy Smoked Pecans

(Ready in about 6 hours | Servings 24)

Ingredients

- 8 cups raw pecans
- 3 tablespoons butter, melted
- 1 tablespoon tamari sauce
- 2 tablespoons Worcestershire sauce
- 1 teaspoons garlic powder
- 1 teaspoon celery seeds

- 1 teaspoon smoked salt, to taste
- 1 teaspoon smoked paprika
- 1/2 teaspoon white pepper

Directions

1. Add all of the ingredients to your crock pot. Stir to coat the pecans evenly.
2. Cover and cook for 6 hours on low, stirring occasionally.
3. Please store smoked pecans in a covered container.

Easy Summer Snack

(Ready in about 2 hours | Servings 16)

Ingredients

- 1 pound raw pistachios
- 1/2 teaspoon ground black pepper
- 2 tablespoons olive oil
- 1 teaspoon seasoned salt
- 1/2 teaspoon cayenne pepper
- 1 teaspoon sugar

Directions

1. Put all ingredients into your crock pot.
2. Cover and slow cook for 2 hours, stirring after 1 hour.
3. Store in an airtight container.

Cajun Nut Mix

(Ready in about 3 hours | Servings 16)

Ingredients

- 2 pounds almonds
- 2 tablespoons olive oil
- 1 pound walnuts, halved
- 2 tablespoons Cajun seasoning blend

Directions

1. Add all of the ingredients to the crock pot. Stir to combine; then cover and cook on low for 1 hour, stirring occasionally. Adjust seasonings to taste.

2. Slow cook for 2 hours longer, stirring after 1 hour.

Spiced Party Pecans

(Ready in about 2 hours 30 minutes | Servings 16)

Ingredients

- 2 pounds pecans
- 2 tablespoons butter
- 2 tablespoons Cajun seasoning blend
- 1 teaspoon salt
- 1 teaspoon freshly ground black pepper
- 1 teaspoon paprika

Directions

1. Place all of the ingredients into the crock pot.

2. Set the crock pot to low, cover with a lid and slow cook your mix for about 2 ½ hours.

3. Let pecans cool completely. Serve and enjoy!

Cinnamon Vanilla Walnuts

(Ready in about 2 hours 15 minutes | Servings 16)

Ingredients

- 1 stick butter, melted
- 1 pound walnut halves
- 1 teaspoon cinnamon
- 2/3 cup powdered sugar
- 1 teaspoon vanilla
- A pinch of salt

Directions

1. Combine all of the ingredients in your crock pot.

2. Cover with a lid and cook for 15 minutes on high.

3. Next, turn heat to low, remove the lid and cook for 2 hours, stirring occasionally.

4. Let stand to cool completely before serving and storing.

Curried Mixed Nuts

(Ready in about 2 hours 15 minutes | Servings 16)

Ingredients

- 3 tablespoons coconut oil
- 2 tablespoons curry powder
- 1 tablespoon chili powder
- 1 tablespoon dried basil leaves
- 1 teaspoon smoked salt
- 3 cups walnuts, halved
- 3 cups pecans
- 2 cups almonds
- 1/2 cups pumpkin seeds

Directions

1. Treat the inside of a crock pot with coconut oil.

2. Place remaining ingredients in the crock pot.

3. Slow cook about 2 hours on low heat setting.

4. Let stand to cool completely before serving and storing. You can freeze leftovers.

Chili Honey Snack Mix

(Ready in about 4 hours | Servings 12)

Ingredients

- 2 teaspoons butter, melted
- 1 cup pecans
- 1/2 cup peanuts
- 1/4 cup balsamic vinegar
- 1/2 cup brown sugar
- 2 teaspoons cinnamon
- 1 teaspoon chili powder
- 1 teaspoon salt
- 2 teaspoons honey

Directions

1. Grease the inside of a crock pot with melted butter.
2. Add remaining ingredients and cook on low for 4 hours.
3. Pour this nut mixture out onto a baking sheet. Allow to cool; then, store in a container with an airtight lid.

Easy Velveeta Dipping Sauce

(Ready in about 3 hours | Servings 12)

Ingredients

1. 1 (15-ounce) can chili
2. 2 roated bell peppers, chopped
3. 1 pound Velveeta cheese, cubed

Directions

1. Add all ingredients to the crock pot.
2. Cover and cook on low for 3 hours, stirring every half hour.
3. Serve with bread sticks or crackers.

Mexican-Style Appetizer

(Ready in about 6 hours | Servings 24)

Ingredients

- 3 pounds lean ground beef, cooked and drained
- 1 medium-sized yellow onion, sliced
- 2-3 cloves garlic, minced
- 1 (15-ounce) can refried beans
- 1 cup tomato paste
- 1/2 cup tomato juice
- 1 teaspoon cayenne peppers
- Salt to taste
- 1 cup salsa
- 2 pounds cream cheese, cut into cubes

Directions

1. In a wide pan, brown ground beef over medium heat for about 10 minutes. Transfer to the crock pot.

2. Add the rest of the ingredients and stir to combine.

3. Cook covered on low for 4 to 6 hours, stirring every 30 minutes.

4. Taste for seasoning and add more spices if needed.

Old-Fashion Chicken Liver Pâté

(Ready in about 3 hours | Servings 16)

Ingredients

- 1 pound chicken livers
- 1/4 cup red onion, finely chopped
- 1 apple, peeled, cored and chopped
- 1/2 cup butter, room temperature
- 1/2 teaspoon paprika
- 1/2 teaspoon ground black pepper
- Salt, to taste

Directions

1. Cook all ingredients in a crock pot about 3 hours.

2. Transfer to a food processor. Puree until creamy and uniform.

3. Serve chilled with crackers.

Smoked Salmon Pâté

(Ready in about 3 hours | Servings 10)

Ingredients

- 1 ½ cups smoked salmon
- 2 cups cream cheese
- 2 tablespoons milk
- 1 tablespoon fresh lemon juice
- 1 teaspoon soy sauce
- 1/2 teaspoon ground black pepper
- 1/2 teaspoon paprika
- Fresh parsley, for garnish

Directions

1. Place all of the ingredients, except fresh parsley, in your crock pot.
2. Slow cook about 3 hours.
3. Sprinkle with fresh parsley and serve chilled.

Vegetarian Lentil Pâté

(Ready in about 2 hours | Servings 8)

Ingredients

- 1 cup dried lentils
- 2 cups vegetable stock
- 3 tablespoons butter
- 1 teaspoon celery seeds
- 1 tablespoon cilantro
- 1/2 teaspoon seasoned salt
- 1/2 teaspoon ground black pepper

Directions

1. Simply arrange all of the ingredients in your crock pot.
2. Cook covered for 2 hours on high heat setting.
3. Serve chilled with the pickles slices, celery sticks or tortilla chips.

Appetizer Meatballs with Barbecue Sauce

(Ready in about 4 hours | Servings 12)

Ingredients

- 1/2 pound ground pork
- 1 pound lean ground beef
- 1 small-sized onion, finely chopped
- 2 cloves garlic, minced
- 1 large-sized egg
- 1/3 cup dry bread crumbs
- 1/2 teaspoon seasoned salt
- 1/2 teaspoon red pepper flakes, crushed
- 1/2 teaspoon pepper ground black pepper
- 2 cups barbecue sauce
- 1 cup orange marmalade

Directions

1. Mix pork, beef, onion, garlic, egg, bread crumbs, salt, red pepper and black pepper. Mix well to combine; shape this mixture into 24 meatballs.
2. Add meatballs to the crock pot. Then, add barbecue sauce and orange marmalade.
3. Cook covered about 4 hours. Serve warm with cocktail sticks!

Hot Pineapple Chutney

(Ready in about 4 hours | Servings 6)

Ingredients

- 1 cups fresh mango, cubed
- 3 cups fresh pineapple, cubed
- 2 tablespoons shallots, minced
- 2 teaspoons garlic, minced
- 1/4 cup balsamic vinegar
- 3 tablespoons lemon juice
- 1/4 cup sugar
- 1 teaspoon honey
- 1 jalapeño, minced

Directions

1. Put all ingredients into your crock pot. Stir well to combine.
2. Turn the crock pot to high and cook 3 hours.
3. Then, uncover and continue cooking for 1 hour on high.

Black Bean Dipping Sauce

(Ready in about 2 hours | Servings 24)

Ingredients

- 1 teaspoon extra-virgin olive oil
- 1 poblano pepper, minced
- 2-3 cloves garlic, minced
- 1 medium-sized onion, chopped
- 1/2 teaspoon cayenne pepper
- 1 teaspoon celery seeds
- 1/4 cup reduced-fat sour cream
- 2 tablespoons lemon juice
- 4 cups canned black beans, drained and rinsed

Directions

1. Heat olive oil in a non-stick saucepan. Sauté the poblano, garlic and onion for about 10 minutes until tender.

2. Add remaining ingredients and stir to combine. Mash the mixture.

3. Add to the crock pot and cook on low for 2 hours.

Hot Corn Bean Dip

(Ready in about 2 hours | Servings 16)

Ingredients

- 1 teaspoon olive oil
- 1/2 cup shallots, minced
- 2 cloves garlic, minced
- 1 jalapeño pepper, minced
- A few drops of hot sauce
- 1/2 teaspoon paprika
- 1/2 teaspoon cumin
- 2 tablespoons fresh lemon juice
- 1/4 cup cream cheese
- 2 cups canned cannellini beans, drained and rinsed
- 1/2 cup corn kernels
- 2 tablespoons fresh cilantro, coarsely chopped

Directions

1. Heat olive oil in a heavy skillet. Sauté the shallots, garlic and jalapeño until soft and fragrant or about 3 minutes.

2. Pour into a large-sized mixing bowl. Add remaining ingredients, except cilantro.

3. Mash with a potato masher. Transfer to the crock pot.

4. Cook on low for 2 hours. Sprinkle with fresh chopped cilantro and serve with tortilla chips or pita chips, if desired.

Vegetable-Rich Dipping Sauce

(Ready in about 1 hour | Servings 16)

Ingredients

- 2 cups cauliflower florets, steamed
- 2 cups broccoli florets, steamed
- 1 medium-sized onion, chopped
- 1 large-sized carrot, chopped
- 1 cup fresh spinach
- 1 jalapeño, minced
- 1 tablespoon Worcestershire sauce
- 1 cup plain yogurt
- Sea salt, to taste
- 1/4 teaspoon ground black pepper
- 1 tablespoon lemon juice

Directions

1. Place the cauliflower florets, broccoli florets, onion, carrot, spinach, jalapeño and Worcestershire sauce in a food processor.
2. Pulse until the mixture is creamy and smooth. Add the yogurt, salt, black pepper, and lemon juice. Pulse again.
3. Pour this mixture into the crock pot. Cover and cook for 1 hour on low heat setting. Serve chilled with soft pretzels or sliced baguette.

Eggplant Dip with Tahini and Cheese

(Ready in about 2 hours | Servings 12)

Ingredients

- 2 large-sized eggplants, sliced
- 2-3 cloves garlic, minced
- 1 tablespoon fresh parsley
- 1/2 teaspoon dried thyme
- 1 teaspoon dried basil leaves
- 1 teaspoon dired oregano leaves
- 1 teaspoon sea salt
- 1/2 teaspoon ground black pepper
- 2 tablespoons lime juice
- 2 tablespoons tahini
- 1 cup Swiss cheese, grated

Directions

1. Arrange eggplant, garlic, parsley, thyme, basil, oregano, salt and black pepper in a crock pot. Slow cook on high for about 2 hours.

2. Allow to cool; then, add lime and tahini. Pulse in a food processor until your desired consistency is reached.

3. Reheat the mixture in a crock pot; add Swiss cheese and allow to melt. Serve warm or at room temperature. Serve with pumpernickel pretzels, raw vegetables or mini pitas.

Seafood Artichoke Dip

(Ready in about 1 hour | Servings 20)

Ingredients

- 2 cups sour cream
- 1 cup reduced-fat cream cheese
- 1 cup leeks, chopped
- 1 tablespoon soy sauce
- 12 ounces artichoke hearts
- 1 cup shrimp
- 1 cup crabmeat

Directions

1. In a food processor, place sour cream, cream cheese, leeks, soy sauce and artichoke hearts.

2. Pulse until everything is well combined.

3. Scrape into a crock pot. Add shrimp and crabmeat; stir well to combine.

4. Cook 40 minutes on low. Garnish with lemon slices and serve with sesame pretzels or baked potato chips.

Pecans with Syrupy Coating

(Ready in about 4 hours | Servings 16)

Ingredients

- 2 cups whole pecans
- 1/2 cup apple cider vinegar

- 1/2 cup brown sugar
- 1 teaspoon allspice
- 1 teaspoon paprika
- 1 teaspoon kosher salt

Directions

1. Arrange all your ingredients in a crock pot. Cook on high until all the liquid has evaporated or about 4 hours, stirring every 15 minutes.

2. Place the pecans in a single layer on the baking sheets that are coated with parchment paper. Let them cool completely before storing. Keep this pecans for up to 2 weeks.

Grandma's Blackberry Compote

(Ready in about 7 hours | Servings 6)

Ingredients

- 2 cups blackberries
- 1/4 cup brown sugar
- 1 vanilla bean
- 1 cinnamon stick
- 1/4 cup lukewarm water
- 6 English muffins or favorite waffles, as garnish

Directions

1. Put all ingredients into a crock pot.

2. At the beginning, set your crock pot to low heat. Cook the compote covered for about 3 hours.

3. Next, remove the lid; increase the heat to high and cook 4 hours longer.

4. Serve warm with English muffins or your favorite waffles. Enjoy this great old-fashioned snack!

Favorite Pear Butter

(Ready in about 22 hours | Servings 12)

Ingredients

- 8 Bartlett pears, cored and quartered
- 1 cup water

- 2 tablespoons fresh orange juice
- 1/2 cup sugar
- 1/4 teaspoon ground cloves
- 1 stick cinnamon
- 1/2 teaspoon mace

Directions

1. Arrange all of the ingredients in your crock pot. Cook covered on low heat setting approximately 10 hours.
2. Then, uncover and cook an additional 10 to 12 hours or until the mixture is thickened.
3. Cool completely and then transfer to a food processor. Purée until smooth and uniform.
4. Keep in clean glass jars. Refrigerate and serve chilled with pancakes, waffles or English muffins.

Hummus with Carrot Sticks

(Ready in about 8 hours | Servings 20)

Ingredients

- Water
- 1 lb. chickpeas, dried
- 3 tablespoons tahini (sesame seed paste)
- 2 tablespoons balsamic vinegar
- 2-3 cloves garlic
- 1/2 teaspoon salt
- 10 large-sized carrots, cut into snack-friendly sizes

Directions

1. Pour water into your crock pot. Add chickpeas and let soak overnight.
2. The next morning, cook for 8 hours on low; drain, but reserve the liquid.
3. Transfer the cooked chickpeas to a food processor; add tahini, balsamic vinegar, garlic, and salt. Pulse until creamy and smooth, adding the reserved liquid as needed.
4. Serve with carrot sticks and enjoy!

Traditional Middle Eastern Spread

(Ready in about 8 hours | Servings 20)

Ingredients

- 1 pound canned chickpeas
- Water
- 5 tablespoons extra-virgin olive oil
- 3 tablespoons tahini
- 3 tablespoons freshly squeezed lemon juice
- 3 cloves garlic
- 1 teaspoon onion powder
- 1 teaspoon cayenne pepper
- 1 tablespoon fresh coriander, chopped
- 1/4 teaspoon kosher salt
- Falafel, as garnish

Directions

1. First of all, soak the chickpeas in water at least 8 hours or overnight.
2. Cook for 8 hours on low heat setting; replace to a food processor.
3. Add the rest of the ingredients, except falafel. Process until the mixture is creamy.
4. Serve with falafel and enjoy!

Cream Cheese Vegetable Spread

(Ready in about 2 hours | Servings 20)

Ingredients

- 2 tablespoons low-fat mayonnaise
- 1 cup cream cheese, at room temperature
- 1/2 cup sour cream
- 1/2 teaspoon garlic powder
- 1/2 teaspoon celery seeds
- 1 teaspoon Worcestershire sauce
- 1 stalk celery, minced
- 3 tablespoons fresh baby kale, minced
- 1/2 head cauliflower broccoli, chopped

Directions

1. Combine all ingredients in your crock pot. Cook for 2 hours on low.
2. Stir before serving; serve with your favorite crackers or croutons.

Strawberry Fruit Dipping Sauce

(Ready in about 1 hour | Servings 18)

Ingredients

- 1 cup cream cheese
- 1/2 cup strawberry purée
- 1 tablespoon brown sugar
- A pinch of salt
- 3/4 cup sour cream, reduced-fat
- 1/4 teaspoon grated nutmeg
- 1 teaspoon vanilla extract

Directions

1. Whisk together all ingredients in a mixing bowl.
2. Pour into a crock pot; cook on low for 1 hour. Stir before serving.
3. Serve with your favorite fruit dippers such as star fruit, banana, etc.

Sun-Dried Tomato Dip

(Ready in about 1 hour | Servings 18)

Ingredients

- 2 cloves garlic
- 2 tablespoons mayonnaise, reduced-fat
- 1 teaspoon onion powder
- 3/4 ounce fresh cilantro
- 2 tablespoons pecans, toasted
- 1/2 teaspoon paprika
- 1/2 teaspoon black pepper
- 1/4 cup sun-dried tomatoes, julienned
- 1 cup reduced-fat cream cheese

Directions

1. Put the garlic, mayonnaise, onion powder, cilantro, pecans, paprika, and black pepper into a food processor.

2. Process until a smooth paste forms. Add the sun-dried tomatoes and cream cheese and pulse until smooth and creamy.

3. Transfer the mixture to the crock pot. Cook on low for 1 hour; stir before serving and serve with baked potato chips and pita chips.

Squid and Scallop Dip

(Ready in about 1 hour | Servings 12)

Ingredients

- 1/2 cup scallions, chopped
- 1/3 cup squid, chopped
- 2/3 cup scallops, chopped
- 1 teaspoon garlic powder
- 1 cup cream cheese, reduced-fat
- 1/2 cup sour cream, reduced-fat
- 1 tablespoon balsamic vinegar
- 1 roasted red bell pepper, chopped
- Sea salt, to taste
- Cayenne pepper, to taste
- 1 tablespoon fresh parsley
- 1/8 teaspoon mustard seed

Directions

1. In a mixing bowl, combine together all of the ingredients.

2. Scrape into a crock pot. Cook until heated through or for 1 hour on low.

3. Serve with croutons and bell pepper sticks.

Mediterranean Seafood Treat

(Ready in about 1 hour | Servings 12)

Ingredients

- 1/2 cup red onions, chopped
- 1/3 cup clams, chopped

- 2/3 cup shrimp, chopped
- 1/2 teaspoon celery seed
- 1/2 teaspoon garlic powder
- 1 cup cream cheese, reduced-fat
- 2 tablespoons mayonnaise
- 1/2 cup sour cream, reduced-fat
- 1 tablespoon lemon juice
- 1 large-sized Roma tomato, chopped
- 1 tablespoon fresh cilantro
- 1/4 teaspoon sea salt
- 1/4 teaspoon ground black pepper

Directions

1. Mix together all of the ingredients in a medium-sized bowl. Transfer to the crock pot.
2. Then, cook covered for 1 hour on low heat setting.
3. Sprinkle with chopped chives; serve chilled with your favorite dippers.

Spiced Date Spread

(Ready in about 6 hours | Servings 24)

Ingredients

- 2 lbs. fresh dates
- 1 tablespoon ground ginger
- 1/4 teaspoon ground cinnamon
- 2 tablespoons orange juice
- 1/2 cup water
- 1/3 cup brown sugar
- 1 tablespoon honey

Directions

1. Combine all ingredients in your crock pot. Stir to combine well.
2. Cook covered on low 2 to 3 hours. Then, remove the lid; cook an additional 3 hours until the mixture is thickened.
3. Place in an airtight container and refrigerate up to 6 weeks.

Amazing Autumn Spread

(Ready in about 22 hours | Servings 24)

Ingredients

- 4 pears, cored and sliced
- 4 apples, cored and sliced
- 1/2 cup pear cider
- 1/2 cup water
- 2 tablespoons molasses
- 1/4 cup sugar
- 1/4 teaspoon ground cloves
- 1/2 teaspoon grated ginger
- 1/2 teaspoon ground cinnamon
- 1/2 teaspoon grated nutmeg

Directions

1. Place all ingredients in a crock pot. Cook for 10 to 12 hours on low.
2. Remove the lid; cook an additional 10 to 12 hours or until your spread is thickened. Allow to cool.
3. Pour into the food processor; purée until uniform and smooth.
4. Refrigerate and keep in glass jars up to 6 weeks.

Nutty Beef Dipping Sauce

(Ready in about 3 hours | Servings 6)

Ingredients

- 1/2 cup beef, shredded
- 2 tablespoons scallions, finely chopped
- 1/2 cup pine nuts, finely chopped
- 1 cup cream cheese
- 2 tablespoons mayonnaise
- 1/2 cup sour cream
- 2 tablespoons water
- 1/4 teaspoon white pepper

Directions

1. Combine all ingredients in the crock pot.
2. Cover and heat on a low setting for 2 to 3 hours. Serve with croutons and enjoy!

Cheesy Crab Dipping Sauce

(Ready in about 3 hours | Servings 6)

Ingredients

- 1 cup cream cheese, crumbled
- 1 cup crabmeat, shredded
- 1 tablespoon water
- 1/2 teaspoon salt
- 1/2 teaspoon ground black pepper
- 1/4 cup pecans, toasted

Directions

1. Put all ingredients, except pecans, into a crock pot.
2. Cover with the lid; heat on a low setting approximately 3 hours.
3. Sprinkle the dipping sauce with the pecans and serve with your favorite dippers.

Pepperoni Cheese Dip

(Ready in about 3 hours | Servings 16)

Ingredients

- 1 pound Cheddar cheese, shredded
- 1 pound Mozzarella cheese, shredded
- 1 sweet red bell pepper, chopped
- 1 sweet green bell pepper, chopped
- 1 teaspoon Dijon mustard
- 1/2 pound pepperoni, sliced
- 1 cup cream cheese
- 1 cup mayonnaise

Directions

1. Combine all the ingredients in the crock pot. Cover with the lid.
2. Heat on low setting for 2 to 3 hours, until all the cheese is melted.
3. Serve with your favorite crackers or veggie sticks.

Rich-Tasting Prosciutto Spread

(Ready in about 3 hours | Servings 16)

Ingredients

- 1/3 pound Prosciutto, chopped
- 2 pounds Cheddar cheese, shredded
- 1 poblano pepper, minced
- 1 teaspoon onion powder
- 1 teaspoon garlic powder
- 1 teaspoon mustard
- 1 cup sour cream
- 1 cup cream cheese
- 1 cup mayonnaise

Directions

1. Put all ingredients into the crock pot.
2. Cover; heat 2 to 3 hours on a low setting.
3. Serve with celery sticks or bread sticks.

Best Cocktail Meatballs

(Ready in about 4 hours | Servings 8)

Ingredients

- 1 (16-ounce) can whole cranberry sauce
- 1 ½ cup chili sauce
- Salt to taste
- 2 bay leaves
- 27 ounces sauerkraut, undrained
- 1 cup water
- 1/2 cup brown sugar
- 1 (16-ounce) package meatballs

Directions

1. In a mixing bowl, combine cranberry sauce, chili sauce, salt, bay leaves, sauerkraut, water, and brown sugar. Mix well to combine.
2. Then, pour sauce and meatballs into the crock pot; stir again.
3. Cook covered for 4 hours. Serve with cocktail sticks.

Saucy Meat Appetizer

(Ready in about 40 minutes | Servings 8)

Ingredients

- Non-stick cooking spray
- 2/3 cup milk
- 1 pound lean ground beef
- 2-3 cloves garlic, minced
- 1 tablespoon tamari sauce
- 1/4 cup Worcestershire sauce
- 1/2 teaspoon ground black pepper
- 1 teaspoon onion powder
- 1 cup tomato paste
- 1/2 cup brown sugar

Directions

1. Begin by preheating the oven to broil. Coat a roasting pan with non-stick cooking spray.
2. In a mixing bowl, combine milk, ground beef, garlic, tamari sauce, Worcestershire sauce, black pepper, and onion powder. Roll the mixture into meatballs.
3. Arrange meatballs on a roasting pan. Broil about 10 minutes, or until the meatballs are cooked through.
4. In a mixing bowl, mix tomato paste and brown sugar. Transfer mixture to the crock pot. Add the broiled meatballs.
5. Cook meatballs for about 30 minutes on high. Transfer to a serving platter.

Chicken Pita Bites

(Ready in about 7 hours | Servings 6)

Ingredients

- 3 tablespoons olive oil
- 1 large-sized onion, chopped
- 2 cloves garlic, minced
- 1 teaspoon celery seeds
- 1 teaspoon allspice
- 1/2 teaspoon cinnamon
- 1 teaspoon paprika
- 1 pound chicken, cubed
- 1 ½ cups chicken stock
- 1 tablespoon apple cider vinegar
- Salt, to taste
- 6 pita bread

Directions

1. In a heavy skillet, heat the olive oil; sauté the onion and garlic until the onion is just tender.

2. Add the celery seeds, allspice, cinnamon, and paprika. Cook a few minutes, stirring frequently.

3. Mix well and cook a few minutes longer.

4. Place chicken in the crock pot. Pour the spiced onion mixture over it.

5. Pour in chicken stock; add vinegar and salt. Cover with the lid and let it slow cook 7 hours on low.

6. Toast pitas about 10 minutes or until crispy. Cut your pitas into small wedges. Serve with cooked chicken.

Juicy Orange Chicken Wings

(Ready in about 7 hours | Servings 8)

Ingredients

- 1/4 cup fruit vinegar
- 1/4 cup tamari sauce
- 3 tablespoons molasses
- 1 clove garlic, minced
- 1 teaspoon ground ginger
- 3 tablespoons orange juice
- 2 lbs. chicken wings
- 4 teaspoons cornflour
- 1 tablespoon water
- 2 tablespoons fresh parsley, chopped

Directions

1. In a measuring cup or a mixing bowl, whisk together fruit vinegar, tamari sauce, molasses, garlic, ginger, and orange juice.

2. Place wings into a crock pot. Pour orange sauce over wings; stir gently to combine. Cook on low heat setting for 6 to 7 hours.

3. In a small-sized bowl, whisk together cornflour and water. Stir in the crock pot.

4. Cover and cook until your sauce has thickened. Sprinkle with fresh parsley and serve warm or at room temperature.

Zesty Chicken Drumettes

(Ready in about 7 hours | Servings 6)

Ingredients

- 1 cup apples, cubed
- 1/2 teaspoon ground black pepper
- Salt, to taste
- 1 tablespoon lemon juice
- 1 teaspoon lemon rind
- 1/4 teaspoon grated ginger
- 1 garlic clove, minced
- 1/2 cup honey
- 1/2 cup soy sauce
- 1 teaspoon Creole mustard
- 10-12 chicken drumettes

Directions

1. To make the sauce: In a medium-sized mixing bowl, combine all ingredients, except chicken drumettes. Mix well to combine.
2. Next, rinse chicken drumettes under cold running water and drain them.
3. Arrange chicken drumettes in your crock pot; pour sauce over it.
4. Cover and cook on low approximately 7 hours. Serve warm and enjoy!

Kielbasa Bites with Tomato-Mustard Sauce

(Ready in about 5 hours | Servings 6)

Ingredients

- 2 cups tomato paste
- 2 tablespoons tomato ketchup
- 1/2 cup honey
- 1 tablespoon soy sauce
- 1 tablespoon orange juice
- 1 teaspoon mustard
- 1 chili pepper, minced
- 1 cup shallots, finely chopped
- 1/2 cup bourbon
- 2 pounds kielbasa, cut into 1/2 inch thick rounds

Directions

1. Arrange all of the ingredients in the crock pot.

2. Cover with the lid and cook on low for about 5 hours.

3. Serve warm with cocktail sticks and some extra mustard.

Amazing Country Bites

(Ready in about 3 hours | Servings 12)

Ingredients

- 2 ½ cups miniature smoked sausages
- 1 pound Polish sausage, cut into 1/2-inch slices
- 2 cups BBQ sauce of choice
- 1 teaspoon dried tarragon
- 1 teaspoon dried basil leaves
- 1 teaspoon mustard
- 2/3 cup orange marmalade

Directions

1. Place smoked sausages and Polish sausage in a crock pot.

2. In a medium-sized mixing bowl, or a measuring cup, whisk together the rest of the ingredients. Pour the sauce into the crock pot.

3. Cover the crock pot and cook until heated through or about 3 hours.

4. Serve with cocktail sticks or toothpicks.

Sweet Hot Bites

(Ready in about 4 hours | Servings 8)

Ingredients

- 1 ½ pounds Mennonite sausage, cut into rounds
- 2 bay leaves
- 1 teaspoon mustard
- 2 teaspoons Sriracha Hot Sauce
- 1 cup apricot jam

Directions

1. Arrange the sausage in your crock pot. Then, add bay leaves.
2. In a measuring cup, combine together remaining ingredients. Whisk until everything is well combined. Add to the prepared crock pot.
3. Cover and cook on high for about 4 hours.
4. Insert a toothpick into each of sausage rounds and transfer them to a serving platter.

Tangy Smoked Sausage

(Ready in about 6 hours | Servings 8)

Ingredients

- 1 (15.25-ounce) can pineapple tidbits, drained and juice reserved
- 2 tablespoons apple cider vinegar
- 1/2 cup maple syrup
- 1/3 cup water
- 1 ½ teaspoon whole grain mustard
- 2 tablespoons cornflour
- 1 pound mini smoked sausages

Directions

1. Drain the pineapple tidbits, reserving the juice.
2. In a medium-sized mixing bowl, blend reserved pineapple juice, apple cider vinegar, maple syrup, water, and mustard; stir in the cornflour.
3. Pour the mixture into the crock pot.

4. Add reserved pineapple tidbits and sausages; stir gently to combine.

5. Cover and cook on low setting approximately 6 hours.

Cheesy Sausage Snack with Mini Pitas

(Ready in about 4 hours | Servings 10)

Ingredients

- 2 ½ pounds smoked sausage, cut into small 1/4 inch pieces
- 2-3 cloves garlic, minced
- 2 pounds cream cheese, crumbled
- 1 ½ cups canned diced tomatoes, drained
- 1 tablespoon ground cumin
- 1 teaspoon smoked paprika
- 1 cup sour cream
- 2 tablespoons mayonnaise
- 1/2 cup fresh parsley, chopped
- Mini pitas, as garnish

Directions

1. In a medium-sized skillet, brown the sausages about 5 minutes. Add minced garlic and sauté an additional 3 minutes.

2. Transfer to the crock pot. Add the rest of the ingredients and stir to coat sausages; cover with the lid.

3. Slow cook for 4 hours on high. Serve with mini pitas and enjoy!

Tomato-Pepper Sausage Dip

(Ready in about 4 hours | Servings 12)

Ingredients

- 1 pound bulk sausage
- 2-3 spring onions
- 1 cup cream cheese, crumbled
- 1 ½ cup canned tomatoes, diced
- 1 jalapeño, minced
- 1 teaspoon dried oregano leaves

- 1 teaspoon dried basil leaves
- 1 teaspoon dried rosemary
- 2-3 heaping tablespoons chopped chives, as garnish
- Potato chips, as garnish

Directions

1. Heat a large non-stick skillet; then, sauté the sausages and spring onions until the onions are tender and translucent.
2. Transfer to the crock pot. Then, add the rest of the ingredients, except, chives and potato chips.
3. Slow cook for 4 hours or until everything is heated through.
4. Transfer to a nice serving bowl and sprinkle with fresh chopped chives; serve with potato chips.

Party Smoked Sausage Bites

(Ready in about 3 hours | Servings 16)

Ingredients

- 16 ounces smoked sausage, sliced into bite-size rounds
- 1 ½ cups barbecue sauce
- 2 tablespoons apple cider vinegar
- 1 cup plum jam
- 1 teaspoon dry mustard
- 1 poblano pepper, minced
- Decorative toothpicks

Directions

1. In a large heavy skillet, cook the sausages until they are browned. Replace to the crock pot.
2. In a mixing bowl, combine barbecue sauce, apple cider vinegar, plum jam, dry mustard and minced poblano pepper.
3. Cook covered on high-heat setting for about 3 hours. Serve these delicious sausage bites with decorative toothpicks and enjoy!

Summer Zesty Party Bites

(Ready in about 2 hours | Servings 12)

Ingredients

- 1/4 cup dry red wine
- 1 cup fresh pineapple juice
- 1 teaspoon cumin powder
- 1 teaspoon garlic powder
- 1 tablespoon dried onion flakes
- 2 tablespoons all-purpose flour
- 1 tablespoon dry mustard
- 1/2 cup maple syrup
- 2 pounds sausage of choice, cut into bite-sized rounds

Directions

1. Arrange all of the ingredients in your crock pot.
2. Stir gently to combine.
3. Cook covered on high at least 2 hours. Transfer to a serving platter and serve with cocktail sticks.

Appetizer Saucy Franks

(Ready in about 4 hours | Servings 20)

Ingredients

- 1 cup barbecue sauce of choice
- 1 tablespoon spicy brown mustard
- 2 cups jellied cranberry sauce
- 1 teaspoon ground cumin
- 1 teaspoon chili powder
- 2 pounds cocktail frankfurts

Directions

1. In your crock pot, place all ingredients and stir gently to coat the sausages well.
2. Set the crock pot to high and slow cook your sausages for 4 hours.
3. Transfer to a serving platter, and serve with sour cream, ketchup or mustard.

Kielbasa Chipotle Dipping Sauce

(Ready in about 4 hours | Servings 6)

Ingredients

- 2 tablespoons olive oil
- 2 Polish kielbasa, crumbled
- 1 medium-sized onion, chopped
- 2 chipotle peppers, minced
- Sea salt to taste
- 1/2 teaspoon ground black pepper
- 1 teaspoon cayenne pepper
- 2 tablespoons flour
- 1 ½ cups half and half
- 1 cup sharp cheese, grated
- 1/2 cup cream cheese

Directions

1. Start by heating the oil in a heavy skillet. Sauté kielbasa and onions over medium heat; cook for about 10 minutes until the onions are translucent and the kielbasa is browned.
2. Transfer to the crock pot. Add the rest of the ingredients and set your crock pot to high.
3. Slow cook about 4 hours or until the mixture is heated through. Serve with your favorite dippers such as crusty bread, crackers, bread sticks or croutons.

Hot and Tangy Appetizer Meatballs

(Ready in about 4 hours | Servings 16)

Ingredients

- 1/2 cup apple cider vinegar
- 1/2 cup water
- 1 teaspoon fine sea salt
- 1 teaspoon ground black pepper
- 1 teaspoon dried tarragon
- 1 teaspoon dried rosemary
- 1 cup brown sugar
- 1 cup tomato ketchup
- 1 tablespoon soy sauce
- 2 tablespoons mustard
- A few drops of hot pepper sauce
- 18 ounces cherry preserves
- 32 ounces meatballs, frozen

Directions

1. In your crock pot, combine all of the ingredients; stir gently to combine well.

2. Set the crock pot to high; cook uncovered for 3 to 4 hours.

3. Serve with decorative toothpicks and enjoy!

Favorite Party Queso

(Ready in about 2 hours | Servings 16)

Ingredients

- 4 cups cans refried beans
- 1/2 canned green chiles, chopped
- 1/2 cup white wine
- 1/2 cup water
- 1 teaspoon dried basil leaves
- 1 teaspoon dried onion flakes
- 1/2 teaspoon garlic powder
- 1 cup beer
- 2 cups homemade cheese sauce
- 1/2 cup fresh parsley, chopped

Directions

1. In a large-sized mixing bowl, combine all of the ingredients, except beer, cheese sauce, and parsley.

2. Mix well until the mixture becomes creamy and smooth. Next, add beer and cheese sauce.

3. Slow cook for 2 hours on low heat setting. Sprinkle with fresh parsley and serve with tortilla chips or crusty bread.

Yummy Super Bowl Dip

(Ready in about 8 hours | Servings 6)

Ingredients

- 2 tablespoons butter, melted
- 2 red onions, finely chopped
- 1/2 teaspoon seasoned salt
- 1 cup sour cream

- 1 teaspoon celery seeds
- 1 teaspoon ground cumin
- 1/2 teaspoon garlic powder
- 1/2 cup mayonnaise

Directions

1. Arrange butter, onions and seasoned salt in your crock pot.
2. Slow cook for 8 hours on high, until onions are tender and browned.
3. Drain any liquid. Stir in remaining ingredients; stir until everything is well blended; enjoy the Super Bowl!

Mom's Crowd-Pleasing Dip

(Ready in about 2 hours | Servings 6)

Ingredients

- 1/2 cup mayonnaise
- 1 teaspoon fine sea salt
- 1 cup cream cheese, crumbled
- 1/2 teaspoon ground black pepper
- 1/4 cup prepared horseradish
- Toasted sesame seeds, as garnish
- 2 tablespoons milk

Directions

1. In a medium-sized mixing bowl, combine together mayonnaise, cream cheese, horseradish, and milk. Mix until everything is well incorporated.
2. Season with salt and ground black pepper.
3. Next, dump the mixture into your crock pot, cook covered 2 hours on low heat setting until cheese is melted and heated through.
4. Sprinkle with sesame seeds and serve with your favorite dippers such as bread sticks or potato chips.

Yummy Game-Day Dip

(Ready in about 4 hours | Servings 8)

Ingredients

- 1 cup cream cheese
- 10 ounces chunk chicken, drained
- 1/2 cup dry white wine
- 3/4 cup hot sauce
- 3/4 cups cheddar cheese, shredded
- Sea salt, to taste

Directions

1. Add all ingredients to your crock pot.
2. Turn on crock pot and cook on low heat setting for 4 hours. Serve with crusty bread or veggie sticks and enjoy!

Sun-Dried Tomato Dip

(Ready in about 2 hours 30 minutes | Servings 18)

Ingredients

- 1 cup boiling water
- 1/4 cup sun-dried tomatoes
- 1 ½ cups canned artichoke hearts, drained and chopped
- 1/2 cup milk
- 1 cup sour cream
- 1 ½ cups cream cheese, crumbled
- 3/4 cup sharp cheese, grated light
- 1/2 cup mayonnaise
- 1-2 garlic cloves, minced
- Seasoned salt, to taste
- 1/2 teaspoon ground black pepper

Directions

1. In a medium-sized bowl, pour boiling water; add sun-dried tomatoes and let soak until soft or for 1 hour. Drain and replace to your crock pot.
2. Add the rest of the ingredients to the crock pot. Cover and cook on low heat setting approximately 1 ½ hour.
3. Serve with dippers of choice and enjoy!

Ground Meat and Olive Queso Dip

(Ready in about 4 hours | Servings 32)

Ingredients

- 1/2 pound ground beef
- 1/2 pound ground pork
- 1 medium-sized sweet bell pepper, chopped
- 2 to 3 spring onions, chopped
- 1 cup canned beans
- 2 cups mozzarella cheese, shredded
- 1 cup salsa
- 2 cups cheddar cheese, shredded
- 1/2 cup pitted olives in oil

Directions

1. In a large non-stick skillet, cook the beef, pork, bell pepper and onion over medium heat; cook until veggies are tender and ground meat is no longer pink; drain.
2. Transfer to the crock pot.
3. Add the rest of the ingredients. Cover and cook for 3 to 4 hours on low; serve with dippers of choice and enjoy!

Mushroom Appetizer with Beer Sauce

(Ready in about 3 hours | Servings 4)

Ingredients

- 1 tablespoon canola oil
- 2 pounds mushrooms
- 2 cloves garlic, minced
- 1 teaspoon seasoned salt
- 1/2 teaspoon ground black pepper
- 1 teaspoon dried dill weed
- 1/4 cup non-alcoholic beer

Directions

1. Arrange all of the ingredients in your crock pot.
2. Cover and cook 2 to 3 hours on high.
3. Transfer to a serving platter, sprinkle with fresh parsley or cilantro and serve.

Herbed Saucy Mushroom Appetizer

(Ready in about 2 hours | Servings 10)

Ingredients

- 3 pounds cremini mushrooms
- 1 pound butter
- 1 teaspoon seasoned salt
- 1 teaspoon dried rosemary
- 1 teaspoon dried basil leaves
- 1 teaspoon dried oregano leaves
- 1/2 teaspoon onion powder
- 1/2 teaspoon garlic powder

Directions

1. Clean cremini mushrooms and arrange them in your crock pot.
2. Add the rest of the ingredients and cook approximately 2 hours on high.
3. Serve with tortilla chips, mini pitas or veggie sticks.

PART FIVE: DESSERTS

Old-Fashioned Cheese Cake

(Ready in about 3 hours | Servings 8)

Ingredients

- Non-stick cooking spray (butter flavour)
- 1 cup cream cheese, softened
- 1 stick butter, softened
- 1 (5.1-ounce) package instant vanilla pudding
- 3 large-sized eggs
- 1/2 cup fat-free half-and-half
- 1 teaspoon pure almond extract
- 1/2 teaspoon grated nutmeg
- 1 (18-ounce) package butter cake mix
- Toasted almonds, as garnish

Directions

1. Treat the inside of the crock pot with non-stick cooking spray.
2. Whip the cream cheese with butter in a medium-sized mixing bowl. Beat in the vanilla pudding, eggs, half-and-half, almond extract, and grated nutmeg.
3. Next step, fold in the butter cake mix.
4. Drop prepared batter into the crock pot; lightly pat it down.
5. Cover with the lid; cook on high for 3 hours or until a fork or a wooden skewer inserted in the center comes out clean.
6. Invert the cake onto a plate, scatter almonds on top and serve.

Bread Pudding with Figs and Cherries

(Ready in about 2 hours | Servings 4)

Ingredients

- 2 cups whole milk
- 2 large-sized eggs

- 1 teaspoon vanilla extract
- 1/2 teaspoon allspice
- 1/2 teaspoon ground cloves
- 1/2 teaspoon cinnamon
- A pinch of sea salt
- 1/2 cup sugar
- 1/2 cup figs, chopped
- 1/2 cup dried cherries
- 2 cups bread cubes
- 1/2 cup hot water

Directions

1. In a measuring cup, beat together the milk, eggs, vanilla extract, allspice, cloves, cinnamon, sea salt, and sugar.
2. Fold in the figs, cherries, and bread cubes.
3. Pour the mixture into a suitable baking dish that will fit on the cooking rack inside of the crock pot.
4. Pour the hot water into the crock pot.
5. Cover and cook 2 hours on high. Turn off the crock pot and serve; you can top it with caramel sauce if desired.

Bread Pudding with Pecans and Fruits

(Ready in about 2 hours | Servings 4)

Ingredients

- 2 eggs, lightly beaten
- 2 cups whole milk
- A pinch of sea salt
- 1 teaspoon pure almond extract
- 1/4 teaspoon ground anise seed
- 1/2 cardamom
- 1/2 teaspoon grated nutmeg
- 1/2 teaspoon cinnamon
- 1/2 cup brown sugar
- 1/2 cup toasted pecans, chopped
- 1/2 cup golden raisins
- 1/2 cup dried cranberries
- 2 ½ cups bread cubes
- 1/2 cup water

Directions

1. In a medium-sized mixing bowl, combine together eggs, milk, salt, almond extract, anise seed, cardamom, nutmeg, cinnamon, and brown sugar. Mix well until everything is well incorporated.

2. Fold in the pecans, golden raisins, dried cranberries, and bread cubes.

3. Transfer the batter to a baking dish. Place the baking dish on the cooking rack inside of the crock pot; then, pour in the water to cover the bottom of the crock pot.

4. Cook covered 2 hours on high. Serve at room temperature and enjoy.

Summer Peach Treat

(Ready in about 3 hours | Servings 8)

Ingredients

- 1 tablespoon canola oil
- 2 cups peaches, sliced
- 1 tablespoon cornflour
- 1/4 cup sugar
- 1 teaspoon vanilla extract
- 1 tablespoon molasses
- 1/2 teaspoon grated ginger
- 1/2 teaspoon cinnamon
- 9 ounces cake mix
- 4 tablespoons margarine, melted

Directions

1. Lightly grease the inside of your crock pot with 1 tablespoon of canola oil; then arrange the slices of the peaches in the bottom.

2. Sprinkle with cornflour; then, toss to coat.

3. Sprinkle with sugar, vanilla, molasses, grated ginger, and cinnamon. Fold in cake mix and drizzle melted margarine evenly over it.

4. Cover and cook on high about 3 hours. Turn off the crock pot; serve and enjoy!

Banana Butter Cake with Coconut and Almonds

(Ready in about 4 hours | Servings 8)

Ingredients

- 1 stick butter
- 1 cup cream cheese, softened
- 1 cup granulated white sugar
- 1 tablespoon molasses
- 3 medium-sized eggs
- 1/2 cup half-and-half
- 1 tablespoon orange juice
- 2 ripe bananas, sliced
- 1 1/3 cup cake flour
- 1 teaspoon baking soda
- 1/2 teaspoon baking powder
- A pinch of salt
- A dash of cinnamon
- A dash of cardamom
- 1/2 cup almonds, chopped
- 1/2 cup grated coconut, unsweetened

Directions

1. Add butter, cheese, sugar, molasses, eggs, half-and-half, orange juice and bananas to a food processor. Process until everything is well combined.
2. Then, in a separate mixing bowl, combine together the cake flour, baking soda, baking powder, salt, cinnamon and cardamom. Stir to mix well.
3. Scrape in the creamy banana mixture. Stir again. Fold in the almonds and coconut.
4. Line the bottom of the crock pot with a parchment paper; pour in the prepared batter.
5. Cover and cook on low for 4 hours.

Country Apple Cake with Walnuts

(Ready in about 4 hours | Servings 8)

Ingredients

- 1 cup cream cheese, softened
- 1 stick butter
- 1 cup granulated white sugar
- 3 eggs, lightly beaten

- 1/2 cup buttermilk
- 2 tart apples, sliced
- 1 1/3 cup fine pastry flour
- 1 teaspoon baking powder
- Sea salt, taste
- 1/4 teaspoon ground mace
- 1/4 teaspoon allspice
- 1 cup walnuts, chopped

Directions

1. Combine cream cheese, butter, sugar, eggs, buttermilk and apples in your food processor. Blend until the mixture is well mixed.
2. Next step, in another mixing bowl, combine together your fine pastry flour, baking powder, sea salt, mace and allspice. Stir to combine.
3. Scrape in the apple mixture. Stir to combine. Fold in the walnuts.
4. Coat the bottom of the crock pot with a parchment paper; pour the batter into the crock pot.
5. Cook covered about 4 hours on low.

Date Pudding Cake

(Ready in about 4 hours | Servings 8)

Ingredients

- 2 ½ cups dates, pitted and snipped
- 1 teaspoon baking soda
- 1 2/3 cups boiling water
- 2 cups packed brown sugar
- 1/2 cup butter, softened
- 1 teaspoon vanilla
- 1/4 teaspoon grated nutmeg
- 1/2 teaspoon cinnamon
- 3 large-sized eggs
- 3 ½ cups cake flour
- 1 tablespoon baking powder
- 1/4 teaspoon salt
- Non-stick spray (butter flavour)

Directions

1. In a mixing bowl, place dates together with baking soda and water. Set aside.

2. In a food processor, place brown sugar and butter; process until creamy and uniform; then, continue to process adding vanilla, nutmeg, cinnamon and eggs.

3. Scrape the mixture into the bowl and stir to mix.

4. Add the cake flour, baking powder, and salt to the mixing bowl; stir to mix.

5. Treat the crock pot with non-stick spray. Next, pour the batter into the crock pot.

6. Cover and cook on low for 4 hours or until the center of the cake is set. Serve with a dollop of whipped cream.

Grandma's Orange Coffee Cake

(Ready in about 2 hours 30 minutes | Servings 6)

Ingredients

- 4 eggs, separated
- 1/4 cup fresh orange juice
- 1 teaspoon grated ginger
- 1 teaspoon allspice
- 1 teaspoon vanilla extract
- 3 tablespoons butter
- 1 ½ cups whole milk
- 1 cup cake flour
- 1/2 cup powdered sugar
- 1/2 cup granulated white sugar
- A pinch salt
- A dash of cinnamon

Directions

1. In a food processor, combine egg yolks, orange juice, ginger, allspice, vanilla extract, and butter; process in order to cream all ingredients together.

2. Continue to process and slowly add the milk.

3. Stir in the rest of the ingredients; stir to mix. Add the egg yolk mixture to the bowl.

4. In a separate bowl, whip the egg whites until stiff peaks form. Fold into the prepared batter.

5. Transfer the batter to the crock pot. Cover and cook on low for 2 ½ hours. Enjoy!

Favorite Winter Compote

(Ready in about 6 hours | Servings 10)

Ingredients

- 2 medium-sized apples, peeled, cored and sliced
- 1 medium-sized pear, peeled, cored and sliced
- 2/3 cup dried cherries
- 1 vanilla bean
- 1 cinnamon stick
- 1/2 cup dried prunes
- 1/2 cup dried apricots, halved
- 1 cup canned pineapple tidbits with juice, unsweetened
- 1/4 cup brown sugar
- 1/2 cup apple juice
- 2 tablespoons orange juice
- 1 (21-oz.) can peach pie filling

Directions

1. Simply place all of the ingredients in your crock pot.
2. Cover and slow cook on low heat setting for about 6 hours.
3. Divide among ten serving bowls and serve warm or at room temperature.

Everyday Dried Fruit Compote

(Ready in about 5 hours | Servings 10)

Ingredients

- 4 cups dried apricots
- 6 ounces dried prunes
- 1 ½ cups golden raisins
- 1/2 cups dried dates
- 1/2 cup dried cranberries
- 1/3 cup dried figs
- 1 teaspoon lemon zest
- 2 cups pineapple juice
- 2 cups orange juice
- 1 cup white zinfandel
- 1 vanilla bean
- 1 cinnamon bean
- 1/4 teaspoon anise seed

Directions

1. Put all ingredients into your crock pot.

2. Next, cover with the lid and cook for 4 to 5 hours on high.

3. Turn off the crock pot. Divide among ten serving bowls; serve with a scoop of vanilla ice cream if desired.

Carrot Cake with Hazelnuts and Golden Raisins

(Ready in about 3 hours 30 minutes | Servings 12)

Ingredients

- 3/4 cup light brown sugar
- 12 tablespoons butter, room temperature
- 3 medium-sized eggs
- 1 tablespoon fresh lemon juice
- 2 cups carrots, shredded
- 1/3 cup hazelnuts, coarsely chopped
- 1/3 cup golden raisins
- 1 ½ cups self-rising flour
- 1 teaspoon baking powder
- A pinch of salt

For Cream Cheese Glaze:

- 1/3 cup cream cheese, room temperature
- 1 tablespoon butter, room temperature
- 1 teaspoon almond extract
- 1 ½ cups powdered sugar
- Milk

Directions

1. Begin by making the batter. In a large-sized bowl, beat brown sugar and butter until fluffy; stir in eggs one at a time, beating well.

2. Stir in lemon juice, carrots, hazelnuts, and golden raisins. Fold in flour, baking powder, and salt.

3. Pour batter into greased and floured springform pan; place on a rack in your crock pot. Set your crock pot on high and cook your cake about 3 ½ hours.

4. Meanwhile, make cream cheese glaze. In a medium-sized mixing bowl, beat cream cheese, butter and almond extract until smooth; add powdered sugar and milk in order to make a thick glaze consistency.

5. Drizzle carrot cake with cream cheese glaze.

Ginger and Walnut Sponge Cake

(Ready in about 2 hours | Servings 6)

Ingredients

- 1/2 cup packed light brown sugar
- 1/4 cup molasses
- 1/2 cup canned pumpkin
- 1/4 cup margarine, room temperature
- 1 large-sized egg
- 1/2 cup ground walnuts
- 1/2 teaspoon grated ginger
- 1/2 teaspoon ground mace
- 1 ½ cups fine cake flour
- 1/2 teaspoon baking powder
- 1 teaspoon baking soda

Directions

1. Combine brown sugar, molasses, pumpkin, margarine and egg in a large mixer bowl; mix at medium speed until everything is well blended.

2. Stir in walnuts, ginger, mace, fine cake flour, baking powder and baking soda; blending at low speed until the mixture is moistened.

3. Pour your batter into two greased and floured cans. Place cans in the crock pot; cover and cook on high until wooden skewer inserted in cake comes out clean or about 2 hours.

4. Allow to cool 10 minutes before cutting and serving.

Winter Gingerbread Cake

(Ready in about 5 hours | Servings 12)

Ingredients

- 1 ½ cups cake flour
- 1/2 cup all-purpose flour

- 1/2 teaspoon baking soda
- 1/2 teaspoon baking powder
- 1 teaspoon lemon juice
- 1/2 teaspoon ground cinnamon
- 1/4 teaspoon kosher salt
- 1/4 teaspoon allspice
- 8 tablespoons margarine, room temperature
- 3/4 cup brown sugar
- 2/3 cup molasses
- 1/2 cup whole milk
- 1 large-sized egg, lightly beaten

Directions

1. Combine cake flour, all-purpose flour, baking soda and baking powder in a large-sized bowl.
2. Combine lemon juice, cinnamon, salt, allspice, margarine, sugar and molasses; microwave on high until margarine is completely melted, about 1 to 2 minutes.
3. Add the margarine mixture to the flour mixture, whisk in milk and egg; mix to combine.
4. Pour prepared batter into greased and floured baking pan; place on a rack in your crock pot. Cover and cook on high about 5 hours or until wooden skewer inserted in center of cake comes out clean.
5. Drizzle with cream cheese glaze and serve.

Applesauce Genoise with Buttery Glaze

(Ready in about 3 hours | Servings 12)

Ingredients

For the Cake:

- 1/2 cup butter, room temperature
- 1 tablespoon molasses
- 1 tablespoon orange juice
- 3/4 cup granulated white sugar
- 1 egg
- 3/4 cup applesauce
- 1 cup pastry flour
- 1/2 cup whole-wheat flour
- 1 tablespoon baking powder
- 1/2 teaspoon grated nutmeg
- 1/4 teaspoon ground cloves

- 1/2 teaspoon ground cinnamon
- 1/2 teaspoon salt
- 1/2 teaspoon baking soda

For Buttery Glaze:
- 1/2 teaspoon butter extract
- 1 cup powdered sugar
- Milk

Directions

1. Beat butter, molasses, orange juice and white sugar in a large-sized mixing bowl until the mixture is well blended; stir in egg and applesauce.
2. Combine the rest of the ingredients for the cake. Add to the bowl.
3. Pour batter into greased and floured 6-cup cake pan; place pan on a rack in the crock pot.
4. Cover and cook on high about 3 hours, until wooden skewer inserted in center of cake comes out clean.
5. In the meantime, combine all of the ingredients for buttery glaze. Mix in order to make a glaze consistency.
6. Invert onto a rack and let cool completely before serving.

Easy Chocolate Peanut Butter Cake

(Ready in about 2 hours | Servings 12)

Ingredients

- 1/3 cup margarine
- 1/3 cup light brown sugar
- 2 medium-sized eggs
- 1/2 cup peanut butter
- 1/2 cup sour cream
- 1 2/3 cups self-rising flour
- A pinch of sea salt
- 1/2 cup chocolate morsels

Directions

1. Beat margarine and light brown sugar in a mixing bowl until fluffy; add eggs and blend well to combine. Stir in peanut butter and sour cream.
2. Add self-rising flour, sea salt, and chocolate morsels.

3. Pour batter into greased and floured 6-cup cake pan; place on a rack in a crock pot.

4. Slow cook on high 2 to 2 ½ hours.

5. Serve with chocolate sauce if desired. Enjoy!

Delicious Apple Streusel Dessert

(Ready in about 8 hours | Servings 8)

Ingredients

For the Cake:

- 6 cups tart apples, cored, peeled and sliced
- 1 teaspoon grated nutmeg
- 1/2 teaspoon ground mace
- 1 teaspoon ground cinnamon
- 1 tablespoon fresh lemon juice
- 3/4 cup milk
- 2 tablespoons canola oil
- 3/4 cup powdered sugar
- 2 eggs, beaten
- 1 teaspoon pure vanilla
- 1/2 cup baking mix

For the Topping:

- 1 cup baking mix
- 1/3 cup sugar
- 1 tablespoon honey
- 3 tablespoons margarine, cold
- 1/2 cup walnuts, coarsely chopped

Directions

1. In a large-sized mixing bowl, toss sliced apples with nutmeg, mace and cinnamon, Drizzle with lemon juice and place in a greased crock pot.

2. In a separate small-sized bowl, combine the milk, oil, powdered sugar, beaten eggs, vanilla and baking mix. Spoon this mixture over the apples in the crock pot.

3. Combine all of the ingredients for the topping in a bowl.

4. Slow cook on low about 8 hours. Serve with whipped cream if desired.

Holiday Pumpkin Pie Pudding

(Ready in about 7 hours | Servings 8)

Ingredients

- Non-stick cooking spray
- 2 cups canned pumpkin
- 1 ½ cups whole milk
- 3/4 cup brown sugar
- 1/2 cup biscuit mix
- 2 medium-sized eggs, beaten
- 2 tablespoons margarine, melted
- 1 teaspoon grated ginger
- 2 teaspoons vanilla extract
- 2 ½ teaspoons pumpkin pie spice
- Whipped topping, as garnish

Directions

1. Coat the inside of a crock pot with non-stick cooking spray.

2. In a large-sized mixing bowl, combine all ingredients, except whipped topping. Transfer to the crock pot. Slow cook on low for 7 hours. Serve with whipped topping.

Cocoa Cake with Vanilla Ice Cream

(Ready in about 3 hours | Servings 4)

Ingredients

- 4 medium-sized eggs
- 1/2 cup butter, melted
- 1/2 teaspoon pure mint extract
- 2 teaspoons vanilla
- 1 ½ cups granulated white sugar
- 1 cup pastry flour
- 1/2 cup baking cocoa
- 1 tablespoon instant coffee granules
- A pinch of salt
- Vanilla ice cream, as garnish

Directions

1. In a large-sized mixing bowl, combine eggs, butter, mint extract, vanilla and white sugar until the mixture is blended.

2. In a separate bowl, whisk pastry flour, cocoa, coffee granules, and salt.

3. Transfer to a greased crock pot. Cook covered on low heat setting for 3 hours.

4. If desired, serve warm cake with vanilla ice cream.

Easy Everyday Cherry Pie

(Ready in about 3 hours | Servings 12)

Ingredients

- 1 (18-ounce) package yellow cake mix
- 1/2 cup butter
- 1 (21-ounce) can cherry pie filling
- A dash of cinnamon
- 1 teaspoon lemon rind

Directions

1. Combine cake mix with butter in a large-sized mixing bowl.

2. Place cherry pie filling in your crock pot. Sprinkle the cake mixture over cherry pie filling. Sprinkle with cinnamon and lemon rind.

3. Cover with the lid and slow cook on low for 3 hours. Sprinkle with granulated white sugar and serve.

Chocolate Candy with Almonds and Pecans

(Ready in about 3 hours | Servings 12)

Ingredients

- 2 cups pecans, chopped
- 2 cups roasted almonds
- 1 (12-ounce) package semi-sweet chocolate morsels
- 1/2 cup chocolate bars
- 32 ounces white almond bark

Directions

1. Arrange pecans and almonds on the bottom of the crock pot.
2. Layer the other ingredients over the nuts.
3. Cook on low heat setting about 2 hours.
4. Next, drop the candy into cupcake pan liners. Allow to cool completely before serving or storing.

Apple Sauce with Pecans

(Ready in about 6 hours | Servings 8)

Ingredients

- 1 tablespoon unsalted butter
- 4 pounds apples, cored and sliced
- 1/2 cup brown sugar
- 1/2 teaspoon grated ginger
- 1/2 teaspoon cinnamon
- 1 cup water
- 1 tablespoon lemon juice
- 1 tablespoon finely chopped pecans

Directions

1. Put all of the ingredients into the crock pot.
2. Cover and slow cook on low for 6 hours.
3. Garnish with lightly sweetened whipped cream.

Family Apple Oatmeal Delight

(Ready in about 2 hours 30 minutes | Servings 8)

Ingredients

- 1 cup oatmeal
- 1 cup sugar
- 1 tablespoon molasses
- 1/3 cup all-purpose flour
- 1 tablespoon fresh lemon juice
- 1 teaspoon allspice

- 1/2 teaspoon almond extract
- 1 teaspoon vanilla extract
- 1/2 cup butter, melted
- 1/2 cup almonds
- 6 apples, peeled, cored and sliced

Directions

1. In a medium-sized mixing bowl, combine oatmeal with sugar, molasses, flour, and lemon juice.
2. Add allspice, almond extract, vanilla extract, butter and almonds to the oatmeal mixture.
3. Put 1/2 of the apples into the crock pot; after that, spoon half of oatmeal mixture on top.
4. Afterwards, place remaining 1/2 of apples and top with the rest of the oatmeal mixture.
5. Slow cook on high 2 to 2 ½ hours. Serve with cool whip and enjoy!

Bananas Foster with Vanilla Ice Cream

(Ready in about 1 hour 10 minutes | Servings 4)

Ingredients

- 1/2 cup butter
- 1/4 cup brown sugar
- 6 fresh bananas, sliced
- 1/4 cup rum
- Vanilla ice cream, as garnish

Directions

1. Melt margarine in the crock pot on low, about 10 minutes.
2. Add brown sugar, banana slices, and rum.
3. Cook on low for 1 hour.
4. Spoon over vanilla ice cream and serve.

Spiced Apples with Currants

(Ready in about 2 hours | Servings 6)

Ingredients

- 6 large-sized apples, cored, peeled and sliced
- 1 cup currants
- 1/4 cup light brown sugar
- 1 cup sugar
- 1/4 teaspoon nutmeg
- 1/2 teaspoon ground mace
- 1 cinnamon
- 3 tablespoons cornflour
- 4 tablespoons butter, sliced

Directions

1. Put all ingredients, except butter, into the crock pot; stir well; then, place slices of butter on top.
2. Cook on high for 2 hours.
3. Serve and enjoy!

Apple Walnut Cobbler

(Ready in about 3 hours | Servings 6)

Ingredients

- 1 (21-ounce) can apple pie filling
- 1 (18 ounce) package yellow cake mix
- 1/2 cup ground walnuts
- 1 teaspoon ground mace
- 1/2 cup melted margarine

Directions

1. Place apple pie filling into the crock pot.
2. Mix remaining ingredients.
3. Place the mixture over apple pie filling in the crock pot.
4. Cook on low for 3 hours.

26. Cherry Cobbler with Custard

(Ready in about 2 hours | Servings 6)

Ingredients

- Non-stick cooking spray
- 1 (21-ounce) can cherry pie filling
- 1 cup all-purpose flour
- 1/4 cup sugar
- 1/4 cup margarine, melted
- 1/2 cup milk
- 1 teaspoon baking soda
- 1/2 teaspoon baking powder
- Salt, to taste
- 1 teaspoon cherry flavored liqueur
- 1 cup toasted pine nuts, chopped
- Custard for garnish

Directions

1. Lightly grease the inside of a crock pot with non-stick cooking spray.
2. Place the cherry pie filling into the oiled crock pot. To make the batter, in a large-sized mixing bowl, combine the rest of the ingredients, except custard.
3. Spread the batter over the cherry pie filling. Cover on high for 2 hours.
4. Turn off the crock pot. Serve with custard and enjoy.

Summer Peach Cake

(Ready in about 8 hours | Servings 6)

Ingredients

- 1/2 cup sugar
- 2 teaspoons butter, melted
- 2 medium-sized eggs
- 1 ½ cups evaporated milk
- 3/4 cup white baking mix
- 2 cups peaches, mashed
- 1 tablespoon fresh lemon juice
- 1/2 teaspoon ground mace
- 3/4 teaspoon allspice

Directions

1. Oil your crock pot with non-stick cooking spray.
2. Combine the rest of the ingredients in a mixing bowl.
3. Pour into the crock pot. Cook on low for 8 hours.
4. Turn off your crock pot; serve and enjoy!

Country Honey-Sauced Pears

(Ready in about 2 hours 30 minutes | Servings 6)

Ingredients

- 6 pears, peeled and cored
- 1/2 cup brown sugar
- 1/4 cup honey
- 1 tablespoon butter, melted
- 1 teaspoon lemon zest
- 1/2 teaspoon ground mace
- 1/4 teaspoon ground ginger
- 1 tablespoon cornflour
- 2 tablespoons lemon juice

Directions

1. Place pears upright in a crock pot.
2. In a bowl, mix remaining ingredients, except cornflour and lemon juice; pour the mixture over pears.
3. Cover with the lid and cook on high heat setting 2 ½ hours or until the pears are tender.
4. Remove the pears from the crock pot and transfer to the dessert dishes.
5. Combine together cornflour and lemon juice; mix to combine; pour into the crock pot. Cover and cook on high until sauce is thickened or approximately 10 minutes.
6. Turn off your crock pot. Spoon sauce over pears and serve.

Apricot Cobbler with Ice Cream

(Ready in about 8 hours | Servings 6)

Ingredients

- Non-stick cooking spray (butter flavour)
- 1 cup brown sugar
- 3/4 cup yellow baking mix
- 2 eggs
- 1/2 teaspoon allspice
- 1 tablespoon orange juice
- 1/2 teaspoon ground mace
- 1 teaspoon vanilla extract
- 1/2 cup whole milk
- 2 tablespoons margarine, melted
- 10 large-sized apricots, mashed
- Ice cream, as garnish

Directions

1. Treat the inside of your crock pot with non-stick cooking spray.
2. In a large-sized mixing bowl, combine the rest of the ingredients, except apricots and ice cream. Mix well to combine all ingredients.
3. Fold in mashed apricots; stir well to combine.
4. Cover with the lid, set the crock pot to low and slow cook for 6 to 8 hours. Serve with your favorite ice cream.

Chocolate Raisin-Peanut Candy

(Ready in about 45 minutes | Servings 15)

Ingredients

- 1 ½ cup milk chocolate
- 1/2 cup white chocolate
- 1 cup raisins
- 1 cup toasted peanuts, unsalted

Directions

1. Place all of the ingredients in your crock pot.

2. Slow cook about 45 minutes on low heat setting.

3. Turn off your crock pot. Drop the mixture into cupcake pan liners; allow to cool completely. Enjoy!

Coconut Chocolate Brownies

(Ready in about 2 hours 30 minutes | Servings 8)

Ingredients

- 2 cups water
- 1 (21-ounce) package brownie mix
- 2 eggs
- 1/4 cup butter, melted
- 1/2 cup chocolate
- Non-stick cooking spray
- 1 cup sugar
- 1 teaspoon allspice
- 1/2 teaspoon anise seed
- 1/2 teaspoon grated nutmeg
- 1/2 cup shredded coconut
- 1/4 cup cocoa powder

Directions

1. Add 1/2 cup of the water, brownie mix, the eggs, butter and chocolate to a mixing bowl; stir to mix well.

2. Treat the crock pot with non-stick cooking spray. Scrape the batter into the crock pot.

3. Add the rest of the ingredients together with the remaining water to a medium-sized saucepan; cook over medium-high heat. Bring to a boil; next, pour over the batter in the crock pot.

4. Cover and cook on high approximately 2 ½ hours. Let your brownie cool slightly before slicing and serving.

Kicked up Lemon Cake

(Ready in about 4 hours | Servings 8)

Ingredients

- 1 (18-ounce) lemon cake mix
- 1 cup sour cream

- 4 eggs
- 3/4 cup butter
- 1 cup milk
- 1 (3-ounce) package instant lemon pudding mix
- 1/4 teaspoon lemon extract
- 1/2 teaspoon allspice
- 1/4 teaspoon ground cloves
- 1 tablespoon butter, melted
- 1/4 cup sugar

Directions

1. Add all ingredients, except 1 tablespoon of butter and sugar, to a mixing bowl. Stir by hand in order to combine.
2. Use the remaining 1 tablespoon of butter to grease the inside of your crock pot. Sprinkle the sugar evenly over the butter.
3. Afterwards, carefully pour the batter into the crock pot. Cover, set the crock pot to low, and cook for 4 hours.

Old-Fashioned Butterscotch Caramel Sauce

(Ready in about 4 hours | Servings 12)

Ingredients

- 2 cups fat-free half-and-half
- 1 stick butter
- 2 tablespoons fresh lemon juice
- 4 cups sugar
- 1/2 teaspoon ground cinnamon
- 1/2 teaspoon grated nutmeg
- 1/2 teaspoon ground cloves
- A pinch of sea salt

Directions

1. Add the half-and-half, butter, lemon juice, sugar, cinnamon, nutmeg, cloves and sea salt to your crock pot.
2. Cover with the lid and cook on high for 1 hour.
3. Then, reduce the heat to low and cook for 2 hours, stirring occasionally.
4. Remove the lid and cook on low for 1 more hour or until the sauce reaches your desired thickness.

Hot Chocolate Fondue

(Ready in about 2 hours | Servings 12)

Ingredients

- 2 sticks butter
- 1 cup heavy cream
- 1/2 cup corn syrup
- Pinch of salt
- 1/2 teaspoon ground cinnamon
- 1/4 teaspoon grated nutmeg
- 2 cups semisweet chocolate chips
- 1 tablespoon vanilla

Directions

1. Add the butter, heavy cream, corn syrup, salt, cinnamon and nutmeg to the crock pot.
2. Cover with the lid and cook on low for 1 hour. Then, stir with a heatproof spatula, cover, and cook for another 1 hour.
3. Add the chocolate chips and vanilla. Whisk until the chocolate is completely melted.

Amazing Coconut Rice Pudding

(Ready in about 5 hours | Servings 8)

Ingredients

- 1 cup long-grain rice
- 2/3 cup sugar
- 3 ½ cups milk
- 1/3 cup shredded coconut
- 1/2 teaspoon vanilla
- 1 teaspoon ground cinnamon
- 1/2 teaspoon grated nutmeg
- 1/2 teaspoon ground cloves
- A pinch of salt
- 1 teaspoon orange rind

Directions

1. Arrange all of the ingredients in your crock pot. Stir.
2. Cook on low heat setting for 5 hours.
3. Serve warm or at room temperature.

Rice Pudding with Whipped Cream

(Ready in about 3 hours | Servings 6)

Ingredients

- Non-stick cooking spray (butter flavor)
- 3 cups milk
- 3/4 cup granulated sugar
- 3/4 cup Basmati rice
- 1 teaspoon allspice
- 1/2 teaspoon ground cinnamon
- A pinch of salt
- 1/3 cup butter, melted
- Whipped cream, as garnish

Directions

1. Grease your crock pot with non-stick cooking spray.
2. Rinse rice thoroughly in a colander, under cold running water. Transfer to the crock pot; add remaining ingredients, except whipped cream; stir to combine.
3. Set your crock pot to high for about 3 hours, and stir once or twice during cooking period; cook until your rice has absorbed the liquid.
4. Spoon the pudding into dessert bowls and top with prepared whipped cream.

Pudding with Cranberries and Bananas

(Ready in about 5 hours | Servings 8)

Ingredients

- 1 cup rice
- 2 cups water
- 2 cups evaporated milk
- 1/3 cup sugar
- 1/2 cup dried cranberries
- A pinch of salt
- 1 vanilla bean
- 1 cinnamon sticks
- 3 bananas, sliced

Directions

1. Combine all ingredients, except bananas, in your crock pot; stir well until everything is incorporated.

2. Cover and cook on low heat setting for 4 to 5 hours.

3. Divide among eight dessert bowls, garnish with banana slices and enjoy.

Rice Pudding with Candied Fruit

(Ready in about 5 hours | Servings 8)

Ingredients

- Non-stick cooking spray
- 1 cup water
- 2 cups skim milk
- 3⁄4 cup white rice
- 3⁄4 cup sugar
- 1 stick cinnamon
- 1⁄3 cup butter, melted
- Candied fruit, as garnish

Directions

1. Place all ingredients, except candied fruit, in your crock pot; stir well.

2. Cover and cook on low approximately 5 hours.

3. Garnish with candied fruit and enjoy!

Aromatic Pears and Apples

(Ready in about 2 hours | Servings 6)

Ingredients

- 3 large-sized pears, cored, peeled and sliced
- 3 large-sized apples, cored, peeled and sliced
- 1 tablespoon fresh orange juice
- 1 cup sugar
- 1 tablespoon maple syrup
- 1 cup raisins
- 1 cinnamon stick
- A few drops of anise flavor
- 1⁄8 teaspoon nutmeg
- 3 tablespoons corn flour
- 4 tablespoons butter, sliced

Directions

1. Put all of the ingredients, except butter, into your crock pot; stir well to coat pear and apple slices

2. Next step, place the slices of butter on top.

3. Cook on high for 2 hours, stirring once. Enjoy!

Berry Dump Cake with Ice Cream

(Ready in about 3 hours | Servings 8)

Ingredients

- 1 (21-ounce) can blueberry pie filling
- 1 (18 ¼-ounce) package white cake mix
- 1/2 cup butter
- 1/2 teaspoon hazelnut extract
- 1/2 cup toasted almonds, chopped

Directions

1. First of all, place blueberry pie filling in the crock pot.

2. In a large-sized bowl, combine dry cake mix with butter and hazelnut extract; spread over the pie filling in the crock pot.

3. Sprinkle the chopped almonds on top. Cover and cook on low for 2 to 3 hours. Serve warm with your favorite ice cream.

Ooey Gooey Chocolate Cake

(Ready in about 3 hours | Servings 8)

Ingredients

- 1 (18 ¼ ounces) package chocolate cake mix
- 1 (4-ounce) package instant chocolate pudding mix
- 1 cup sour cream
- 3 large eggs, beaten
- 1/3 cup butter, melted
- 1 teaspoon hazelnut extract
- 3 cups milk

- 3/4 teaspoon ground cinnamon
- 1/4 teaspoon grated nutmeg
- 1/2 teaspoon grated ginger
- 1/2 cup chocolate cook-and-serve pudding mix
- 1/2 cup toasted peanuts, chopped
- 1 ½ cups miniature marshmallows
- 1/2 cup chocolate morsel

Directions

1. Beat cake mix, chocolate pudding mix, sour cream, eggs, butter, hazelnut extract and 1 cup of milk with an electric mixer about 2 minutes, at medium speed.
2. Pour prepared batter into a lightly greased crock pot.
3. In a saucepan, over medium heat, cook remaining 2 cups of milk. Stir often and do not boil.
4. Sprinkle cinnamon, nutmeg, ginger and cook-and-serve pudding mix over your batter. Pour hot milk over pudding. Cover and cook on low about 3 hours.
5. Turn off your crock pot. Sprinkle cake with toasted peanuts, miniature marshmallows, and chocolate morsels. Let stand until marshmallows are slightly melted.
6. Spoon into nice dessert dishes, serve warm and enjoy!

Halloween Caramel Apples

(Ready in about 1 hour 30 minutes | Servings 8)

Ingredients

- 1/4 cup water
- 2 (14-ounce) packages caramel candies
- 8 Granny Smith apples

Directions

1. Place water and caramel candies in a crock pot.

2. Cover and cook on high about 1 ½ hours on high, stirring often. Remove stems from the apples and insert stick into them.

3. Set the crock pot to low; dip apples into the hot caramel sauce.

4. Place the apples on a greased wax paper to cool completely.

Baker Days Zucchini Cake

(Ready in about 4 hours | Servings 8)

Ingredients

- 1/4 cup applesauce
- 1/4 cup margarine
- 3/4 cup sugar
- 1 large-sized egg, lightly beaten
- 1/4 cup low-fat buttermilk
- 1 ¼ cups pastry flour
- 2 tablespoons cocoa powder
- 1 teaspoon baking powder
- 1/2 teaspoon anise seed
- 1 teaspoon ground cinnamon
- A pinch of salt
- 1 cup zucchini, peeled and shredded
- 1/4 cup semisweet chocolate, coarsely chopped
- Icing sugar, as garnish

Directions

1. Beat applesauce, margarine, and sugar in a large-sized bowl until uniform and smooth.

2. Stir in egg and buttermilk; then, mix in combined flour, cocoa, baking powder, anise seed, cinnamon and salt.

3. Stir in zucchini and chocolate.

4. Pour prepared batter into greased and floured cake pan; place cake pan on a rack in the crock pot. Cover and slow cook 3 to 4 hours.

5. Transfer to a wire rack for 10 minutes in order to cool.

6. Sprinkle generously with icing sugar and cut into serving-sized pieces.

Cocoa Cake with Coffee Glaze

(Ready in about 4 hours 30 minutes | Servings 12)

Ingredients

- 1 ¼ cups sugar
- 1 tablespoon molasses
- 6 tablespoons butter, room temperature
- 2 medium-sized eggs
- 1 pinch of salt
- 1 cup cake flour
- 1/3 cup cocoa powder
- 1/2 teaspoon baking soda
- 1/2 teaspoon baking powder
- 1/3 cup sour cream
- 1 tablespoon instant espresso powder
- 2 tablespoons strong brewed coffee
- 3/4 cup powdered sugar
- 1 tablespoon butter, melted

Directions

1. In a small-sized mixing bowl, beat sugar, molasses and butter until fluffy; add eggs one at a time, and continue to beat.

2. Add salt and combined flour, cocoa powder, baking soda and baking powder. Stir to combine. Add sour cream and instant espresso.

3. Then, pour prepared batter into greased and floured cake pan; place pan on a rack in the crock pot.

4. Cover and cook on high until a wooden toothpick inserted in center of cake comes out clean, or about 4 ½ hours.

5. In the meantime, make the coffee glaze by mixing coffee, powdered sugar and melted butter.

6. Drizzle your cake with coffee glaze and serve.

Sinfully Delicious Mocha Mousse Cake

(Ready in about 3 hours | Servings 8)

Ingredients

- 3/4 cup sugar
- 1/2 cup Dutch process cocoa

- 3 tablespoons fine pastry flour
- 2 teaspoons instant espresso powder
- A pinch of salt
- 3/4 cup milk
- 1 teaspoon hazelnuts extract
- 1/2 bittersweet chocolate, coarsely chopped
- 1 whole egg
- 3 egg whites
- 1/3 cup granulated sugar
- Powdered sugar, as garnish

Directions

1. In a saucepan, over medium-low heat, cook sugar, Dutch process cocoa, flour, espresso powder, and salt; gradually whisk in milk and cook until the mixture is hot.
2. Remove saucepan from the heat and add hazelnuts extract and chocolate, stirring until it is melted. Add whole egg and cool to room temperature.
3. Beat egg whites to stiff peaks, gradually adding granulated sugar. Add egg whites to the chocolate mixture.
4. Pour batter into greased cake pan; place on a rack in your crock pot. Place 3 layers of paper towels under the lid and cover the crock pot; cook on high about 3 hours. The cake will look moist.
5. Sprinkle top of the cake generously with powdered sugar. Serve chilled.

Orange-Glazed Chocolate Cake

(Ready in about 4 hours | Servings 8)

Ingredients

- 3/4 cup low-fat buttermilk
- 1/2 teaspoon baking soda
- 1/2 teaspoon baking powder
- 6 tablespoons butter, room temperature
- 1 teaspoon orange extract
- 1 cup granulated sugar
- 1 egg
- 1 ½ cups cake flour
- A dash of ground cinnamon
- A dash of grated nutmeg
- A pinch of salt
- 1/4 cup semisweet chocolate, melted
- 3/4 cup powdered sugar
- 1/2 cup orange juice

Directions

1. Mix together buttermilk, baking soda and baking powder. In a large-sized bowl, beat butter with orange extract and granulated sugar until fluffy.
2. Then add whole egg, blending well. Stir in flour, cinnamon, nutmeg, and salt. Add egg mixture to the buttermilk mixture.
3. Reserve about 1 ½ cups of prepared batter; add melted chocolate to remaining batter.
4. Next, spoon batters alternately into greased and floured cake pan; you can swirl gently with a knife.
5. Place cake pan on rack in the crock pot; cover, set the crock pot to high and cook about 4 hours.
6. Meanwhile, make orange syrup in the following way. In a small-sized pan, heat 3 powdered sugar and orange juice, stirring frequently. Cook until sugar is dissolved.
7. Pour orange syrup over prepared cake and allow to stand in order to cool before serving time.

Chocolate Almond Pound Cake

(Ready in about 4 hours | Servings 8)

Ingredients

- 3/4 cup low-fat buttermilk
- 1 teaspoon baking powder
- 6 tablespoons margarine, melted
- 1 cup sugar
- 1 teaspoon almond extract
- 2 medium-sized eggs, lightly beaten
- 1 ½ cups all-purpose flour
- 1/2 cup almonds, chopped
- 1 teaspoon allspice
- 1/2 teaspoon grated ginger
- A pinch of salt
- 1/4 cup bittersweet chocolate, melted
- 1/2 cup powdered sugar

Directions

1. In a medium-sized bowl, combine buttermilk and baking powder.

2. In another bowl, beat margarine with sugar for about 10 minutes or until fluffy. Stir in almond extract and whole eggs. Add flour, almonds, allspice, ginger, and salt. Add this mixture to the buttermilk mixture in the bowl.

3. Then, reserve about 1 ½ cups of your batter; add bittersweet chocolate to remaining batter.

4. Alternate batters into greased and floured cake pan; you can swirl gently with a knife.

5. Place your pan on a rack in the crock pot; cover and cook about 4 hours on high. Dust the cake with powdered sugar and enjoy.

Orange Rice Pudding with Raisins

(Ready in about 3 hours | Servings 6)

Ingredients

- 1/2 cup sugar
- 4 cups low-fat milk
- 2 tablespoons orange juice
- 1/2 cup rice, uncooked
- 2/3 cup raisins
- 2 teaspoons orange rind
- 1/2 teaspoon ground cloves
- Chocolate curls for garnish

Directions

1. In your crock pot, combine all of the ingredients, except chocolate curls.

2. Cook on high about 3 hours, stirring occasionally.

3. Spoon into the serving bowls; before serving, scatter chocolate curls on top.

Peach Hazelnut Cobbler

(Ready in about 2 hours | Servings 8)

Ingredients

- 2 (21-ounce) cans peach pie filling
- 1 stick butter, melted
- 1 (18-ounce) package yellow cake mix
- 1/3 cup hazelnuts
- Whipped cream, as garnish

Directions

1. Dump peach pie filling into the crock pot.
2. Combine butter with cake mix until crumbly. Evenly spread over pie filling in the crock pot.
3. Sprinkle with hazelnuts.
4. Cook 2 hours on high heat setting. Serve warm with whipped cream. Enjoy!

Amazing Fudge Pudding Cake

(Ready in about 2 hours | Servings 6)

Ingredients

- 1 cup fine cake flour
- 1/2 cup packed brown sugar
- 6 tablespoons unsweetened cocoa powder
- 1/2 teaspoon baking soda
- 1 teaspoon baking powder
- 1/2 cup milk
- 2 tablespoons canola oil
- 1/3 cup granulated sugar
- Light whipped topping, as garnish

Directions

1. Wrap bottom of the cake pan in aluminum foil.
2. In a medium-sized bowl, combine cake flour, sugar, 3 tablespoons cocoa, baking soda, and baking powder.
3. Add combined milk and canola oil to the flour mixture; mix well.
4. Spoon batter into greased and floured cake pan. Combine together remaining 3 tablespoons of cocoa and granulated sugar; sprinkle over batter in the cake pan.
5. Place cake pan on a rack in the crock pot. Cover and cook on high about 2 hours. Serve with light whipped topping.

Warm Pudding-Style Cake

(Ready in about 6 hours | Servings 12)

Ingredients

- Cooking spray
- 1 package (1-ounce) instant butterscotch pudding
- 1 package (18.25-ounces) spice cake mix
- 1 cup water
- 1 cup sour cream
- 3/4 cup canola oil
- 1 egg
- 1 teaspoon allspice
- 1 cup pineapple, crushed

Directions

1. Lightly grease a bottom and side of your crock pot with cooking spray.
2. Combine remaining ingredients, except pineapple, in a bowl of an electric mixer. Mix at medium speed until everything is combined, or about 2 minutes. Add pineapple and stir to combine.
3. Pour into the crock pot; cover and cook on low about 6 hours.
4. Spoon warm cake onto serving platter.

Pear and Apple Oatmeal Pudding

(Ready in about 4 hours | Servings 6)

Ingredients

- Non-stick cooking spray
- 3 pears, cored, peeled and diced
- 3 apples, peeled and diced
- 3 eggs
- 1/2 cup fine pastry flour
- 3/4 cup oats
- 1/3 cup powdered milk
- 1 cup sugar
- 2 teaspoons baking powder
- 1/2 teaspoon ground cinnamon
- 1 teaspoon vanilla extract

Directions

1. Lightly oil your crock pot with non-stick cooking spray.
2. Arrange pears and apples in your crock pot. Then, place the rest of the ingredients.
3. Mix well to combine. Cover and cook for 4 hours on low.
4. Serve chilled and enjoy.

Rice Pudding with Prunes and Pistachios

(Ready in about 3 hours | Servings 18)

Ingredients

- 1 tablespoon canola oil
- 1/2 cup agave nectar
- 1 cup rice
- 1/2 teaspoon anise seed
- 1 teaspoon ground allspice
- 1/2 cup dried prunes, chopped
- 8 cups soy milk, unsweetened
- 2 tablespoons pistachios, chopped

Directions

1. Treat the bottom and sides of a crock pot with canola oil.
2. Then, add remaining ingredients, except pistachios.
3. Cook for 3 hours on high; stir once or twice.
4. Sprinkle with chopped pistachios and serve warm.

Pudding with Dried Cherries and Walnuts

(Ready in about 3 hours | Servings 18)

Ingredients

- Non-stick cooking spray (butter flavor)
- 1/3 cup sugar
- 1 tablespoon honey
- 1 cup rice
- 1/2 teaspoon ground mace

- 1 teaspoon ground allspice
- 1 vanilla bean
- 1 cinnamon stick
- 1/2 cup dried cherries, chopped
- 8 cups skim milk
- 2 tablespoons walnuts, chopped

Directions

1. Oil the inside of your crock pot with cooking spray.
2. Then, add remaining ingredients, except walnuts.
3. Cover and slow cook for 3 hours on high, stirring once or twice.
4. Sprinkle with chopped walnuts and serve warm or at room temperature.

Easiest Tapioca Pudding

(Ready in about 2 hours | Servings 6)

Ingredients

- 1/4 cup small pearl tapioca
- 2 cups milk
- 1 teaspoon green tea powder
- 1/4 cup agave nectar
- 1/4 cup brown sugar
- 1 large-sized egg

Directions

1. Add all of the ingredients, except eggs, to the crock pot; then cook about 1 ½ hours on low.
2. Whisk in the egg. Cook an additional 1/2 hour; serve warm.

Spiced Challah Pudding

(Ready in about 5 hours | Servings 10)

Ingredients

- Cooking spray
- 4 cups cubed challah bread

- 1/3 cup dried cranberries
- 2 ½ cups fat-free milk
- 2 medium-sized eggs
- 1/3 cup sugar
- 1/2 teaspoon pure banana extract
- 1 teaspoon allspice
- 1/2 teaspoon ground ginger
- 1/2 teaspoon ground cloves

Directions

1. Grease a crock pot with cooking spray. Add the cubed challah bread and dried cranberries. Then, stir to combine.
2. In a medium-sized bowl, whisk the rest of the ingredients.
3. Pour the mixture over the cubed challah and dried cranberries in the crock pot.
4. Cook covered for 5 hours on low.

Luscious Chocolate Bread Pudding

(Ready in about 5 hours | Servings 10)

Ingredients

- Cooking spray
- 4 cups bread, cubed
- 2 eggs
- 2 ¼ cups fat-free evaporated milk
- 1/3 cup light brown sugar
- 1/4 cup cocoa
- 1 teaspoon ground cinnamon
- 1 teaspoon almond extract
- 1/2 cup miniature marshmallows, as garnish

Directions

1. Spray a crock pot with non-stick cooking spray. Arrange the bread cubes in the crock pot.
2. In a mixing bowl, or a measuring cup, combine the rest of the ingredients, except miniature marshmallows. Pour the egg mixture over the bread cubes.
3. Cook for 5 hours on low, until the bread pudding is no longer liquid. Scatter miniature marshmallows on top and serve warm or at room temperature. Enjoy!

Pudding with Raisins and Walnuts

(Ready in about 5 hours | Servings 8)

Ingredients

- 1 tablespoon butter, melted
- 3 ½ cups bread, cubed
- 1/4 cup sugar
- 1 tablespoon honey
- 2 medium-sized eggs
- 1/2 cup golden raisins
- 1/2 cup ground walnuts
- 2 ¼ cups soy milk
- 1/4 cup cocoa powder

Directions

4. Treat the inside of your crock pot with melted butter. Layer the bread cubes into your crock pot.
5. In a measuring cup, combine the rest of the ingredients; pour the mixture over the bread cubes in the crock pot.
6. Then, cover and cook for 5 hours on low heat setting. Serve warm or at room temperature.

Favourite Apple Brown Betty

(Ready in about 2 hours 20 minutes | Servings 6)

Ingredients

- 1 tablespoon margarine, melted
- 6 apples, peeled, cored and cubed
- 1 tablespoon fresh orange juice
- 1 tablespoon maple syrup
- 1/2 teaspoon grated nutmeg
- 1/4 teaspoon allspice
- 1/4 teaspoon ground mace
- 1/2 teaspoon cinnamon
- 1 ¾ cups bread cubes

Directions

1. First of all, treat the inside of the crock pot with melted margarine.

2. Add the apples, orange juice, maple syrup, and spices. Stir well to combine ingredients. Cook on high approximately 2 hours.

3. Preheat your oven to 250 degrees F. Spread the bread cubes on a baking sheet and bake until browned, or about 10 minutes.

4. Place the toasted bread cubes over the mixture in the crock pot. Cook on high heat setting for 10 minutes longer.

Easiest Orange-Vanilla Custard

(Ready in about 8 hours | Servings 8)

Ingredients

- 1/2 teaspoon orange extract
- 1 teaspoon vanilla extract
- 2 cups fat-free milk
- 5 medium-sized eggs
- 1 tablespoon cornstarch
- 1/3 cup sugar
- A pinch of kosher salt

Directions

1. Combine all ingredients in a large-sized mixing bowl. Whisk until everything is well incorporated and blended.

2. Pour into your crock pot.

3. Cook for 8 hours on low, until the center of your custard looks set. Serve with vanilla ice cream if desired.

Apple-Carrot Pudding Cake

(Ready in about 6 hours | Servings 8)

Ingredients

- Non-stick cooking spray
- 1 ounce instant butterscotch pudding
- 1 package (18.25-ounces) carrot cake mix
- 1 cup cold water

- 1 cup sour cream
- 3/4 cup margarine, melted
- 1 egg
- 1 cup apples, chopped

Directions

1. Lightly grease the bottom and side of your crock pot with non-stick cooking spray.
2. In a large-sized mixing bowl, combine the rest of the ingredients; beat with your electric mixer at medium speed until everything is well blended, or about 2 minutes.
3. Replace the mixture to the crock pot; cover and cook on low 6 hours. Spoon warm pudding cake onto plates and enjoy!

Cosy Winter Morning Apple Pudding

(Ready in about 4 hours | Servings 6)

Ingredients

- 4-5 large-sized apples, cored, peeled and sliced
- 1/2 cup granulated sugar
- 1/2 teaspoon grated nutmeg
- 1/2 teaspoon allspice
- 1/2 teaspoon ground mace
- 1 teaspoon ground cinnamon
- 1/4 teaspoon kosher salt
- 1 ½ tablespoons pearl tapioca
- 1 cup boiling water
- 1 lemon, juiced
- 1/2 cup walnuts, chopped

Directions

1. In a large-sized mixing bowl, combine together apple slices, sugar, nutmeg, allspice, mace, cinnamon, salt, and pearl tapioca; toss to coat apples.
2. Transfer the mixture to a crock pot. In a separate bowl, combine boiling water with lemon juice. Pour over the apples in the crock pot.
3. Set the cooker to high and cook 3 to 4 hours. Sprinkle with chopped walnuts. Serve warm and enjoy your winter morning!

Orange Tapioca Pudding

(Ready in about 3 hours | Servings 8)

Ingredients

- 1/2 cup sugar
- 4 cups milk
- 2 teaspoons orange extract
- A pinch of salt
- 1/2 teaspoon allspice
- 1/2 cup small tapioca pearls
- 3 egg yolks
- Oranges, sectioned

Directions

1. Place sugar, milk, orange extract, salt, allspice and tapioca pearls in a crock pot. Whisk thoroughly until the sugar has dissolved.
2. Turn the crock pot to high, cover and cook for 2 hours.
3. In a small-sized mixing bowl, whisk the egg yolks until frothy. Pour about 1 tablespoon of the hot tapioca pudding from the crock pot into the egg yolks; mix until combined.
4. Then, gradually add hot pudding to the egg yolks until you get about 2 cups of the pudding-yolk mixture.
5. Slowly pour this mixture into remaining tapioca pudding in the crock pot; mix until everything is well blended, or 4 to 5 minutes.
6. Slow cook for 1 more hour on low. Serve warm with oranges and enjoy.

Rum Bananas Foster with Pecans

(Ready in about 2 hours | Servings 4)

Ingredients

- 4 ripe bananas, sliced
- 1 cup packed light brown sugar
- 4 tablespoons margarine, melted
- 1/4 cup rum
- 1 tablespoon orange juice
- 1 teaspoon vanilla extract
- 1/2 teaspoon allspice
- 1/4 cup pecans, chopped

Directions

1. Arrange the slices of banana at the bottom of your crock pot.

2. In a medium-sized mixing bowl, combine sugar, margarine, rum, orange juice, vanilla and allspice; pour over banana slices.

3. Cover and cook for 2 hours on low. Scatter chopped pecans on top and serve warm.

Coconut Bananas Foster

(Ready in about 2 hours | Servings 4)

Ingredients

- Non-stick cooking spray (butter flavor)
- 4 ripe bananas, halved
- 1 tablespoon maple syrup
- 1 cup granulated sugar
- 3 tablespoons butter, melted
- 1/4 cup water
- 1 teaspoon almond extract
- 1/2 teaspoon ground cinnamon
- 1/4 teaspoon ground cloves
- 1/2 teaspoon grated ginger
- 1/4 cup coconut, shredded

Directions

1. Treat the inside of your crock pot with cooking spray.

2. Place bananas in the bottom of your crock pot.

3. In a mixing bowl, mix together the rest of the ingredients, except coconut; pour over banana slices. Cover with the lid and cook for 2 hours on low heat setting. Sprinkle with shredded coconut and serve warm.

Download a FREE PDF file with photos of all the 500 recipes by following the link:

Download a FREE PDF file with 200 Bonus Recipes:

Made in the USA
Lexington, KY
15 October 2016